DEAR WILLIE

THANK YOU FOR YOUR LOVE, LEADERSHIP & LIGHT. WE ARE THE ICONIC LEADERS WE HAVE BEEN WAITING FOR; CURATORS OF THE CHANGE WE'RE SEEKING TO SEE!

LOVE,
SHAWN

#ITOOAMAMERICA

AVAILABLE 1/6/2022

I TOO AM AMERICA

ON LOVING AND LEADING BLACK MEN & BOYS

BY SHAWN DOVE AND NICK CHILES

FOREWORD BY SUSAN L. TAYLOR

I TOO AM AMERICA

ON LOVING AND LEADING BLACK MEN & BOYS

BY SHAWN DOVE AND NICK CHILES

FOREWORD BY SUSAN L. TAYLOR

Published in the United States by The Corporation for Black Male Achievement.
For information address Corporation for Black Male Achievement
6 Crestwood Street, Piscataway, NJ 08854.

Hardback ISBN: 978-1-73731-150-8
Paperback ISBN: 978-1-73731-151-5
Ebook ISBN: 978-1-73731-152-2

Cover photograph and design: Salahadeen Betts
Shawn Dove author photo ©Nick Chiles
Nick Chiles author photo ©Danielle Earles
Cover model photograph: Sahdeeq Betts

www.dovesoars.com

Printed in the United States of America.
First Edition.

Praise for *I Too Am America: On Loving and Leading Black Men & Boys*

"*I Too Am America* is a special book written by special men. Shawn graciously shares his lessons of leadership, love, and sacrifice for the world to see and learn from, and we all should be truly grateful. This book should be read, analyzed, and copied to make our world a better place."

—**Wes Moore**, NY Times bestselling author

"*I Too Am America* is engaging, relevant, and timely; and as a Black woman, I saw myself in the narrative as well."

—**Minda Harts**, bestselling author of *The Memo*

"Shawn Dove and Nick Chiles' *I Too Am America: On Loving and Leading Black Men & Boys* is essential reading for anyone concerned with the future of Black men and boys—and anyone concerned with the future of America as a whole. Dove and Chiles bring unparalleled experience, compelling stories and a deep bedrock of empathy to this book, giving readers unique insight into the lives and stories of Black men and how what impacts one of us impacts us all. Read this book, savor it and share with a friend—I can't recommend it heartily enough!"

—**Joshua DuBois**, CEO of Gauge, Founder of Values Partnerships, Inc, and bestselling author of *The President's Devotional: Daily Readings that Inspired President Obama*

"*I Too Am America* is a story that needs to be told and needs to be read. Shawn's story is a testament to the power of love and determination to lift up every soul who longs for expression and validation. America's work is still not done and perhaps never will be (since all our work is to grow and evolve). But stories like these show a path forward—a path of love—which we must continue working on for the sake of our children and our children's children."

—**Maria Rodale**, author, former Chair and CEO of Rodale, Inc.

"In *I Too Am America* Shawn Dove illuminates the challenges of being a young Black man in America with grace and wisdom—but more than that, he sets a path forward that is clear-eyed, realistic, and also relentlessly hopeful."

—**Christina Lewis,** philanthropist and founder of Allstar Code

"Shawn Dove is one of the nation's top leaders in Black male achievement. His sacrificial work and service was a catalyst for igniting a movement that developed and empowered Black leaders like myself to bring healing to our communities. Learn from him, this is the blueprint for loving and leading Black men and boys."

—*Jason Wilson,* CEO of The Yunion & Founder of The Cave of Adullam; bestselling author of *Cry Like A Man* and *Battle Cry*

Love & Dedication

To my divine mate, Desere, my wife whose love and compassion
continues to change my life for the better.
To my children, Nia, Maya, Cameron and Caleb, who remind me
daily that the Dove Nest is for growing our collective roots
and wings.

To my mom, Deanna, for infusing me with creativity, courage,
love and the superpower of reinvention.

To Black men and boys, and the people who love them, for your
bravery, beauty and brilliance. May you always love, learn
and lead.

—Shawn Dove

To Mazi, Miles, Cole, Tyre, Riley, Tristan, and all the Black men
and boys who have inspired my steps and enlivened my days: your
fight is my fight; your love is my oxygen.

—Nick Chiles

I, Too

BY LANGSTON HUGHES

I, too, sing America.

I am the darker brother.
They send me to eat in the kitchen
When company comes,
But I laugh,
And eat well,
And grow strong.

Tomorrow,
I'll be at the table
When company comes.
Nobody'll dare
Say to me,
    "Eat in the kitchen,"
Then.

Besides,
They'll see how beautiful I am
And be ashamed—

I, too, am America.

Table of Contents

Foreword

Over several decades, seeking and assigning powerful writing has been central to my life. For 27 years I worked as the chief editor of *Essence,* as the magazine's editor-in-chief and publishing director; and now for 15 years I have served as the CEO of the National CARES Mentoring Movement, founded as Essence CARES to help secure our oft-forgotten children growing up in disinvested communities and schools. In all that time, working in service to the Black community, I have read, edited, and published compelling writings that would offer insight into the world of Black people, widening the lens when leading the magazine for Black women to include the voices of our men and boys and stories about supports for African Americans struggling in poverty. First, for the understanding of millions of Black women, my own understanding included.

And now, as the leader of CARES, a national nonprofit, I continue with efforts to elevate my and my colleagues' awareness of the pathologies and impacts of racism and poverty. A goal is to pool the collective knowledge and wisdom of those who are similarly dedicated to dismantling Black poverty, held fast by the centuries-long injustices made legal that continue to destroy African American lives. My library is filled to overflowing with manuscripts and books that delineate the challenges.

However, the book you are holding in your hands, Shawn Dove's *I Too Am America: On Loving and Leading Black Men & Boys,* is of a different kind. Co-written with Pulitzer Prize-winning journalist and author Nick Chiles, it is a master course, one I didn't know I needed, delving deeply into the masked lives of today's Black boys and men. Crafted with exceeding care and painful honesty, it pierces to the heart of their lives, to the root of the challenges so many face; many living in generational poverty, many aching from the absence of fathers and worry for mothers overwhelmed with struggle on every front. Here we feel unspoken frustrations, witness acquiescence and adaptive response to the chronic stress of systemic assault and a history of brutality against African Americans that often damp down our tenderness, early on among Black boys. Under unrelenting environmental pressure, conditioned to fight for the right to exist, without intervention, they may grow in the image and likeness of an uncaring, uncompromising nation. Pitted against their own, Black boys quickly learn that compassion is a weakness to be trained out or die in the theater of urban colosseums. The code in the streets is to never back down. Be hard if you want to survive. So many have not. And some would say that is in fact the point.

This too is America. Its new-world life-and-death gladiatorial games sublimated on the field, in the ring, in the do-or-die competition of capitalist corporate America and glorified in our media for the entertainment of a culture long addicted to violence at the expense of the enslaved, their descendants, immigrants, and the poor. Labor stolen, talents plundered, lives lost, and communities laid waste.

Shawn Dove has earned his place as a prophetic voice for Black men and boys. Community leaders, parents and teachers, aunties and sisters, and also the brothers themselves—all of us who care deeply about rebuilding the village—will be deeply moved and enlightened by this needed work. This book lays out in chapter and verse the longing Black men have to emerge from the pain that blankets them like a toxic fog and often leads to self-harming behaviors. This, in part, was Shawn's story.

Over the course of the years recounted, the turning of leaves and pages, Shawn traces the paths taken, the times he wandered lost, and the forks that forced a choice to live in the lie or to love himself, his family (whom he endearingly calls the Dove Nest), Black men and boys, their families and communities.

I Too Am America is an impassioned portrait not just of Shawn's story, but the collective, curated story of Black people—what we have had to overcome and continue to endure in this America. It is equal parts memoir, historical account of the Campaign for Black Male Achievement under his leadership, and manifesto for the journey ahead. He brings to bear a wealth of perspectives from the phenomenal souls that have contributed to the work of the Campaign for Black Male Achievement.

The memoir reveals the Shawn Dove I have come to love and treasure. With gut-wrenching vulnerability and God-given courage, Shawn's story mirrors that of so many Black men and boys in our nation. One recent winter evening, after a long call and listening to Shawn, I was compelled to write in response to something he had shared with me—a painful period in his younger days when he had contemplated ending his life.

"My dear Shawn," I began, "what a blessing that the voice of Spirit spoke and was heard, that you didn't throw yourself before a barreling train. How fortunate are we and so many more you will never know that you chose life over death!" And isn't that the choice each of us must make?

It is vitally important, I wrote, that in the quiet that sits at the center of our being, we acknowledge the good we have given the world. But for Shawn's life, there would be no Nia or Maya, Cameron or Caleb—his beloved children—and all that they are bringing to life, the good they will extend into the world beyond him, because of him and his Desere. Without him, there would have been no *Proud Poppa* magazine, which brought him to me at *Essence*, no Campaign for Black Male Achievement for the healing and elevation of the tens of thousands of Black boys and men he has already touched. But for Shawn's vision and effort, there would be no My Brother's Keeper; Shawn was the Obama administration's inspiration. He made it safe for Black men to unmask, to feel, to have their say. But for the visionary Shawn Dove, National CARES would not have been able to build strong our *Rising* program. He was the sole funder at the time who understood the need for healing the traumas sustained by Black children growing up in poverty, the first funder to invest in it.

I Too Am America, at its very essence, is all about love. My hope is that this book Shawn and Nick have delivered to us at this divine right moment will inspire us to lead the change we need to see for Black men and boys, Black families, and our communities. As I wrote years ago in one of my own books, *All About Love,* I hope all who read this powerful testimony are inspired to hold fast to their spiritual rudder. We need our individual and collective wisdom to guide us home to ourselves, to a better way of living, a renaissance, away from catastrophe. Join the vanguard of visionaries who are redefining success and the purpose of work from solely making money to making a better society. Pursue your purpose, your highest aspiration, as Shawn Dove continues to do, and by the power of our trust and faith, the walls will tumble and the way open wide for all to proclaim proudly, in the words of Langston Hughes, I too am America.

—Susan L. Taylor

Introduction

Whilst at Poetry in Motion I stopped to look
For a brother with ways to write a book.
Arranged round me with a story to tell,
A billion brothers who know all too well.
Bout unwritten words that unwillingly die,
Before bred and bound and able to fly.
Why do my brothers' words wear weights of woe?
My ears to the ground...I'm dying to know.
We must give our words wings so they can sing,
A song for all brothers they will bring.
The ability to dream, to fly and to soar,
It's to you my brothers these words are for.
To give your words a life you must sit and write,
Your story with tales of what life is like.
Do me a favor and set your words free,
Cuz I need to hear them...do it for me.

—Shawn Dove, 1988

Poetry In Motion

Poetry, writing, and publishing have long been my salvation, my healing balm—my go-to when nothing else seems to cease whatever is ailing my heart and soul. As a 16-year-old boy on a prep-school campus in the boonies of Massachusetts and far from my New York City neighborhoods, I discovered my penchant for writing and reciting poetry. A strange man in a strange land, poetry centered my inner compass and allowed me to cope with my life. Poetry provided an escape hatch to free me from the tightening grips of adolescent flailing, depression I didn't know I had, and a deepening addiction to drugs and alcohol. Poetry nudged with a fuzzy, liminal feeling that I had a purpose for my life, one I worried I would never find. Poetry allowed me to put those fragile feelings and unexplored emotions, first on paper and then spoken out loud into my world. That self-expression—my spoken word—saved me from myself. I didn't know it at the time, but poetry saved my life.

With profound respect for poets and life-saving reverence for the often grueling process of producing poetry, we borrow the title of this book from the venerable Harlem Renaissance poet, Langston Hughes. The moment my co-author, Nick Chiles, suggested the title, *I Too Am America: On Loving and Leading Black Men & Boys,* I knew it perfectly captured the story I wanted to share in this book. This is a story of a Black baby boy born in 1962 in New York City during the Civil Rights Movement who comes of age and grips with the paradox of promise and peril for most Black boys and men in America.

When Langston Hughes penned his prophetic poem in 1926, he portrayed what it meant to be Black in America. "I, Too" profoundly depicts the paradox of promise and peril in just sixty-two words. Sadly, almost a century later, the "tomorrow" he foretells has yet to become "today." Hughes wrote his poem during the Harlem Renaissance, a seminal movement to claim our culture and proclaim our worth in this country. We wrote this book in 2019-2020, during the equally powerful emergent movement for Black lives. In the wake of the murders of George Floyd, Breonna Taylor, and Ahmaud Arbery (among too many others) and amid a global pandemic, this country wrestled with what many have been calling a "racial reckoning in America." Such a declaration is premature for this era of American history as still, I too, sing America.

It is in reverence to Langton Hughes and the many voices, translators, and amplifiers of the Black American experience that we present, *I Too Am America: On Loving and Leading Black Men & Boys*. Though equal parts memoir, historical account of the Campaign for Black Male Achievement (CBMA), and a manifesto for a hopeful path forward, it is offered as a protest against America's continued racism, anti-Blackness, and systemic oppression of Black Americans, with a unique lens on the impact on Black men and boys. Courage, Resilience, and Vision are characters in this book, as are young men like Jamare Winston and Romero Wesson. My story is their story; our stories are yours. These stories of loving, learning, and leading for and by Black men and boys epitomize the work described by Judy Touzin, author of *Exceptional: Black Men Leading, Living, and Loving*, in her mini-manifesto contribution to the book:

> "*We need visionaries who can inspire us to reimagine and believe in what's possible. Finally, we need builders who can help create and sustain the infrastructure needed to guarantee that the Black boys born today inherit a more just world than we did. This is the work. It is big, and it is important.*"

Leading the Campaign for Black Male Achievement and working alongside courageous and committed men and women in the Black male achievement field over the past dozen years has been the highlight of a career devoted to youth development, community-building, and racial justice. When we launched the Campaign in 2008, many experts and well-intending partners warned me that a field for Black male achievement simply did not exist. Fortunately, I was not smart enough not to listen to them and just began to call it such. Be careful what you declare because it just might appear.

The Moment We're In

> "The barriers to success that Black men face have been in plain sight for decades, so it's particularly heartening to see a movement taking shape that is specifically crafted to address these challenges and change the odds of one of the most disenfranchised populations in America."
>
> —Geoffrey Canada

What does it take to help an entire population achieve the long-promised American Dream? What does it take to make that possible while also counteracting systemic obstacles built over generations that work to hold back that same population?

These were two of the overarching questions that fueled the Campaign for Black Male Achievement launch in the Summer of 2008 at the Open Society Foundations (OSF). CBMA began as a three-year campaign in the backdrop of President Barack Obama's historic surge to the democratic nomination for President of the United States of America. Our mission was to ensure the growth, sustainability, and impact of leaders and organizations committed to improving the life outcomes of Black men and boys.

We recognized that eliminating the disparities facing Black men and boys takes strong leaders and organizations, sustained attention and investment, a change in perception of Black men and boys from the typical deficit-based narratives to an asset-based narrative, and a coordinated effort by a cross-section of leaders. But as we have witnessed in the political landscape of late, it will take an honest racial reckoning that reaches beyond the pledges and platitudes we saw in the wake of the horrific public lynching of George Floyd on May 25, 2020.

In order to change the life outcomes of Black men and boys, we must deeply invest in leaders and organizations like Joe Jones, founder of the Center of Urban Families in Baltimore, which is doing ground-breaking work on the west side of Baltimore to accelerate the social and economic upward mobility of Black fathers and their families. We need to invest in leaders like David Banks, founder of Eagle Academy Foundation, a network of seven all-boys public schools in New York City and Newark, NJ. And then there is Anthony Smith, who leads a national organization called Cities United, which is tackling one of the thorniest issues in this country with its commitment to cut in half the homicide rates of Black men and boys by 2025. The list of organizations and leaders is long—more are listed in the appendix—and their stories amplify the loving, learning, and leading desperately needed at this moment we are in as a nation, which I hope will inspire you to learn more about these movement builders and support them.

Over the years, I've created and curated countless "mission mantras" that I share with our network. They serve as necessary self-talk that all leaders and change agents require to weather the many storms and keep on keeping on. One such mission mantra over the past decade is *There is no cavalry coming to save the day in Black communities. We are the iconic leaders that we have been waiting for, curators of the change we're seeking to see.* We hold fast to the vision of an America that sees Black men and boys as assets full of potential with an equal opportunity to obtain the American dream, the opportunity to say, "I, too, am America."

What Had Happened Was...

> "Historically, pandemics have forced humans to break with the past and imagine their world anew. This one is no different. It is a portal, a gateway between one world and the next. We can choose to walk through it, dragging the carcasses of our prejudice and hatred, our avarice, our data banks, and dead ideas, our dead rivers and smoky skies behind us. Or we can walk through lightly, with little luggage, ready to imagine another world. And ready to fight for it."
>
> —Arundhati Roy

It has taken me all 59 years of my life to birth this book. Brene Brown professes that "owning our story and loving ourselves through the process is the bravest thing we will ever do." In many ways, telling my truth, being transparent about my journey, and sharing it with you, has been an act of bravery. My time in therapy over the years has helped me to realize that two things can be true at the same time – in this case, writing and publishing this book has been an example of me being both brave and afraid.

The process of writing and publishing includes a stage of thinking the book is finished over and over again. After my third declaration that "It is finished!" Althea Dryden, a mini-manifesto contributor and a leader with Cities United, asked me if it was finished or if I was just done? What had to happen in the year since I declared my book was done for my book to be finished? The disruption and tumult of 2020 had to happen for sure. Oprah reminds us at the outset of her Super Soul podcasts that the greatest gift we can give ourselves is the gift of time. Time had to happen; both the forward-focused rhythmic ticking of a celestial clock and the sequencing of days, nights, and seasons had to happen.

The wayward wandering through a wilderness that the time travel of memory and manuscript invited me into had to happen, both the meandering of the years gone by and realizing that time does not heal all wounds, healing heals all wounds—and accepting that healing hurts had to happen.

Realizing the book of my life will never be finished and the perpetual unfolding of untold stories will persist even long after I leave this planet had to happen. Wooing, cooing, and seducing the writing and publishing process had to happen too. I am still learning to embrace, love, and "trust the process" of writing, planning, climbing, celebrating, and crying that this process has evoked. I am also learning to love the fear, bravery, and everything else that comes with such an endeavor as this. All of that had to happen.

Ushering in the 2020 New Year in Ghana, my first trip to Africa, had to happen along with a return to the dank, damp dungeons where my ancestors' souls were stolen and amassed for the slave trade. AfricanAncestry.com had to happen and discovering that my ancestral lineage lay forever rooted in the soil of Sierra Leone with the Mende Tribe and their rebellious spirit that transformed the Amistad into a freedom journey somewhere along the Middle Passage.

My near-death sleep experience in January 2020 during a leadership retreat in Belize had to happen. The news from the Campaign's financial consultants that they were premature in declaring we had eliminated an operating deficit of $400K in restricted funds—they had made a mistake, and we were still in the hole. Realizing that deficit seemed like so much more then than it does now, had to happen. Understanding God created this deep cavern for me to let go of one world and to reimagine my world anew—had to happen.

The pandemic had to happen. Painfully, yet purposefully, sunsetting the Campaign for Black Male Achievement in December 2020 had to happen. A virtual Rumble Young Man, Rumble 10, one final gathering in honor of the humanitarian spirit of Muhammad Ali that had served as a catalyst for movement-building, healing, loving, and leading for a decade at the Ali Center in Louisville, Kentucky, had to happen.

An Old Shore had to happen. A New Shore had to happen. Longstanding relationships reframed had to happen. Fully discerning the mountainous terrain that I was called to climb had to happen.

Forgiveness had to happen. Trust had to happen. Fifty-year pent-up tears had to happen. Therapy had to happen. This free-flow writing attempt to shake and submit to the anchors and shackles of writing deadlines had to happen.

Birthing the Corporation for Black Male Achievement had to happen. The "pandemic is a portal" had to happen, as did this portrait of me in mid-portal as a love light in flight had to happen. Dove Soars had to happen.

The *100 Days of Believing Bigger* devotional by Marshawn Evans Daniels had to happen. It had to happen again. And again. And again, and again. Read. Write. Pray. Repeat.

My father's unexpected gift on my 58th birthday had to happen. His own book, *It Ain't Over Until I Say It's Over: Don't Listen To Naysayers* by Bernard Dove first felt like a thunder-stealing offering until it lovingly turned into legacy inspiring mission fuel to complete this book.

George Floyd had to happen. Breonna Taylor had to happen. The pain of writing the last sentence had to happen.

Resurrected poetry had to happen.

Discovering and discerning the Sherpas in front of me with their guiding mountain moonlight had to happen. Learning that even Sherpas need Sherpas had to happen.

Meditating and meandering through "The Labyrinth Within" had to happen—a commitment to an ongoing journey of radical self-discovery and inquiry. Everything had to happen. God wastes nothing, and as the prophet Isaiah reminds us, "This is the way, walk in it." Isaiah 30:21.

Everything had to happen in the year since my book was "done" for me to be genuinely finished and able to offer it to you now. *I Too Am America: On Loving and Leading Black Men & Boys* is more than my memoir and story. Trabian Shorters, founder of BMe Community, a national network of Black leaders from all walks of life committed to amplifying the assets of Black people in America, says, "We lead the lives of the stories we tell about ourselves."

This book was written for Black men and boys and those of us committed to seeing them realize their full potential even in a place where so much is systemically designed for their demise and a life lacking dignity. This is a story to all of you loving, learning, and leading Black men and boys across this country. Our stories of resilience, redemption, and reconciliation have to be told so that Langston Hughes' American poetic prophecy will someday soon come true.

They'll see how beautiful I am and be ashamed—I, too, am America.

Chapter 1: Jamare

"Everybody says that Jamare was brought up right. You know the way he talks, the way he carries himself...You can't convince him to do dumb stuff, 'cause he grew up around it. I've always been proud of that because that takes a lot of courage."

—*Juansha Winston*

Whether he realizes it or not, Jamare Winston holds within his slender, muscular frame the hope of generations. When he walks down the blighted streets of Detroit's Westside neighborhood, just a few blocks from the first Nation of Islam temple where Detroit Red became Minister Malcolm X, he carries the prayers of millions that came before him. He is awash with the whispered dreams of his ancestors when he slides into his aunt's car in the morning's wee hours and leaves Detroit, passing not far from the small Motown building where American popular music was germinated, so they can drive 40 minutes to the public schools of Gibraltar, Michigan, a nearly all-white town that he and his family believe will unlock academic success.

In his bright, toothy grin and earnest, ebullient charisma, Jamare is the bedeviling paradox of the Black boy in America—suffused with boundless talents and promise but surrounded by seemingly unrelenting waves of peril. At 17, Jamare is everything that we want our boys to grow into, and he embodies all the fears that keep us awake at night.

Jamare's plight has been pondered by Black writers and thinkers for most of the past century.

"I, too, sing America," Langston Hughes started his 1926 poem "I, Too."

"I am the darker brother/ They send me to eat in the kitchen When company comes, But I laugh And eat well, And grow strong/ Tomorrow, I'll be at the table When company comes/ Nobody'll dare Say to me, 'Eat in the kitchen,' Then/ Besides, They'll see how beautiful I am And be ashamed/ I, too, am America."

"When a Negro child is fourteen, he knows the score already," James Baldwin said in 1961. "There is nothing you can do. And all you can do about it is try...is pray really that this will not destroy him. But the tension this creates within the best of the Negro men is absolutely unimaginable, and something this country refuses to imagine, and very, very dangerous."

Malcolm X wrote in his 1965 autobiography, "America's most dangerous and threatening Black man is the one who has been kept sealed up by the Northerner in the Black ghettoes—the Northern white power structure's system to keep talking democracy while keeping the Black man out of sight somewhere, around the corner."

Those who know him well say Jamare has always been different, always his own man, able to resist the aggressions of peer pressure and the sinister entreaties of the streets.

"Everybody says that Jamare was brought up right. You know the way he talks, the way he carries himself," says his father, Juansha Winston, 44, with whom Jamare has lived for most of his teen years. "That was all through trials of his own that he learned to overcome and realize what type of person he wanted to be. Especially growing up in this kind of environment. You see a child his age getting high doing everything that they shouldn't be doing. And he's always been straightforward. You can't convince him to do dumb stuff, 'cause he grew up around it. I've always been proud of that because that takes a lot of courage."

But still, he is far from assured of a safe passage out of adolescence. He is trying to figure out how to navigate one of the most complicated periods in a Black boy's life—and to do it in Detroit, a city that has long been considered one of the most dangerous places in America. It held the top spot during several recent years in the FBI rankings of the cities with the most violent crime. Although Detroit was overtaken by St. Louis in 2017, dropping to number two, its violent crime rate actually increased between 2016 and 2017.

Every report on the state of Black boys in America uses a long list of depressing statistics to make the case for peril. But the numbers, while mind-numbing evidence of problems, mask the everyday challenges and triumphs that boys like Jamare log, typically with no recognition. Black males in America are so much more than statistics. But until we do a much better job of telling their individual stories, the crushing narrative that swirls around them won't budge even an inch.

The Campaign for Black Male Achievement was created to change this paradigm, to affix a spotlight on both the challenges and the successes of Black males—to create many more pathways for them to negotiate around and through the peril. But it's an overwhelmingly daunting mission. When you shoulder the task of reversing 400 years of intentional destruction, you will have many sleepless nights and crises of aching self-doubt. However, we've never had any choice but to keep moving forward. There are millions waiting for the fruits of our exertions; millions more who will come behind those.

We study Jamare to get a keen idea of the mission we face. Jamare was chosen for this reflective revealing because of his promise, not because of the peril. And please don't assume the peril is just a synonym for poverty. One of the most alarming aspects of the struggle testing Black boys in America is how thoroughly it cuts across socioeconomic lines. A long-accepted maxim among educators is the strong correlation between family income and academic success. Wealthier kids do better than poor kids. But that probability should be tossed aside when examining Black males. It doesn't apply. Black parents from every region of the country, from every socioeconomic class—the richest to the poorest—are deeply concerned about the problems their boys are exhibiting. In fact, *concerned* may be too mild. They are *terrified*. And their terror was amplified in March 2018 when researchers from Harvard, Stanford, and the Census Bureau, led by Harvard's Raj Chetty, released a study revealing that the income inequality between Blacks and whites was entirely because Black boys are likely to end up in poverty as adults—no matter what kind of family they were raised in.

"White boys who grow up rich are likely to remain that way. Black boys raised at the top, however, are more likely to become poor than to stay wealthy in their own adult households," said a report in the *New York Times* summarizing the study. "Even when children grow up next to each other with parents who earn similar incomes, Black boys fare worse than white boys in 99 percent of America. And the gaps only worsen in the kind of neighborhoods that promise low poverty and good schools...Though Black girls and women face deep inequality on many measures, Black and white girls from families with comparable earnings attain similar individual incomes as adults."

These kinds of statistics hover like a storm cloud over the heads of boys like Jamare. Bursting with talent and potential, Jamare knows there are no guarantees that things will work out for him. He needs only to glance around him to see that even when Black males don't succumb to the streets, their lives are often still difficult, the failures coming at a rapid pace, the next day never promised. He is surrounded by cousins, uncles, friends who have shown him the many hazards that might pop up in his path. While he has lived mostly with his dad over the last few years, Jamare has also stayed with his mother, his grandmother, a friend, and an aunt. He counts eight different homes; he has seen his share of instability.

His mother, Tamisha, was only 15 when he was born, just 14 when she got pregnant—by a man almost nine years her senior. But Tamisha says her pregnancy didn't cause dissension in her family.

"When I was born, my mom was 16 and my dad was 27," she explains. Her situation had already been normalized.

Both Tamisha and Juansha have faced job layoffs, poverty, alcoholism (mom and dad), drug abuse (mom), and relationship drama over the years, each episode affecting Jamare and his two younger siblings in different ways.

"Seeing is believing. So, if you see people struggling with drugs and addiction and bad mistakes, you pick up on that," says his father, who has battled alcoholism for more than a decade. "Jamare is tough, he's got a good heart, and he's real forgiving. So, as he got older, he started to understand the stuff we go through."

Juansha, born in 1978, was thrust into the crucible of Detroit's mean streets as soon as he emerged from the womb—his father was a drug dealer who was killed before Juansha was even born. With his grandfather providing a strong, guiding hand, Juansha made it through high school. But by the time he was 25, just after Jamare was born, Juansha says he had embraced a lifestyle he now calls "wild." Running the streets, drinking, making lots of bad choices.

Jamare says the early years with his mother weren't easy. She was young and stressed and she often took out her frustrations on her children. He says he sometimes would get a beating merely for asking where they were going—though Tamisha says Jamare only got occasional "whuppings." As he got older, he found that he had a rage inside of him that he didn't really understand. The engaging smile he is quick to offer can sometimes be a shield, hiding what lies beneath.

"I get mad really fast, and a lot of stuff honestly irritates me," he says.

When Jamare was in middle school, he and his mother got into an actual fistfight that resulted in Tamisha getting charged with assault and battery—which led to her losing her license as a certified nursing aide.

"It was over something stupid," Tamisha recalls. "They went on a field trip, and I was picking him up. He kept talking back. Then he swung on me in the car. I said, 'If you wanna fight, then let's fight.' So, he swung open the door and jumped out. I got out and we went at it. It wasn't our first altercation."

After the fistfight, Jamare went to live with his dad. He was fortunate that he had Juansha greeting him with open arms; most Black boys don't have that option when adolescence brings conflict with Mom.

Jamare says on two occasions, once in eighth grade and once in ninth grade, he punched a wall with such force that he broke his hand. He has also used his fists to punch other boys. The anger outbursts have gotten him in trouble in school. Usually, he can control it. But sometimes he can't.

It's not hard to understand why a Black boy growing up on the West side of Detroit might be angry; why he might wake up some mornings and question why his life must be so hard, why the world cares so little about him and his future. The crumbling structures and desolate lots that surround the house where Jamare has lived with his father clearly send a message—you don't matter.

Juansha says by the time you reach Jamare's age of 17, and certainly, when you get to Juansha's age of 43, you can't help but feel grateful to be alive.

"Most of my friends are dead," Juansha says with a sigh as he sits at his dining room table next to a stack of mail.

Does that make him worry more about his son, as well as his daughter, Rain, 14, and his younger son, Alex, nine?

"I worry all the time," he says. "Like I said, it's good that Jamare is not like, 'Oh, I want to go party at somebody's house.' Because that stuff turn sideways real quick. So, I'm lucky my boy ain't in the streets. But bullets don't have no name. You could be standing at a bus stop—you know what I'm saying?"

One of the men who had a huge influence on Juansha was his older brother—a solid guy who had successfully navigated a path to middle-class stability after the challenges of their early life. The brother operated a forklift for years, watching over his family and being a good father to his six daughters. But three years ago, when he was 45, the streets came back to get him.

"He had a nice truck. Somebody thought he was a drug dealer or whatnot. They jacked him, shot him twice in the head," Juansha says, shaking his head. "He was a successful Black man, and somebody tried to take advantage. This is my life—every time I look up, somebody dies."

Jamare's middle name is Gerald, named after one of Juansha's closest friends, who was killed right before Jamare was born—shot five times with an AK. In the wrong place at the wrong time. But Juansha wasn't done. He listed several other friends, grown men around his age, who were victims of random violence. One was killed when the shooter was aiming for someone else and hit Juansha's friend twice in the back. Another was killed when he let somebody he knew into his house—and when he turned his back, the man, intent on robbery, shot him in the back and in the head, then went upstairs and killed his girlfriend.

In the late 1990s, researchers found a strong correlation between the number of adverse childhood experiences (ACEs) a person had undergone and the likelihood that as adults they would participate in risky behavior, have significant health challenges, and contract disease. The researchers, who studied more than 13,000 adults in California, asked respondents a series of questions about their childhoods: whether they had been psychologically, physically, or sexually abused by a parent or other adult in the household; whether they ever lived with anyone who abused alcohol or used illegal drugs; if anyone in their household had a mental illness or attempted suicide; was their mother treated violently; whether a family member went to prison.

The more childhood exposures a person had, the more likely they were as an adult to be dealing with alcoholism, drug abuse, depression, smoking, having more than 50 sexual partners, sexually transmitted diseases, suffering from severe obesity and diseases such as cancer, heart disease, and liver disease. In other words, they were more likely to be facing premature death.

When I look at the list of adverse childhood experiences, I am saddened by how common so many of them are in the Black community. Painfully, too many of our children are a walking ACEs checklist. For young men like Jamare, the challenge is to face down the ACEs list and somehow live a life that robs ACEs of its predictive value. In many neighborhoods in Detroit, that challenge can seem almost insurmountable.

Detroit is a city of incredible history but one whose visage can bring tears to your eyes. So much blight, so much dilapidation, vast stretches of vacant plots, dotted with collapsing houses, the grandness of their former glory just barely detectable in their ghostly frames. But always in Detroit, there are signs of hope, bright flowers bursting through the weeds and cracks in the cement. Black people coming together to push back against collapse, to remake and reawaken the city. This is one of the places that birthed the Black middle class in America—yet it feels like a city the middle class deserted long ago, left it to rot. In 2013, the city filed for bankruptcy, the largest city in the country ever to do so. There is evident trauma flowing through its streets like a raging river. But everybody isn't gone. And everybody hasn't given up. There is still pride here, innovation, folks working themselves to exhaustion to bring about elusive change and rejuvenation.

"There are issues in the city, but there's so many, so many more people involved in bringing about solutions," says educator and longtime Detroit native Quan Neloms. "I grew up not even knowing that Detroit was the blackest city in America. I thought all cities were like this. So, it wasn't till I left the city to visit other places where I'm like, *oh, where are all the Black people*"?

"Growing up, I was in a city that had a Black mayor, Black city council, Black school board, Black superintendent of that school board. I was seeing Black excellence all around me. So, it wasn't out of the realm of possibility that I could become a mayor, or I could become a principal, or I could become a superintendent. I saw it every year of my life growing up here. That's why I think you have so many solution-oriented people, cause it's not out of the realm of possibility to say, 'Yo, we can help ourselves.'"

Even after everything he's seen, Juansha believes that conditions in his city are improving. He says the local community center has managed to stay open and clean, transformed by local residents. Many of the old, collapsing houses are being torn down, removing a significant threat—over the years, he says many people would be pulled into vacant buildings to be raped or even killed. A 2014 study found that 50,000 of the city's then 261,000 structures were abandoned.

"You don't want those old buildings near your house where you're trying to raise a family," he says.

Juansha gazes out the window. "It ain't going to happen overnight. But it's going to be better for them when they grown, as opposed to how it was for us. It's a lot quieter over here now than it used to be. You used to hear gunshots every day. But it's been better for at least a couple of years now."

Jamare is trying to figure out how to bank on his evident talents. Does American society have any use for an energetic, bright, creative, charismatic, young Black male with clear leadership abilities? He's the kind of kid whose path to prosperity would be all but guaranteed in other communities. As he thinks about his future, Jamare has latched onto some form of counseling work as a path, perhaps psychology. But the idea of all those years in school gives him pause. School has not always been his favorite place. While he has fond memories of his four years at Frederick Douglass Academy, his time in elementary and middle school was much more unpleasant.

When Jamare runs through the narrative of all the problems he's had in school, it sounds like a microcosmic case study of the educational challenges of Black boys in America. The first few years were fine. But when he got to fourth grade, the trouble started. This is a common tale in America's public schools— Black boys in fourth grade transforming from cute and cuddly to the teacher's enemy. Jamare says much of it was his own doing.

"The bad kids got a lot of attention, and I kind of felt left out," Jamare remembers. "Doing good jobs, finishing my work on time, not getting in trouble, I wasn't getting recognized enough."

Even bad recognition was better than no recognition. He had a hard time sitting quietly and doing his work. And then there were his friends.

"People I hung out with, that kind of determined who I was, 'cause I would follow them," he says.

He pauses, then delves deeper into self-analysis. "I figured since I didn't know myself, I thought that like maybe I could be like them. Follow after somebody else. The older I got, I kind of like hit a place where I wasn't doing so good. From being a good child as a baby to like lying and being suspended from school. I felt like that transition really changed my life a lot."

By the time he moved to middle school, Jamare was performing so poorly that he had to repeat seventh grade. His family signed him up for football, thinking that might give him an outlet for his aggression. But eventually, he lost interest. Things began to look up for Jamare when he followed several of his uncles and cousins and enrolled at a progressive all-boys school in Detroit called Frederick Douglass Academy for Young Men (FDA), which goes from sixth to 12th grade. The only all-boys public school in the state of Michigan—which became possible only after the state legislature passed a law in 2006. FDA officials recognized the precarious plight of Black boys in school and endeavored to change the dynamic. For the first time, Jamare encountered Black male teachers who seemed to understand him, teachers who cared about him. Jamare started liking school; he started doing much better.

Quan Neloms, who was a teacher at FDA when Jamare arrived there, explains how a Black male teacher can make a difference to boys like Jamare. Neloms says he was able to recognize situations when students like Jamare are releasing pent-up anger and frustration. He believes perhaps it's easier for a Black man to really see and understand someone like Jamare.

"I think that to know his background, to know who he is as a person, that's important to know. As a man, being able to relate to him is important," Neloms says. "Jamare gravitates toward men. When I look at his family, I see a lot of men. Some of the men may not make the greatest decisions, but Jamare has the uncanny ability to pull out the positive aspects of people. I think that, in turn, we owe it to him to do the same. So, when he has those outbursts, instead of reacting right away, it's better to talk to him, to be able to pull out the positivity in him, just like he does. If he's able to do it, I think we have to ask the adults in his life to reciprocate that."

FDA was stocked with adults that Jamare felt close to, but the school still strains to pull the young men up to proficiency on measures such as state standardized tests. It also has struggled of late to attract students. Its enrollment at the close of the 2018 school year was just 88 students—with seven students enrolled in sixth grade, 10 students in seventh grade, and four students in eighth grade.

Jamare decided he needed a change of scenery. That's how, in September of 2019, he found himself at Carlson High School in Gibraltar, Michigan. Jamare's aunt hits I-75 every morning and drives 20 miles to Gibraltar to drop off her 13-year-old son at Shumate Middle School and 17-year-old Jamare at the adjacent Carlson High School.

Gibraltar is a fairly tiny, non-descript town of modest split-level homes and green lawns, sprawling easily near the shores of the Detroit River and Lake Erie. It is a place that can provide a comfortable existence to the several thousand families connected to the nearby Flat Rock Ford Assembly Plant, which currently makes Mustangs and Lincoln Continentals.

Gibraltar is one of those places where political reporters go to get the pulse of the Midwest—and to ask why they support Donald Trump. Trump won Michigan in 2016 by just 11,612 votes; Trump won Gibraltar handily, receiving 1,443 votes to Clinton's 916. (Those numbers flipped in 2020 with Biden winning the state by 154,188, thanks largely to vibrant organizing and turnout by Black voters in Detroit.) Gibraltar is far enough away from Detroit its denizens can root for the local sports teams without interacting with the blight and Black people. This is where Jamare has come to find his salvation.

Jamare's is a quintessential Black American story—Black students and their parents trying to navigate the minefields, looking for solace and safety outside of the city. A place where perhaps they can concentrate on school without distractions, away from random violence and the hazards of streets that devour children—especially boys. A place where perhaps children can forge paths that work for Black families who can no longer count on the Midwest manufacturing plants that used to provide a solid middle-class life. Now it's all about education. With knots in our stomachs, we try schools like Carlson High School—just six percent Black and five percent Hispanic. Painfully, Tamisha says, Jamare was specifically looking to transfer to a "white" school. We pray that things will work out, that the struggles of racial isolation won't prove insurmountable.

Jamare's dad is a potent illustration of what happens when manufacturing is severed from the American success story. After every layoff from an auto plant—first, he built car seats, then he built rear bumpers for GMC trucks—he struggled, he drank, he worried how he was going to keep the lights on and keep his son safe. So mainly Jamare stayed indoors. Sometimes Jamare didn't have enough food to stop the growling in his belly or adequate light to do his homework. His father had to find anything that would work. He washed dishes at a local restaurant, but it wasn't enough. Now he's trying construction.

"Plants close, contracts get moved," Juansha says, shrugging. "It's cheaper for the work to go to Mexico. So, you understand that you can't blame somebody else for something Big Brother is doing. All you can do is go look for another job."

Juansha and Jamare have formed a steely bond over the years. Jamare appreciates that though things have been hard for his father, Juansha never gave up. Not when he had to contend with relationship drama with Jamare's mom. Not when he got pulled into the criminal justice system for failing a pee test after receiving a summons for driving without a license. Now that Jamare is staying with his aunt most of the time, to make the morning commute easier, Juansha admits that he sometimes gets lonely.

"You come home, and you're used to doing stuff, saying, what are we going to eat? What movie we about to watch? So, the first week it was like, this sucks! My right hand is literally gone. And then with this job, I can't be on the phone as much, so I can't text him. And the new school is way more advanced than the previous school, so he don't have time to text. I look up after working 12 or 14 hours and I just get a 'good morning' and a 'good night' from him."

Does that make him sad?

"Nah. We got holidays. We got weekends. It's not like I'm off somewhere goofing off and he off somewhere goofing off. We're both trying to get somewhere. We both understand what's going on. That school will help him hopefully get into a better college, be prepared better."

Carlson High School sits on a sprawling campus, a vast network of gleaming hallways and bright white faces. Jamare seems at once overwhelmed, excited, and nonchalant about his new school. He is eager to serve as a tour guide, proudly showing off the two gyms, the swimming pool—FDA had a pool, but they couldn't use it because of problems with the pipes—and the trophy case, displaying recent championships in tennis, golf, and competitive cheer. Jamare had never heard of competitive cheer. He has moved from a school in Detroit constructed to deal with the challenges of convincing Black males that they should care about school—to now sitting inside a school constructed to ensure white success. When Black students attend these schools, there is often some kind of trade-off, either cultural or emotional. Jamare initially found the students a bit more standoffish than he expected, more reluctant to make friends. He doesn't seem inclined to assign their standoffishness to anything as dramatic as racial animosity. Besides, Jamare says he has gotten somewhat accustomed to being around white people because his last two girlfriends have been white.

Jamare says his grades at Douglass were less than impressive, but paradoxically he says that's because the classes weren't challenging enough.

"I was a B, C student at Douglass. I could have had all A's, but I didn't apply myself because I felt like it was boring," he says. "I felt like if I could do it with ease or if it was simple to me then why would I give it my all. I don't know..."

While at Douglass, Jamare came across a fascinating program called Lyricist Society. Founded by educator Quan Neloms, Lyricist Society uses music and hip hop as a tool to connect with and inspire young people. It is here that Jamare found a home for his creative talents, a program that would allow him to start seeing the world outside of Detroit and, in founder Neloms, a mentor who devoted himself to molding the young teenager.

There is no doubt—finding Neloms and Lyricist Society changed the course of Jamare's life.

Chapter 2: Romero

"Every day there's hope. There's a reason why we still wake up. There's hope for the next generation. I believe that."

—*Romero Wesson*

Romero Wesson stands at the front of the small church wearing an easy smile. He is in front of the pulpit, not in it, as if he has decided that a 16-year-old isn't quite pulpit-ready. The loud ovation of the 25 people scattered in the red cloth chairs, lined up like pews, seems to give him a surge of energy. He is here to deliver a message to the congregation on this Sunday afternoon. The church is stuffy, moist, belying the chill in the air outside that is common to Oakland at the end of summer. The ceiling fans and the rotating fan plugged into the wall at the back of the church aren't enough to break through the heat. Some women are fanning themselves as they prepare to be moved by this young man's pastoral gifts.

"I had a good day today," he begins, a smile brightening his handsome face. "I got a reason to bless Him."

The women respond to this familiar ministerial overture with shouts.

"I woke up this morning in my right mind," he says, his voice rising. "I woke up with strength in my body."

In his crisp, blue suit, dark bow tie, and white patterned shirt, Romero looks like he belongs at the front of a congregation. When the rousing gospel anthem "Breakthrough" by Jermia Cannon starts to blast through the church speakers, Romero curiously begins acting out the words of the song in a creative combination of praise dancing and pantomime. To an outsider, it is an odd sight, almost comical, as if he is going for a laugh. But that clearly is not how it's being received by the congregation. They have seen this before. The women cheer vigorously, their appreciation seemingly adding more energy to his intriguing movements. This is Romero's happy place, his safe place.

But Romero is a 16-year-old Black male in Oakland, California. Once he walks out the wide doors of the church building, Higher Ground Pentecostal Assembly, he doesn't often come upon feelings of safety. He is a young man of uncommon gifts, able to influence and inspire his peers with the power of his words and his example. But sometimes, he's not sure whether that's enough to successfully navigate the minefields scattered in his path.

Like Jamare's Detroit, Oakland is one of those American cities that has become a national symbol of the dwindling opportunities for Black people. But more than that, it is a city that holds a mythical place in the Black American consciousness. This is the headquarters of the Black Power movement, the birthplace of the Black Panther Party, the spiritual home of Black progressive thought over the last half-century. But one out of every four Black residents of Oakland lives below the federal poverty level. Subsisting amidst this totemic Black history has not insulated the residents of Oakland's Black community from the traumas that seem such an endemic part of being Black and poor in America.

Sitting in the crosshairs of that trauma is Romero Wesson. Like Jamare in Detroit, Romero is another vibrant example of that hazardous state in which so many young Black men find themselves—full of promise but feeling relentless peril. Perhaps it's no surprise, given the nation's history of exploiting and abusing Black bodies, that the path for young men like Romero would be filled with land mines. Nothing is ever easy. Now that high school is over for him, he is trying to figure out adulthood without life exploding in his face.

As I travel the country in my role as a leader in the Black male achievement movement and get an opportunity to spend time with young men like Romero, I'm inspired by their perseverance and optimism. Their hope. It is the same resiliency that has rumbled in the souls of Black folks for generations, pushing us forward over a path that always has been perilous. Peril seems as if it has been spliced into the Black genome by the persistent generational injustices of systemic racism. But we have no choice but to persevere. That also seems part of our DNA. Sometimes we even prosper. I, too, am America.

Romero has grown up in an environment where life is devalued. Especially Black male life. His brother was murdered when Romero was five. Two bullets to the back of the head. Violence is commonplace. Deadly violence is not unfamiliar. Just this summer, one of his friends from the church was gunned down.

Romero has three younger brothers, all struggling to stay on the path Romero is trying to walk in front of them. He worries about his brothers a lot. They're a big reason why he chose to stay in his mother's house after he graduated from high school instead of attending college somewhere that would allow him to get far away from Oakland. Like Romero, they too have been troubled by the lack of a consistent father in their lives. Still, when I ask Romero if he ever feels like Black boys are doomed, he shakes his head vigorously, almost offended.

"No!" he says. "I'm glad to say that. No! Because there's still hope. Every day there's hope. There's a reason why we still wake up. There's hope for the next generation. I believe that."

What Romero says next could have been lifted from a Campaign for Black Male Achievement (CBMA) brochure.

"I don't have my dad, but I have five male figures in my life that kind of... not *replace* my dad, but kind of stand in the gap for my dad," he says.

"I might not have my dad," he continues, "but I still have other men—successful Black men, intelligent Black men—that can teach me how to become a Black man. And teach others."

As in Black communities across America, as in Detroit, families in Oakland are perpetually doing battle against familiar foes— concentrated poverty, police brutality, community violence, and poor health care. It's been a common refrain in urban America for generations. As long as Black men continue to run into dead ends and cold indifference when they try the more acceptable routes to prosperity, the fast money and excitement of the streets will keep reeling them in.

That's what happened to Romero's oldest brother, James. He was a smart, talented kid, going to high school, getting good grades. But as he got older, his mother, Renita Wesson, saw his attention begin to move away from school, away from his family. It was like watching a train wreck happen in slow motion. He got involved with a woman who was several years older—a woman who was spending time with shady characters herself, according to Renita, who could feel her son slipping away from her.

She knew she had lost him when she was driving down the street one day near their home at the time, in North Oakland, and she witnessed her own son robbing someone on the sidewalk. She couldn't believe what her eyes were telling her.

"I'm minding my own business, and I look over and see my son with his friends. Then I see my son hit somebody upside the head," she says, her large, brown eyes widening at the memory. "I stop the car. I'm like, *Give that back!*"

By the time James was 16, Renita—who was only 16 when James was born—had already had three more boys and was pregnant with her fifth. She was becoming a reluctant expert on the travails of Black boy life in America. As

James started to descend further into street life, Renita was trying to be an effective mom for the young boys who still clung to her—Eric, Romero, and SirVante. Renita by then had left behind her own hard-partying lifestyle and had given herself to the Lord, finding much-needed solace and support in the comforting embrace of the church—a place where she had spent considerable time with her family when she was growing up. Church was an ecosystem she knew well. Curiously, though James was not keen on joining her there, he did at times reach out to her for spiritual covering.

"Sometimes, when he didn't want to come home, he would call me on the phone. Or he would come and talk to me before he was about to go out. And he'd want prayer," Renita says. Her voice drops as if she's still stunned by his request.

"That blessed me. Because I remember being on the street selling dope myself," Renita says. "When I was coming home, or when I was out there doing something, I would pray. I'd be thankful to God that nothing has happened to me, that He has kept me safe. He got me through it. So, it just inspired me that James was doing the same thing."

He was bouncing between Renita's house, Renita's mother's house, and also the home of his girlfriend, who now was pregnant at the same time as Renita. His mom saw him intermittently, mainly when he needed some type of rest from the street hustling. Not only was he selling drugs, he also was taking them. By now, James' father—who had been 17 when James was born—was himself in jail, another Black male who had fallen prey to the streets. There were few people in the family or around Renita who could reach out and pull James back in.

On the morning of May 20, 2006, Renita got the call that haunts the psyche of every parent. It came from her mother, who told her that James had been shot. By the time Renita got to the hospital, her first-born son was gone. James, who was listed in the hospital registry as "John Doe" after his crew had dropped him off the night before and then split, was already brain-dead, shot in the back of the head at close range. It had been a drive-by, the bullets coming from the gun of another young Black male with whom James and his crew had been engaged in some sort of beef. James was sitting in the backseat. His seatmate got a bullet in the arm.

No one was ever arrested for the shooting. But a year or so later, word on the street filtered back to Renita—the shooter likely was a young man who had been close to James when they were little boys. So close that Renita used to braid and twist his hair. It was yet another reminder of the destructive code that swirled around these boys, which placed the importance of respect and mis-placed male pride above the value of a former friend's life.

The decorative urn containing James' ashes sits prominently in the fami-ly's living room, a constant reminder to Renita to stay vigilant, to keep her boys as close to her as possible. James' death undoubtedly had a deep effect on the lives of his younger brothers, even if they weren't aware of it at the time. Renita was reluctant to let them go outside—especially when the family moved to the infamous Hillside Street, a neighborhood ruled by a Mexican gang known as the Hillside Boys, who announced their affiliation with prominent "Hillside Boys" tattoos on their necks. Renita put up a basketball hoop in front of the modest one-story house they rented, envisioning their home as the draw for other kids in the neighborhood.

"If they all come here, my kids won't have to wander the streets," she told herself. "And I can monitor them." It was an instinct most any parent could understand—especially one who already has lost a child.

She says she didn't allow cussing or any disrespectful behavior at their little neighborhood hangout. She began to see this as part of her mission and her life's calling—a guardian angel of Black boys.

"There's a lot of broken men out here. Broken women, too. I wanted a daughter at some point, but instead, I got six boys. I believe God blessed me with boys for me to heal the next generation of boys. That's really my assignment.

"You have to be your brother's keeper, the babysitter, your sister's keeper... If it takes a village, you have to be the village keeper. *Somebody* has to monitor our children."

Renita shakes her head. "We can't afford to be selfish."

Many Black boys start out in church, carted there every week by devout mothers, committed grandmothers, dedicated aunts. By the time they hit ado-lescence, most of them are gone, drawn to the worldly pleasures they see danc-ing before their eyes outside the church doors.

But Romero never left.

Even when he was a baby, Renita could tell Romero was going to be dif-ferent. Before the baby was two, he had already started preaching.

"He would be on the floor just praying. *Hallelujah, hallelujah, hallelujah,*" Renita recalls. "He would take the extension cord and go out on the porch and be out there, just preaching. It got to the point where people in our house who smoked weed—we stayed with my mom at the time—they would be, like, convicted. Even now, they tell him, 'I remember when you would be on the porch preaching.' So, it was just something different about him all along."

In fact, Romero sent his mother running back to the church before he was even born. She was sitting in the backseat while her uncle was driving the family back from Las Vegas. The uncle and her cousin had been up all night drinking and snorting cocaine. Renita was chugging Hennessy while watching with alarm as the speedometer went higher and higher. Even though she was in a daze—she had also been smoking weed—she started praying.

"Lord, just let me survive. Just let me walk away."

The speedometer hit 110, 115. Her aunt started fussing at the uncle, telling him he was going too fast.

"I'm not going to hurt my niece," he said angrily.

Renita heard a really loud bump like the car hit something. She doesn't remember the point of impact, but there was pandemonium in the car.

"I got out immediately. The car was bent up like tissue paper. I helped everybody else out. My cousin, who was sitting next to me, had a broken ankle and broken nose. He was choking on his own blood. I was the only one who wasn't hurt."

Her doctor told her the baby inside of her was fine. She couldn't sprint to church fast enough. He had saved her and her baby. She wanted to render thanks with her abiding devotion.

"I remember saying, 'God, whatever it is, I'm going to love it.' Because I know what I had done to my body. The drinking. The smoking weed. The accident. The recklessness. I knew the state that I was in. That was my turning point."

One of the church elders lay hands on her belly, fervently and loudly praying in front of the congregation.

"She literally said that I was not going to want for anything for this child. She said that God gave me this child to turn *my* life around. Those were her literal words. And so, when he came out, that's what it was."

Romero learned to love the church and cherish the Lord, but he still had to negotiate life on Hillside. Gunshots regularly rang out when dark came. It was a tough, unforgiving place, particularly during his elementary and middle school years. He says things began to calm down a bit in the last few years. Romero had to figure out how to balance his Christian teachings with the code of the streets around him, which said that he must never back down from a confrontation. Never show even a glimmer of weakness.

In third grade, Romero became the target of a bully, a larger boy he felt was picking on him because he was small. One day, Romero reached his breaking point. He looked the boy in the eye and delivered a message.

"I'm going to kill you," he hissed.

When he got home that afternoon, he found the biggest knife in the kitchen and stashed it securely in his backpack. He placed the backpack at the foot of his bed so nobody in the crowded household would mess with it. With a mother and a pack of little boys roaming the house, you couldn't be too careful. Romero dressed for school before he got into bed, then he woke up two hours early and quickly got ready for school, leaving the house before anyone could notice he was gone. He arrived at school an hour early. The school doors were still locked. So, Romero just waited.

Romero showed the knife to his best friend and told him about his plan to commit murder. He clearly was not thinking about consequences. He was just thinking about taking out his enemy. His friend went and informed the bully that Romero would soon be killing him.

"I *thought* he was my friend," Romero says with a smirk.

The bully bolted to the main office to inform the authorities that his bullying soul was in danger. Romero found out that they would soon be coming for him, so he went into the bathroom to try to hide the knife. But he got busted.

"I realize my friend did me a favor, and I thank God for that. Because I was focused."

When Romero moved on to Frick Middle School, he ran into problems with one of the kids in the neighborhood during his eighth-grade year. Romero was with his cousin, who started talking trash to the neighborhood kid. Romero laughed because he found the trash-talking funny. But the next day, his cousin wasn't with him. The kid, who was with his crew, ran up behind Romero and pulled him down. They started punching and kicking him as he tried to protect himself. There were too many of them for him to fight back.

Romero limped home, vowing to exact revenge. That night, he prayed for strength, asking God for assistance. He went the entire day at school, avoiding his friends so that he could stay mad. He didn't want anyone lightening his mood.

"I wanted enough anger in me to really whup him."

After school, he moved around the neighborhood with the stealth of a ninja as he sought out his target. He spotted the kid by himself this time. Romero ran up on him and threw him to the ground. While he punched him, Romero told him that he would need a whole gang if he was going to beat Romero Wesson.

"People look at me and think, *Oh, he's so skinny*," Romero says.

To ensure that looks would be deceiving, Romero studied martial arts when he got to high school—karate and a bit of capoeira. He really liked the way it made him feel, the confidence. He was not to be messed with now.

"People feel like because I'm a preacher or a community leader that I'm soft, or I'm a punk. And I was insecure about being skinny. But I mean, don't test me. I got skills. But I don't want to use them. Cause I know what I can do to you."

Even a boy who has spent his entire life inside the warm folds of the church family still has to present a hard, prickly, outer shell to the world to ward off threats like a swaggering porcupine. It's a daily reality for almost every young Black male in cities across America. Can't look soft.

Hillside Street is lined with compact and brightly colored one-story stucco and aluminum siding homes typical of East Oakland. Several blocks over, parallel to Hillside, sits International Boulevard, also known as 14th Street, based on the city's grid-like design. Where International intersects with the avenues in the 80s—80th Avenue to 89th Avenue—is known to many locals as the "Shady 80s." It doesn't take long to understand why. The stretch is overwhelmed with visible markers of urban distress. Unsightly spreads of discarded trash scattered in every direction, as if a fleet of garbage trucks exploded on the scene. Middle-aged and elderly drug addicts staggering about, many laying out on the concrete sidewalk or sitting along fences staring blankly at passing cars. Heroin and crack tend to be their drugs of choice. And a profusion of tents and cardboard coverings crowding the sidewalks, the makeshift homes for a staggeringly large homeless population—about as visceral an emblem as you might find of the Bay Area's exorbitant housing prices. Between 2015 and 2017, Oakland's homeless population increased an astounding 47 percent, according to published reports. The average monthly apartment rental in Oakland in 2019 was

$2,674. Though African Americans make up just 11 percent of the Alameda County population, they are 47 percent of the homeless in the county that includes Oakland.

Along with homelessness, Oakland is grappling with violent crime. Oakland was ranked as the 12th most dangerous city in the nation in 2019, according to FBI statistics. As recently as 2014, Oakland was ranked second, right behind Detroit. Oakland finished 2019 with 78 murders, 10 more than in 2018.

Romero says the visually painful sights along International Boulevard broadcast quite clearly to him that the power structure in his city doesn't care about neighborhoods like his.

"I have to see this every day," he says, shaking his head as he watches an elderly Black woman nearly wander out in front of oncoming traffic.

This is a vital point that shouldn't be underestimated. When Black boys across America look at the conditions of their neighborhoods, their schools, their parks, their surroundings, what other conclusion are they supposed to reach than that their country couldn't care less what happens to them? How far is it from that conclusion to the calculation so many boys make that it doesn't matter how or what they do in school—all they have waiting for them is a short, violent life on unforgiving streets?

Andre Daniels knows that Romero's connection to the church isn't a promise that he will avoid the pitfalls pulling down so many Black males around him—what I've come to call "ghetto gravity." Daniels was also a church boy when he was a teenager, reveling in the warmth and support of this environment introduced to him by his grandparents—his parents at the time were both drug addicts. But after his grandparents died, Daniels, at age 18, turned away from the church, lured by the decidedly unholy enticements he saw his older brother and cousins engaged in. His foundation was gone, replaced by the thrill of fast money. It didn't take long for it to catch up to him. He participated in a fight that turned into a robbery. Somebody got pistol-whipped and was seriously injured. Daniels took a plea and spent the next five years in jail.

Daniels, now 31, has seen the church-to street-to prison pipeline from every twist and turn of the pipe. After he got out of prison eight years ago, he went back to the church—and he hasn't strayed since. Now he's a church elder, a college graduate, a father to seven kids, and an administrator in a church-based program called Men of Valor, started by Bishop Bob Jackson, senior pastor of the Acts Full Gospel Church of God in Christ. Men of Valor works with formerly incarcerated men to help them re-adjust to life outside.

Men of Valor is another strand in the safety net that the African American community is forced to weave for Black men. It often becomes like hospital triage—take on the worst cases, knowing that many will plunge through the cracks and crevices that go uncovered. These programs exist in cities and towns all over America. Some might have found a way to obtain government funding; a few are fortunate enough to have the consistent backing of private foundations and nonprofits; most are held together with masking tape, elbow grease, and lots of prayers. It is into this breach that CBMA has stepped over the years, trying to serve as a vital lifeline providing the funding and support to keep these programs alive and thriving.

Daniels says that though there are some signs of hope in Oakland, in the battle for the souls of young Black males, it feels like the streets are winning. Romero is one of those signs of hope. Daniels is keeping a close eye on Romero, who works with him several days a week, helping the men at Men of Valor figure out the structure of their new lives.

"I believe Romero will not take the route I took because he got a lot of people in his life looking out for him," Daniels says. "He has a good relationship with one of my cousins, Michael, who told me Romero is real serious about not doing what he sees being done out here in these Oakland streets. I'm talking to him, and I'm sharing with him my experience in life without having a father. Come to find out, he has that same story. But he's taking a different route than the route that I took."

The conversations, the analysis, the pain always seems to wend their way back to the same topic—fatherlessness. Romero admits that at times the aching absence of his father has bubbled up like bile and catalyzed into a seething rage that he didn't even understand.

"It's a big issue," he says. "Most of the young men that I know are in the same situation. I deal with it. I mean, I didn't see my dad since I was nine, but every now and then, I might feel some kind of way. But I'm always busy, so I don't have time to think about it."

Two years prior, when he was a high school junior, Romero started getting what he calls "flashes." Normally a genial, level-headed kid, Romero found himself easily frustrated by things that didn't bother him before, annoyed by people who previously didn't affect him.

"Anything would tip me off," he recalls.

One time he got so angry that he shook the refrigerator in the midst of a temper tantrum in the house. Another time he picked up the table and shook it as a way to release his rage. His grades dipped at Castlemont High School. It took months before he connected the dots and located the source of his anger.

"I'd see a few of my friends who have their dads around, and I'd think, 'I got a dad, too, but I don't even know where he is," he says. "I guess the anger just built up."

It's a pain I can understand so acutely because I went through the same thing myself, albeit four decades before Romero—as I will discuss in the next several chapters. His mother, Renita, watched Romero grapple with his anger and frustration, but there was only so much she could do to ease it. She had seen it before in each of her boys—anger and frustration manifesting themselves in different ways. Both Renita and Romero openly voice their concern over the anger that the youngest boy in the family, Israel, seems to carry around with him every day. Renita says it has already caused difficulty in school for the fourth-grader in the form of fights and violent episodes. Over the course of a few hours, I witnessed Israel go after his older brothers, Nelson and SirVante, on several occasions, biting and swinging in a barely controlled rage. I started to get concerned for him, too, wondering how that anger would play out over the next few years.

"The lack of fathers in the home is definitely detrimental," Renita says. "The lack of the leadership, the head, the king role, the protector role. It's not there. So, then you have women playing both roles, and it's very weighty. It's a very heavy weight because it's like we have to nurture and be the disciplinarian and watch out for them, and we're doing like, literally, everything. The young men see us doing all of this, and they have to try to figure out their identities. I don't want to be like Mommy. I want the strength of my mom, but I don't want to be my mom."

She says she's gone out of her way to try to make sure her boys are surrounded by strong, male figures, whether in her family or in the church. She was raised around strong men—her father, her grandfather, her great-grandfather—so she believes from an early age she and her sister saw and understood the importance of male strength in a family.

"I've seen the man work hard, then come home and play with the kids and love the kids," she says, smiling at the memory. "I've seen the man discipline the kids. You know what I'm saying?"

She wanted that for her boys as well, but her life had different ideas. With the birth of each boy, she fully expected the boy's father to become a life partner. But eventually, the relationship would fray.

"I was 16 when I had my first, James—15 when I got pregnant. The father was 17," she says. "I was naïve; the relationship was premature. I was 21 when I had Eric. Twenty-seven when I had Mero [Romero]. I wasn't married to any of their fathers. But I loved each and every one of them."

Finally, Renita did marry the father of her youngest three boys, who all share the same surname of Jones. But that relationship eventually collapsed as well.

Though she's only 46, Renita is now extremely wary of entering into another serious relationship. She is afraid of bringing more potential trauma into the boys' lives. And she's not exaggerating when she uses the word *trauma*. A few years ago, a former boyfriend got so upset when Renita decided to end it that he became violent and tried to break into the house—in her eyes, surely to do her harm, in front of her sons. Maybe harm them, too.

"I explained to him that there were things going on in my family, with my kids, that he couldn't handle. He was a younger guy, an athlete. He tried to break in my house to get at me because he was mad I didn't want to be with him anymore. He was walking around the house, banging on the windows. Then he broke the window out on the front door. When he did that, I just snapped. A man should respect when a woman says that's enough."

Huddled with her boys, upon the sound of the glass smashing, Renita sprang into action. She went to her closet, where she keeps her two 9 mm handguns locked up. She quickly retrieved one of them, loaded the gun, and came back into the living room.

"I started shooting at him," she said. "I literally tried to kill the man."

The man had removed himself from her porch, but Renita shot at him on the street. She missed.

She rises from the couch to demonstrate, leaning halfway out the front door and directing her index finger toward the street as if she were still holding the gun. She adds that she's licensed to carry the guns but says she needs to work on her aim.

"I had shot it before. That's okay—if I'm close enough, I'll get it. But I need to go to a range now because I want to hit my target. I don't want to leave nothing standing."

Renita sits back down.

"That's trauma. Trauma to my family, to my kids," she says, shaking her head.

I point out to her the profusion of studies revealing that too many educational professionals don't recognize trauma in Black kids, illogically believing that they are somehow more impervious to it than other children. Renita nods in agreement.

"They see dope deals. They see bodies dead on the street. They seeing women being abused on these streets. They seeing all this stuff. That's traumatic! Hell, when I walk out the door, it's traumatic for *me*. There are some things I walk out, and I see, and I'm like, 'My God!' It's traumatic. When you have these images in your head. You have the internet, you know, you have all these influences, all these voices, even soft porn and things like that. There's so much more that they are exposed to than it was even for us. So, you got kids coming to school dealing with all this."

Though it's tempting to affix a halo to Romero's head, his mother is quick to point out that her son isn't perfect. She believes he's exceptional, but her instinct is not to burden him with the expectation of perfection.

Once in middle school, Romero went into her purse and stole $500.

"I was saving for something, and I had a purse full of hundreds, right? Romero is under the radar, but he has that side of him, too. A lot of times, he's ostracized because church people will see him do something and be like, you know, he's supposed to be this perfect thing. And I'm like, no, you have to remember, he's still a human. He's still a young man. He's still a *boy*; he's becoming a *man*. He didn't ask for this thing that's on his life. He has to learn how to live with this thing that's on his life, but yet be reachable to other people, and yet be relatable and yet be able to function in life."

Romero eventually paid the money back when he got a job. Renita struggled to understand why he did it; he never gave her a satisfactory answer.

"Mero never really asked for nothing, and I think he just wanted some money," she says. "He's never stolen from me again."

She remembers something. "Oh, but he did take my car one time."

She goes on to explain the time when Romero "stole" her car to impress some girls. They all went on a short joy ride—until he got busted when his grandmother just happened to drive by and see them.

"I would have never known had nobody seen him. So, this was like in 11ᵗʰ grade last year. I was like, *Oh, okay. I gotta watch that.*"

Romero grins broadly when I ask him later about the car "theft." His boyish side shines through.

One of the themes I've consistently encountered over the years—something that's fully investigated in the research—is how much the personality, the aura, the basic nature of so many Black boys abruptly changes when they enter the school building. They can feel so misunderstood and mistreated in school that they give up even trying—often at far too early an age.

In Romero's case, his charm and leadership abilities were evident to most of the people in the school building. After all, he was elected as the student body president. But somehow, someway, he still developed a deep dislike for school. For a young man with Romero's gifts, school should be a place of undeterred achievement. He should have been acing school. But he wasn't. Why not? This question gets to the crux of the challenge facing millions of Black boys—what happens to them when they walk into the school building?

As we sit outside Castlemont High School one afternoon, less than four months after he has graduated from the school, Romero starts recounting all the incidents of racism he experienced from teachers there. Castlemont's racial makeup is about 64 percent Hispanic, 28 percent Black, two percent Pacific Islander and two percent Asian.

Romero says most of his problems were with white, female teachers—though he points out that one of the teachers who seemed to hate Black students most was actually a Black man. As Romero is in midsentence, yet another car races by the school at full speed, the third car within 10 minutes to fly by at a speed easily exceeding 60 mph. In an obvious school zone, speeding with impunity.

"All day, all you hear is people flying down this street," he says sadly. "We hear it sitting in class."

He points to darkened traffic lights. "There are lights over there—but they don't even work. They're just there. The thing is, the police don't care. The teachers...they don't care either."

While he was traveling to conferences and impressing adults with his public speaking abilities, Romero says at one point his GPA at Castlemont was barely above 2.0.

"I was always focused on what I *like* to do, instead of what I *need* to do," he says. "I like preaching. I like traveling and speaking at conferences. I like doing that kind of stuff. And I was more focused on that because I was failing in school. That's like so backwards. How can I speak life into you and give you all this good information on all the different work that's going on in my community, and I gotta go back to school to a 1.0 or a 2.3 GPA? It's embarrassing."

He says he had a hard time focusing on the things he knew he needed to do to ace school. One of the main reasons was because he just didn't like being in the building.

"I don't like school, to be honest. I really hate school. So, if I was failing, I didn't really trip."

He pauses. "I know how our system works. In order to make good money, you gotta go to school, and you gotta get an education. And so, I made sure that I did what I had to do to finish. Because if I want to make six figures a year, let me go ahead and get this education under my belt. I can't live in no nice house and drive a nice car if I ain't got no money."

Romero isn't quite sure what his next steps are, now that he has survived high school. He is thinking of some type of career in sports medicine or kinesiology. Or maybe politics. In the meantime, he has enrolled in some courses at Merritt, the local community college. He says he's taking paralegal studies and sociology his first semester. He doesn't have a clear idea of what the next few years will look like.

Romero quiets for a few seconds. Then he makes a confession, almost as if he's afraid to give it a voice.

"I haven't said this in a long time, but I always wanted to be the president. When I was a kid, that was my number one goal. Even before Obama. Especially when I was in kindergarten. When they ask you what you want to be when you grow up, that was the first thing I said. Besides a preacher, I said I want to be president."

He stares off, a wistful look in his eyes.

It can be painful to hear Romero's indecision, his uncertainty about his future. When I saw him for the first time, I was impressed by his self-assurance, his evident leadership abilities. I was certain that his future was about as bright as the North Star. But his current predicament is a vivid example of the vulnerability too many Black males in America face, the precariousness that accompanies every step in their journey. If they don't have buoys that can help guide their path, Black males can so quickly lose their way—just like Andre Daniels of the Men of Valor program did when he stepped away from the church.

Right now, the church is still a strong buoy in Romero's life. He also has a team of mentors still watching over him, men he came upon when he joined a unique Oakland initiative called the Office of African American Male Achievement (AAMA). It is a program that transformed Romero's life, from the moment in seventh grade when he walked into a class and for the first time saw a Black male teacher staring back at him—a man by the name of John Muhammad. Muhammad was placed there through the efforts of AAMA—one of the most remarkable public school initiatives in America.

Helping AAMA and its indefatigable leader, Chris Chatmon, thrive and survive in Oakland has been a source of incredible pride for me. But as I watched Chatmon hold on through a rollercoaster ride of peaks and valleys over the past decade, I am constantly reminded that our work of improving life outcomes for Black men and boys in the Black Male Achievement field isn't close to done.

Chapter 3: My Path

The moment you start to embrace how you have been formed and fashioned is the moment you step into the very purpose you were created for.

    —T.D. Jakes, *When Power Meets Potential*

When I hear the details of stories like Jamare's and Romero's, I am overcome with resonant reflection. Because their stories are my story. Their lives are my life. We have walked the same path, breathed the same distressed air of promise and peril. Indeed, as I survey the travails that Black males in this country often endure, I encountered so many of them in my early life that has infused me with an essential degree of empathy and perspective in my leadership and community-building journey.

Just like Jamare, my mother and father were never married. I did not burst forth into the world as the glorious end result of some meticulous family planning. My mother and my father were both professionals in the world of dance—my mother a beautiful, young woman barely in her 20s, my father a smooth dancer, producer, and dance instructor. They were members of a troupe called the Ned Williams Dance Company, founded by Ned Williams, a groundbreaking Black dance instructor. My mother, Deanna Durham, had immigrated to the United States from Jamaica at age 18, a creative and talented force of nature looking to make a splash in the big city. The New York dance scene in 1958 was extremely racially segregated, forcing Black professionals to forge their own paths. Just two years earlier, Arthur Mitchell—who would go on in 1969 to form the incredibly influential Dance Theater of Harlem—had broken major ground when he was chosen as a principal dancer with the New York City Ballet, one of the first Black dancers to receive that sort of mainstream recognition.

In New York, Deanna met Bernard Dove, a suave, handsome man who bore a resemblance to Sammy Davis Jr. in face and form. Bernard was taken with the lovely Deanna—her large, almond-shaped eyes and cocoa-brown skin would later evoke comparisons to actresses Pam Grier and Diahann Carroll. I haven't been given many details about their relationship and courtship. I'm not even sure their coupling rose to the level of "relationship." I just know that my early interactions with my father were minimal and not very satisfying. I have a black-and-white picture that I sometimes gaze at, looking at every detail for some clues that I might have missed. My mom, in leotards, is crouched over a large conga drum, pretending to play while looking into the camera with a bemused expression on her pretty, heart-shaped face. Next to her is my father, also in leotards, a slight smile on his handsome face. But my father is also toting a dancer on his right shoulder, a lovely Black woman who is smiling and inexplicably holding up an open umbrella, like one of those fashionable parasols. In the dance studio picture my parents aren't touching; there is no intimacy between them. Not that there necessarily should have been in the picture – just something that I would have wanted to see. From a distance one might imagine the woman on his shoulder was more likely to be a lover. But I suppose there's much I can't see. For all I know, that might have been the day I was conceived.

I had a stronger relationship with my father's parents than I did with him. I looked forward to visiting them in Crown Heights, Brooklyn, because I felt their powerful love for me. Children can quickly sense when an adult cares for them. It's as important to a young person as food and oxygen. In Crown Heights, I could bask in their adoration, which was vital to my upbringing since there's only so much adoration an over-stressed single mother can provide. Their names were Charner and Lucy Dove; I called my grandfather "Goo-Goo." Every few months or so, they would drive uptown and pick me up for the weekend. Even the trip to Brooklyn was a source of excitement for me because our ritual was to stop at a White Castle on Brooklyn's Flatbush Avenue that was on the way to Crown Heights. I would gorge on those tasty little burgers—which unfortunately, during weak moments, are still hard for me to resist. The time with them provided me with rare glimpses into what family stability looked like.

I don't recall ever thinking about my parents as a couple. I never saw them together, so it never crossed my mind to yearn for them to be united. In their living room, my grandparents hung a poster of a dance event at the Apollo Theater where my father had produced a show in 1969, when I was seven. It was a red-and-white poster. There was a picture of my father in a tux and bowtie at the top center of the poster, below his image the words "Bernard Dove Presents." The poster gave me an image of my father as a man of importance, who did things like plan big shows at the Apollo. This image was important to me at the time as a symbolic stand-in for an actual relationship with my dad. I think I had a deeper relationship to that poster than I did to the actual man. But to my mother's credit, she never spoke ill of my dad, letting me form my own judgments about him. That's such a crucial behavior, one that many mothers aren't able to adhere to. I don't remember feeling anger directed at my father; it was more like a curiosity about this distant figure.

Instability often is one of the inescapable consequences of poverty. My young mother worked during the day and was desperate for someone to watch me in my preschool years while she was gone. She found that someone in Harlem, at the home of a caretaker named Lillian Smith, who was known as "Lel." I would stay with my mom at our apartment in the South Bronx on the weekends but during the week I would stay with Lel at her apartment in Harlem. Lel was a stone-cold hustler, cobbling together whatever schemes she could to make money. She was a numbers runner, she ran a boarding house, and she operated an informal daycare center. I stayed with her from ages four to nine. The numbers would change according to the circumstances, but there were usually at least two other children there—kids whose mothers also were single parents who needed help. Lel's was an old-school Harlem apartment with at least eight rooms, so there was enough space for the children and also for other people to live there, such as Mr. Archie, who was from Barbados, and Doc, who was a chauffeur. Because she ran numbers with Roy Barnes, the father of the infamous Harlem drug kingpin, Nicky Barnes, people from the neighborhood were constantly coming by the apartment to place their numbers. The constant stream of traffic gave Lel's place a communal feel. To me, it felt like I was part of a large village of people who cared about me. I had a strong feeling that Lel loved me and wouldn't let anything happen to me. When we were out on the street playing, we were tagged—all anybody needed to know was that we were "Lel's kids" and they wouldn't mess with us. She had stature in the community; that stature extended to us since we were in her care.

Lel was a strict disciplinarian with Southern roots, meaning she wasn't about to spare the rod. In retrospect, the punishment she doled out would definitely fall into the category of child abuse if it were to occur today. But in the 1960s, no eyebrows were raised. When we did something that Lel thought warranted punishment, she would bring out the ironing cord and go to work. On one occasion, I got whupped so viciously that I had pieces of copper from the ironing cord embedded in the welts on my arms. In another sign of the times, Mrs. McLeod, my elementary school music teacher at PS 144, which sat at 122nd

Street between Seventh and Lenox Avenues in Harlem, on more than one occasion used the two 18-inch rulers she had lashed together with rubber bands to spank me in front of the classroom. One morning I was leaning back in my chair too far and I fell backwards with a loud crash, an offense that warranted physical abuse in Mrs. McLeod's estimation. Though, paradoxically, we felt Mrs. McLeod's deep care and concern for our well-being.

At Lel's, the playroom where most of the action took place during the day would become my bedroom at night. One of my earliest memories of staying in Harlem occurred on the evening of April 4, 1968, when the community was on the verge of explosion following the assassination of Martin Luther King Jr. I didn't know what was going on, but I knew my people were in distress. Many observers give Mayor John Lindsay credit for tamping down an impending explosion by wading into Harlem and expressing his outrage over King's murder—as if the Black people couldn't control themselves without the kindly white man cautioning them to behave. While I was supposed to be in bed asleep, I looked out my window facing Lenox Avenue and could see three blocks south to my right where there was mayhem and looting of the Woolworth's store on the corner of 116th street.

I was painfully shy and introverted, riddled with insecurities. Luckily, I was a cute kid, with a big afro, long eyelashes, dimples and a face that people were always saying resembled Michael Jackson's. On more than one occasion when I was very young, I'd be out with my mother and a stranger would come up to her at the bus stop or on the subway and say, "That's a pretty little boy!" Or "Is that a boy or a girl?" There was something innocent about me that drew people in and made me likable. Maybe it was God's way of protecting me because I was so insecure and felt vulnerable.

Though it was clear to me that Lel loved me, she was still capable of doling out shattering emotional abuse. A lot of my early trauma revolved around my bedwetting. Being publicly ridiculed by Lel for wetting the bed was about the most horrible thing in the world to me. My shame was deep, overwhelming. One day when I was outside playing a game of freeze tag with my friends, Lel went out onto the fire escape and hung up my sheet that she had just washed out. The other kids knew what was up right away.

"Shawn peed the bed! Hahaha! He wet the bed!" They pointed, laughing. The ridicule rained down on me; I wanted to sink into the tar and disappear.

Clearly, Lel was not reading any child-rearing manuals. Her idea of getting me to stop the bedwetting was to threaten to beat me if I did it again, as if the fear and stress of impending physical abuse was the answer. Lel was determined to beat it out of me. Beating was the go-to solution for everything. In her book, *Spare the Kids: Why Whupping Children Won't Save Black America*, Dr. Stacey Patton traced the predilection of Black parents to use physical abuse for punishment back to slavery, noting it was a behavior adopted from European slave masters—in many ways as an attempt to save Black children from much more brutal beatings at the slave owners' hands. It chokes me up now to imagine myself as a seven- and eight-year-old boy, terrified to go to sleep, staring at the ceiling and praying that somehow I could be strong to prevent my bladder opening up.

"All you know how to do is sleep, eat, and pee the bed," Lel said to me, loudly, one day when she was upset at me for something. I knew Lel cared about me, but I did see things when I was with her that couldn't have been helpful in a young child's healthy development.

The late 60s and early 70s were the height of the heroin epidemic in Harlem. Everywhere I turned, I saw grown folks nodding off on the corner, like zombies. According to the National Institute on Drug Abuse, from 1969 to 1974 the number of heroin addicts in the United States rose from 242,000 to 558,000—with a disproportionate percentage of those addicts living in New York City. Indeed, by the mid-1970s the New York City Health Department was reporting more than 650 heroin-related deaths a year.

While we were outside playing one day when I was about eight, a man was pushed off the roof of an apartment building across the street and plunged to his death. I'm pretty sure it was drug-related. Right after it happened, we ran across the street to view his lifeless form up close. He was face down, obviously dead, with a huge pool of blood growing around his smashed face. On another occasion, a woman was pushed over the railing in our seven-story building and fell through the center of the stairwell to the ground floor. She survived, but she was screaming in agony.

"My leg! My leg!"

I didn't run up to investigate that time, but I can still hear the sound of her screams echoing throughout the building. The scene did not stop me from going outside to play. I don't recall internalizing any particular trauma from these events, but perhaps I papered over my reactions by desensitizing myself. I think too many Black boys deal with a lot of trauma that doesn't really get acknowledged, investigated, or analyzed. Black girls do as well, but because of the nature of how girls have traditionally been more closely monitored than boys, boys are more likely to be out in the world at a relatively young age, free range, often seeing things they probably shouldn't be seeing. Perhaps this contributes to the phenomenon many people describe in adolescent boys, when they have built up so much emotional scar tissue that they have difficulty accessing their emotions, difficulty even acknowledging that they *have* emotions. In essence, they have learned how to shield themselves—otherwise they wouldn't be able to cope with the many painful things they witness.

I had an important event in my development take place at Lel's when I was about eight. Because I slept in the playroom, I wasn't far away when people would come to the apartment at night to drop off the number they were playing that day. One night after I had gone to bed, two older Black women were talking to Lel while they were looking at the magnet map that I liked to play with that was hanging up on the wall. It was a map of the United States that I would have to put together like a puzzle, with magnets on each piece. They were admiring the map when one of the women said, "Shawn did that. Shawn really loves to read!"

They thought I was asleep, but I could hear everything. There was a note of pride in the woman's voice when she said it, letting me know she was impressed with my love of reading. Up to that point, I never really knew I loved to read. I knew I enjoyed losing myself in a book, but I didn't realize it was something noteworthy or made me different from any other kid. But from that moment on, I began to see myself as a reader. Just hearing that one sentence from that woman, spoken out loud, transformed my self-perception. I often recall that moment in amazement, at the power of a timely, well-placed word to alter a child's life.

During these years, there were two scenes with my father that stand out vividly in my memory, I suppose because they also played a role in my development. One fall weekend when I was staying with my grandparents in Crown Heights, my father came to pick me up to take me to the store. I was about nine at the time. I don't remember which store we were going to, but we were walking down Brooklyn's Kingston Avenue. It was evening because the streetlights had come on. He was wearing an amazing, long, brown leather coat. The coat had a belt, but he had it open and it was flying behind him as he walked. He had on pitted bell-bottom pants with a bright pattern and cuffs, and platform shoes. I think he also was wearing a brim. After all, it *was* the early 70s. He looked like a character out of the blaxploitation movies of the time, like Super Fly or Shaft. He had his wavy hair slicked down, like the suave player he thought he was. He was only 5'7" (considering that my mom is only five foot-three, God must have added the extra inches to make me 6'2" because He thought, "This brother is going to need all the help he can get!") but he had an aura that really impressed me, like he was the coolest dude on the planet. But at the same time, he was walking so fast that my nine-year-old legs couldn't keep up. I was at least five feet behind him, wondering, *why is he walking so fast? Why won't he wait for me?* I was literally walking in his footsteps. Deep down, I had a sense that he was doing this out of a sense of obligation, not love—a drive-by Dad moment. But while that couldn't have felt good, I was also thinking, *Damn, he's cool!* The memory of that poor, confused, little boy can bring tears to my eyes every time I conjure him up.

But it's interesting to note the importance of cool for a little Black boy, how large it loomed even in the midst of my distress. Black boys obsess over cool, investigate and interrogate cool all day every day, like its presence will magically introduce joy into their lives. Black boys respect cool more than any other human trait, worship it like a deity, try to bathe in it like it's a bath salt. When I saw the extent of my father's cool, the enormous shadow it cast, the heights that it rose to on the horizon, it went far to assuage my confusion on Kingston Avenue. I couldn't be sure he loved me or cared about me, but the fact that I came from such impressive stock meant a great deal. It was a sort of corrective balm for just that moment.

The other father memory also took place during a weekend when I was with my grandparents, at their brownstone apartment on President Street. I was playing in the backyard with my friend Dennis, who lived next door. I think it was in the same year as the Kingston Avenue memory. I didn't know my father was coming over, so I was surprised when he came into the backyard and called me. When I got to him, he was already talking to me. But I didn't know what he was talking about.

"You know, sometimes things just don't work out between two people," he said. He turned and headed back into the house, with me on his heels. "Things just don't work out."

We walked into the living room and I was greeted by the sight of a pretty, dark-skinned woman I had never met, holding two babies, one in each arm. Somebody told me they were my twin brother and sister. Apparently, my father, in his haphazard way, was trying to prepare me, his first child, for what I was about to confront by explaining that it was unfortunate things didn't work out with my mother. At least that's my guess. It was head-spinning for me, but I took it all in stride. I had been an only child for a decade. Now I had two siblings. Wow! Okay. Let me go back outside to play with Dennis.

It wouldn't be until a full decade later, when I was in college, that these insufficient early interactions with him would manifest themselves so strongly as a growling Daddy Hunger that I was compelled to track him down the summer between my junior and senior year of college.

My sexual awareness began to bloom at Lel's, though it was far too soon for me to engage in actual sex. There was a cute girl who lived in Lel's building named Vanessa, who was slightly older than me and who took a liking to me. One day, she pulled me into an empty room at Lel's place, laid down on top of me and started grinding against my crotch. I'm not even sure at age eight whether I was capable of an erection, but I was sure I had just had sex, even though we never removed our clothes. That's how clueless I was about sex. In fact, I later bragged to several kids on the street that she and I "did it." As soon as he heard my brags, one of the older boys, whose name was Carlie and who was one of my primary tormentors, dragged me over to the building, right under Michelle's window on the fourth floor. He called up to her and she opened the window.

"Did you and Shawn do it?" he asked her, point blank.

An incredulous expression spread across her face.

"No!" she said.

"Yes, we did," I said to her in a pleading, pitiful voice. "Don't you remember?"

She shook her head and looked down at me.

"What are you talking about? You never had me," she declared. I was mortified as Carlie's laughter, along with the older boys who were with him, rained down on my head.

When I was at Lel's, there was a man who served as a role model of sorts for me. His name was DeWitt Thompson, and he was Lel's son-in-law. His daughter, Lydia, also lived with us; she was a couple of grades ahead of me. DeWitt was also a hustler; he worked with Lel as a numbers runner. But most importantly for me, DeWitt was kind, protective, and loving. He loved his daughter deeply, and it felt like he saw the rest of us as an extension of Lydia. He would take us on trips to places like the amusement park, where he would spoil us. On Christmas of my fourth-grade year, he bought fur coats for me and Michael King, another little boy a couple of years older than me who lived with us. No, a fur coat was not the most practical gift in the world for a nine-year-old, but his heart was in the right place. He was one of the first of a long line of Black men over the years who would step into the void left by my father.

I knew the coat was unusual and special for a little boy—I would quickly find out how special, in the worst way imaginable. The weekend right after Christmas, my mother, after my persistent prodding, decided to let me travel on the subway by myself for the first time. I had to go from our apartment in the Bronx down to Lel's place in Harlem to pick up my dress shoes, then come back. My mother gave me clear instructions: Take the 2 train to 116th Street, get out and walk the few blocks to Lel's building. She gave me an incentive to not linger—when I got home we were going to watch a James Bond movie, *Diamonds Are Forever*. I was a big James Bond and Sean Connery fan—though that fandom soon would fade a bit when Shaft exploded onto my consciousness. Like I said, I was all about the cool.

I successfully maneuvered down to Lel's place and retrieved my shoes, which I carried in a shopping bag along with the Sunday Daily News which had comic strips that I loved to read. I was feeling good and grown. I walked back to the subway station at 116th Street. But instead of going down the steps on the uptown side, I went down on the downtown side. The train's first stop was supposed to be 125th Street. Instead, I looked out and saw that we were at 110th Street. I panicked. Anybody who is familiar with the NYC subway system knows that all I had to do was get off the train, go across the platform to the other side and take the uptown train up to the Bronx. But I wasn't thinking clearly in my panicked state. Before I could make a decision, the doors closed, and the train continued downtown. Next stop, 96th Street. Once again, the smart move would have been to walk across the platform to the uptown side. Hell, I could have asked somebody what to do. Instead, I did the worst thing I could possibly do in that situation—I exited the subway and decided to walk back uptown to 116th Street and Lenox Avenue. Twenty blocks. I was familiar with my immediate Harlem neighborhood and Lenox Avenue, but I was on Broadway and I was far further south than I had ever been by myself. My internal compass was strong enough to propel me in the right direction—helped substantially by the fact that the streets are numbered. I toted my little shopping bag containing my fancy shoes and I headed north and east, walking through Morningside near the Columbia University campus. My mind was single-mindedly focused on my destination. I wasn't about to be distracted by anything I saw on the way. Somehow, I made it back to my starting point, the subway station at 116th Street and Lenox. I put another token in the turnstile and walked to the platform. This time I made sure I was on the uptown side, heading to the Bronx. I was anxious, knowing that I was taking far longer than my mother expected.

"Hey. Where you going?"

I turned and saw that the question was directed at me. It came from a Black man. He was brown-skinned, about my complexion, with serious skin problems—I could see the bumps on his face from a distance. Actually, he looked a little bit like NBA star Spencer Haywood, who was tearing up the league that year with his turnaround jump shot. Maybe that's why I was inclined to see him as a non-threatening presence. I knew talking to strangers was a huge no-no, but I wasn't exactly filled with certitude at the moment.

"I'm going home," I said. I'm sure I was about as conspicuous as a shiny red apple, a nine-year-old boy alone on a subway platform at 116th Street—wearing a glistening new fur coat. If I was the shiny red apple, this man was the serpent, slithering in my direction. When the train came, he stepped on alongside me.

"You know you're on the wrong train, right?" the man said as the train pulled away. He convinced me that the train we were on would not take me to the Bronx. I still wasn't sure if he was telling me the truth, but he had introduced enough doubt in my mind that I was inclined to believe him. We got off at 149th Street and Grand Concourse Avenue and crossed over to a train that was headed back downtown toward Harlem. While we were on the train, I spotted one of the boys who also stayed with Lel on the train with his mother. I could see her staring at me and the stranger with a quizzical look on her face, as if she were wondering, *Who is that man talking to Shawn?* That was my chance to speak up, to go over to her and tell her I didn't know this man, that it would be great if I could stick close to them. But I didn't do any of those things. I was frozen into paralysis and indecision, but I didn't outwardly appear to be in distress. I guess she decided to mind her business. So, when the train stopped at 135th Street and the man told me to come with him, I dutifully obliged.

We started walking up Lenox Avenue and I began to feel that I was in some sort of danger. The man could sense my growing resistance, so he grabbed me by the hand and started pulling me up Lenox.

"No! No. I'm not supposed to go with you!" I said to him. I began to cry. I was being abducted, but to bystanders on the street perhaps we looked like a father trying to discipline an unruly, protesting son. We walked a few blocks up Lenox and then we made a left, I think on 137th or 138th street. He dragged me into a building and quickly we went into the first apartment on the left. As soon as we burst into the apartment, another Black man who had been laying on a bed jumped up.

"What's going on?" the man asked.

But my abductor ignored him and instead grabbed me and stripped off my fur coat. He pushed me into a different room. I started screaming and crying, terrified at what might happen to me. It's the scene I should have been making on the train when I was surrounded by people—though I didn't know then that my life was in danger. Now my only witness was another man who didn't seem too interested in helping me.

"I'm sorry!" I said to him, now begging. "I'm sorry! I'll be your friend! I'll be your friend!"

In the middle of my screams and pleas, the man lifted his right leg and kicked me in the chest. He kicked me so hard that he left a dirty footprint on the light-blue shirt I was wearing. My abductor exited the room and slammed the door shut, leaving me in the dark. I froze, not sure what to do, what was going to happen next. After several minutes, the door opened. It was the other man.

"Get out of here!" he said to me, gesturing toward the door. He didn't have to tell me again. I ran out of the room and out of the apartment, my heart already about to explode with relief. I suppose my abductor had left with my fur coat, surely to sell it for his next drug high. I wasn't thinking about that damn coat anymore. When I got into the hallway of the building, I saw a few people peeking from around their doors, investigating what all the screaming was about. I stumbled out into the cold in my blue shirt with the dark footprint and ran back to Lenox, hurriedly turning north in case my abductor was still around. My mission now was to get back to the Bronx and my mother by any means necessary. By this point, my mother had called Lel and been told that I had left quite a while ago. So panic was starting to set in with the people who loved me. Nobody knew where I was.

I had walked several blocks in the cold up Lenox, crossed the 145th bridge which ushered me from Manhattan and into the Bronx, and kept instinctively walking toward my Bronx neighborhood. I spotted one of those red fire chief station wagons; something told me I might find help inside that car. I knocked on the window and told them I was lost. I said I needed to get to 174th Street and Bryant Avenue in the Bronx. They wanted to be helpful, but they weren't in the business of dealing with lost children. They called the cops. When the squad car arrived, the officers brought me back down to 135th Street, *away* from the Bronx. At the precinct, I was interrogated like I was a crime suspect.

"Who are you?"

"Who do you belong to?"

I answered their questions and tried to explain what had happened, but for some reason they were not happy with me.

"You're lying!" one officer yelled at me. "You better tell the truth, or I'm going to stick this blade up your ass!"

Eventually, the officers brought me uptown to my mother. She was distraught when I explained to her what had happened to me. I was thoroughly shaken, disturbed by the jarring realization that I wasn't nearly, at nine years-old, as street smart as I had thought I was. I blamed myself for being stupid and not simply walking across the platform to catch the uptown train when the train doors opened at the 110th Street station. But I also began to get this feeling, one that's been repeated many times over the years, that I had some sort of guardian angel watching over me. After all, the scene in the junkie's apartment could have been much worse. It could have led to molestation; he could have decided to slit my throat to keep me from screaming; he could have tied me up and left me there. Instead, his roommate was in possession of an actual conscience and felt sorry for me. If he had the same spirit as my abductor, that all would have turned out really bad for me.

There was no counseling, no therapy, no talking things through – who did that back then? *You survived, Shawn*, I must have thought, *so let's get ready for school.* When I returned to my fourth-grade class after the Christmas break the news of me being "kidnapped" had spread, making me the center of attention. My nine-year-old classmates associated kidnappings with ransoms, so when my classmate Gwen's declaration from across the classroom, "who would kidnap you, Shawn, you're not worth anything?" silenced the buzz in the classroom it also silenced something inside of me.

When I entered fifth grade, my life radically changed when my mother moved us from the South Bronx to the Upper West Side of Manhattan and determined that I was now old enough to take care of myself after school—my subway debacle notwithstanding. At age 10, I changed from PS 144 in Harlem to PS 9 on 84th Street and Columbus Avenue on the Upper Westside. And most significantly, I became a latchkey kid.

I went with her to search for an adequate apartment and walked through a place on Riverside Drive, between 84th and 85th Street, when she decided it would be our new home. Overnight, my script totally flipped—I went from an all-Black school at PS 144 to a school that had a large number of white kids, in addition to some Blacks and Hispanics. Those 40 blocks from Harlem to the Upper West Side thrust me headfirst into the reality of New York's intensely segregated school system. Black activists had been protesting the inequities in the city's segregated schools throughout the 1960s, but the city never made diminishing it a priority.

The latchkey kid has become an emblem of societal dysfunction and family dissolution in America, with many people blaming women for leaving children alone and vulnerable. But it's really just another visible marker of the economic strains that have been fraying American families for at least two generations now. I'm sure my mother would have loved for a team of childcare professionals to be waiting for me when I got home from PS 9. But she had to work with what she had. In her mind, I was mature enough to handle it. I remember the day when I got my own key to our apartment. It was my first key; it was red.

It was during those years walking to and from PS 9 that I was introduced to drinking, drugs, and all manner of risky behavior. Between age 12 and 14, not only did I begin smoking weed but I snorted cocaine, took LSD and even smoked Angel Dust. If I had lived in a different place, my adolescent misadventures might have consisted of smoking cigarettes under the bleachers or killing frogs in the woods (clearly I have no idea what bad-ass kids in the suburbs or the country do when they want to invite trouble). But on the Upper West Side of Manhattan in the mid-1970s, I had access to an entire illicit drug bazaar. I was hanging out with a crew of guys who went around tagging our neighborhood with graffiti. We even had a name—The Pearls, named after lead organizer, Fat Phil, whose graffiti tag was "Pearl." I guess if we had our own name, outsiders would probably want to call us a gang. There were about a dozen of us; I was a couple of years younger than many of the guys. I got an early start to me making a spiral of bad choices.

One of the group's frequent activities was something we called "gapping." We called money "gap," so gapping meant to go out and get our hands on some money. No, it was not by means of employment. We took a shortcut—we took other people's money. The guys liked to go to Central Park at night, which was just a few blocks away, and rob the gays who were cruising in the park.

I hesitate to use the word "we" to describe this behavior because I only participated on two occasions. In retrospect, there was a clear homophobic aspect to the activity, and one of our leaders, Phil, may well have been suppressing feelings he was having and using the violence as a way to exorcise them. Years later, he wound up dying of AIDS. While we were robbing the guys in the park, a few members of the group also would be mocking them and beating them. I was extremely uncomfortable with what was going on. I tried to hang in the back and pretend that I was participating. The second time, when I realized that I might be called out for not fully engaging, I hit a guy in the head with a stick. But my moral compass was deeply disturbed by what I was doing, and I pledged to myself that I would never again participate in this gay-bashing masquerading as robbery.

When I witnessed the incredibly painful saga of the "Central Park 5" more than a decade later in the late 1980s—how those young boys were rounded up, wrongly accused by the police, and sent to jail for years—I knew that something like that easily could have happened to me. I broke down when I watched Ava DuVernay's searing four-part series on Netflix, *When They See Us*. If one of those gay guys had been seriously hurt or worse, I could have been swept up into the criminal justice system and my life snatched away. But again, my guardian angel was making sure that the stakes for me never became that high.

These were the years when something else came along that fortuitously took up much of my energy and focus—basketball. When I was living in the Bronx and Harlem, I was a socially awkward little boy. But when we moved to the Upper West Side and I began playing basketball, I started to develop a stronger self-identity. It was the birth of the cool, to borrow a phrase from Miles Davis. This was a process with which many generations of boys, particularly Black boys, can easily identify—using sports as a way of establishing our place in the world. Our importance. When I began to get really good by junior high school, you couldn't tell me nothing. I was a star player on a team that played in the famous Rucker Tournament, which in New York was a publicly identifiable symbol of basketball prowess. If you played in the Rucker, you had game. I had one jersey that had "Rucker Tournament" printed on the front. I wore that thing damn near every day to announce to the world that I had skills.

Finding role models for "cool" became all-important in those years. It's why Black boys often become so attached to the local sports stars, rappers and drug dealers, because they always seem to have street cred in abundance. I've spent many years thinking about the importance of cool to Black boys, pondering why and how we attach so much social capital to it, spend so much time trying to cultivate it, expend so much mental energy envying those who have oodles of it. The academy first began analyzing the importance of cool decades ago. Dr. Richard Majors, a psychologist at the University of Wisconsin at Eau Claire, back in 1992 published a book, entitled *Cool Pose: The Dilemmas of Black Manhood in America*, written with Dr. Janet Mancini Billson, an executive officer at the American Sociological Association in Washington. It was partly an attempt to explain Black urban youth and their problems to white people. The book came out of a six-year study of 60 Black teenagers in Boston by a team of researchers from the Harvard School of Education in the 1980s. Majors described the cool pose as a set of language, mannerisms, gestures and movements that "exaggerate or ritualize masculinity. The essence of cool is to appear in control, whether through a fearless style of walking, an aloof facial expression, the clothes you wear, a haircut, your gestures, or the way you talk. The cool pose shows the dominant culture that you are strong and proud, despite your status in American society." [1]

Some of the descriptions in the book sound as if Black boys were examined and analyzed like animals in an African safari—the Black boy walk is described as "a distinctive swaggering gait, almost a walking dance, which can include tilting the head to one side while one arm swings to the side with the hand slightly cupped while the other hand hangs to the side or is in the pocket." But Majors' point still resonates, accurately characterizing what I was going

1   Goleman, Daniel (1992, April 21). Black Scientists Study the 'Pose' Of the Inner City. *New York Times*. Retrieved from https://www.nytimes.com/1992/04/21/science/black-scientists-study-the-pose-of-the-inner-city.html

through in the 1970s. According to Majors, the cool pose can be seen as a psychological coping mechanism, which was definitely the case for me as I grappled with my identity and sense of purpose. Dr. Alvin Poussaint, the famous psychiatrist at Harvard Medical School, called the cool pose a way for Black boys to show maleness in an environment where fathers are often absent and grown male figures are scarce. It's telling that Poussaint connected the cool pose to father figures because, as I said earlier, my father's coolness, in my mind, went far in acting as a sort of substitute for his absence in my life.

When I lived with Lel, her stereo was off-limits to us children. If one of us dared touch it, that would surely be grounds for a whupping. That meant we were captives to Lel's music choices—endless loops of Brook Benton singing "Rainy Night in Georgia," Clarence Carter crooning "Patches," Ray Charles and "Hit the Road Jack." But things changed when we moved to our own place. I was now old enough and free enough to have my own music playlist. I would spend countless hours not only playing Isaac Hayes' *Shaft* album but staring at the images on the album cover, with Shaft in his fly black leather outfit firing a gun at the bad guys. It was almost like I was trying to memorize every detail, as if I could become that person if I just stared at it long enough—like the Shaft swag could jump off the album cover and be absorbed into my cells.

Shaft was a mythic character, helped immensely by the magnetism of the Isaac Hayes soundtrack. But Hollywood had to take the essence of Shaft—a larger-than-life Black hero—and turn it into painfully stereotypical vehicles like *Superfly, The Mack, Blacula, Cleopatra Jones* and *Foxy Brown*. I absorbed them all, picking up bits and pieces as I formed my own idea of the substance of cool. I also took much from my sports superheroes who were undoubtedly cool—athletes like Dr. J, Muhammad Ali, Walt Frazier, Earl Monroe, Reggie Jackson, Vida Blue, and Kareem Abdul-Jabbar.

The obsession with cool almost wrecked me in middle school. The saga began when I moved from PS 9 to Intermediate School (IS) 44, which was across the street from the Museum of Natural History on West 77th Street. Somehow, I fortuitously got placed in a sixth-grade class that was called "Creative Cluster," taught by Mr. Shaller. Perhaps it was through a standardized test score, or my grades in fifth grade, or divine intervention—I have no idea how I wound up in a classroom with a white teacher so progressive that he had us closing our eyes and doing meditation in 1975. He'd talk to us, tell us a story while our eyes were closed, push us to delve deep into our subconscious—then he would clap his hands and say, "Wake up!" At times I felt like I was having out-of-body experiences. I'll never forget those sessions with Mr. Shaller, exposing me to experiences I had never before encountered. It was obviously stuff that wasn't in the state-mandated curriculum—and maybe would have gotten him fired if they heard about it down at Board of Education headquarters.

Toward the end of the school year, all sixth graders were required to declare a "major" for seventh and eighth grade. At IS 44, there were only two choices— major math-science or major gym. In major gym, the students would have hockey tournaments, play basketball, and spend a part of the day immersed in adolescent boy heaven, at least in the mind of the young Shawn Dove. When I discussed it with my boys Chris, Dave, and Lenny, it was a no-brainer—we were all about that gym major. Playing sports all day? Are you kidding me—sign me up! More than four decades later, I ask why in the world "educators" thought major gym was a good idea for anybody.

When I came home toting the permission slip for me to be assigned to major gym, my mother looked at me like I had two heads.

"You got to be crazy, boy! You ain't going to no major gym. You're going to major math and science."

For two years, I held a great deal of resentment toward my mother for that decision. It was a resentment that was fueled every day by the extreme dichotomy of my experience versus that of my homeboys. I was in a classroom at one end of the hallway, surrounded by white and Asian kids, with a sprinkling of Blacks and Latinos, learning how to use Bunsen burners, dissecting frogs and rabbits. Less than 30 yards away at the other end of the hallway, my buddies were in a class that was almost exclusively Black and Latino, having what sounded like a grand time doing a lot of "playing." Their class was taught by math teacher Mrs. Jones, a heavyset, Black woman who was in the classic Big Momma mold. Let me just say that classroom management was not her strong suit. It would be common to be walking down the hall and see a chair come flying out of her classroom; it seemed to be all chaos, all the time. And that's exactly where I wanted to be.

Though my mother and I weren't wealthy by any stretch, I think there was some kind of class division that was occurring in those two years. My mother was savvy enough to understand that allowing me to major in gym was a decision that could have serious long-term repercussions. But my boy Dave forged his mother's signature on the form. Dave had already experienced a significant amount of trauma by middle school—he had witnessed his father get stabbed to death in the Amsterdam Projects, a public housing community about 20 blocks away from where I lived. His mother was a single woman raising six kids; when I went to his house, she often seemed despondent and distant. I now recognize that as depression. Dave didn't really have anyone paying close attention to what he was doing, in school or on the streets.

This pivotal crossroads in my life stands out to me because I know it's a precarious moment that many Black boys across America still face. Somehow, I had wound up in the "Creative Cluster" class in sixth grade, perhaps due to some sort of tracking, separating kids based on previous performance. I hadn't been exceptional in any way, getting B's and C's in elementary school, and I certainly didn't see myself as particularly smart. But I think others saw things in me that I didn't see in myself. Just like hearing those two Black women at Lel's call out my affection for reading changed the way I saw myself; my friends began to verbalize the idea that I was somehow different than them. It's the same thing that happened to Romero in Oakland—his friends keeping an eye out for him and proclaiming that he was different. Luckily, I had someone at home who also saw it and steered me away from an academic path that held much less potential for eventual success. Many Black boys with unlimited potential languish because they had no one around them to steer them in the right direction at pivotal moments. Walk into most AP classes in America and you will likely find that the number of Black boys in the class lags far behind the percentage of Black boys in the school—even though there are likely many Black boys in the school who could do the work if somebody pushed them. In 2014, according to the U.S. Department of Education, Black and Latino students made up 37 percent of high school students in the nation, but only 27 percent of students taking an AP class and 18 percent of students passing AP exams. In addition, the Black and Latino students in those courses are far more likely to be girls.

Eddie Fergus, a professor and researcher at Temple University, told me that by middle school, Black boys have figured out that if they have been placed in the lower tracks, the school is telling them they aren't going to make it. And, perhaps more importantly, the school's teachers and administrators have already given up on them. Why should they care about school if the school doesn't care about them?

Along with researchers Pedro Noguera and Margary Martin, Fergus conducted a three-year study of seven single-sex schools in New York City, Chicago,

Houston, and Atlanta that are made up of predominantly Black and Latino boys. The study was the centerpiece of their book, *Schooling for Resilience: Improving the Life Trajectory of Black and Latino Boys*. The researchers found that Black and brown boys needed to have meaningful relationships with the adults in the school—relationships that feature care and trust—in order for these boys to perform well academically. When they had formed a bond with at least one adult in the school, when they could walk into the building in the morning and know that there was at least one adult who cared what happened to them, they would have enough trust to push themselves to excel. For instance, one of the teachers they studied who got great results with Black boys would get down on her knees when they were doing group work so that she would be at their eye level when she talked to them. Fergus said such little things mattered.

It was another example of a guardian angel watching over me that my mother chose an apartment on Riverside Drive instead of something on Amsterdam Avenue, where we also looked, and which was a much more dangerous neighborhood. Those couple of blocks made a huge difference, which is one of the peculiarities of city living. New York City in the mid-1970s was considered the epicenter of urban blight in America, replete with panhandlers, heroin addicts, ubiquitous graffiti, and wanton violence. The number of murders in the city passed 2,000 for the first time in 1972. I learned that Amsterdam Avenue, especially in or near the Amsterdam Houses, was where I could find a great deal of that urban blight. Of course, that doesn't mean I stayed away from Amsterdam, but I'm sure I benefitted from living on Riverside, which was more upscale, more high-status and a great deal safer. For instance, one of my friends was a chubby white kid named Benji who lived around the corner and whose parents were actors. Benji is now known to the world as Ben Stiller, movie star and director.

But money didn't always translate to social class. One of my homeboys, Lenny Collins, lived in an impressive, upscale building on Riverside in an apartment near the actor/comedian Robert Klein, who was married to the opera star Brenda Boozer. Lenny later told me when he went out to eat with me and my mother, it was the first time he learned how to properly use a knife and fork and place the table napkin on his lap.

The importance of cool loomed dangerously large for me at this time. Unfortunately, I gleaned too many lessons about cool from some of the unsavory characters around me, like the neighborhood drug dealers. My boys and I started buying weed, rolling it into joints, and selling "looseys" out on the corner of 80th and Amsterdam. I didn't really need the money; my mother was working hard as an employee of the Social Security Administration in Queens to give me mostly everything I needed at the time. But selling the joints wasn't really about the money. It was about that toxic mix of street cred, street cool, and twisted ideas of masculinity that seeps into the brains of young Black boys like me and turns us upside down. I could have easily been sucked into the prison pipeline and eventually sitting in a cell, ruminating about all the "potential" that I had stupidly squandered.

At the most fortuitous of times, I stumbled upon an intervention, a program, a mentor, that changed the trajectory of my life and forcefully yanked me away from that pipeline to nowhere. It was called The DOME Project and the place that would soon become my home away from home.

Chapter 4: Finding a Home at The DOME

Community can create a container for natural abilities that can find no place in a world defined by economics and consumerism.

—Malidoma Patrice Some, *The Healing Wisdom of Africa*

The first time I got high was at the precious age of 11, ironically at a house party my mother brought me to in the Bronx. Before you get alarmed, my mother had nothing to do with it. She was a single mom, so when she wanted to hang out, sometimes it was easier to just bring me along. She had my friend Lenny come with us, I suppose for me to have a playmate.

"Come on, let's collect these roaches from the ashtrays!" Lenny said to me, talking about the leftover butts from the joints the adults were smoking at the party.

"Roaches? What's that?" I asked.

I quickly found out. Lenny was my wise sensei, leading me into a world of thrilling mind-altering substances. A world that would grab hold of me and not let go for many years.

We went around the party and collected all the roaches we could find, two little boys who were basically about to walk out into oncoming traffic. But the adults were too busy partying and getting high to notice what we were up to and pull us back to safety. Barry White was playing on the stereo and they were dancing and laughing in a haze of weed smoke. We went downstairs into a hidden corner of the massive apartment complex and we got high, pulling the last bit of life out of those little butts. I swiftly fell in love with the feeling of being in another state of mind, savoring the freedom and lack of inhibition.

In short order, Lenny and I came up with a plan to go from smoking joints to selling them. We scraped together our dollars and bought a dime bag for $20. We got rolling paper and produced a bag of loose joints. We went down to the corner of 80th Street and Amsterdam Avenue and began selling our wares—two scruffy middle-school drug kingpins. It was like an open bazaar at that corner, where we might be standing next to a couple of other guys also selling loose joints. Our customers were primarily a diverse mixture of residents from the neighborhood. I even had a little rhyme that I would croon to potential buyers:

"Pass me by, you won't get high."

What's interesting is how different that Amsterdam market was from the drug dealing going on in other parts of the city, where turf battles and proprietary protection of territories reigned supreme. Needless to say, our safety would have been seriously challenged if we tried to sell on some drug gang's street corner in Harlem or the Bronx. Fortuitously, we were basically working in the Sesame Street version of the drug market.

I wasn't selling drugs to make money to eat or to feed my children, as former dealers like Biggie Smalls notoriously claimed. My mother provided me with a full plate and everything I needed. No, it was about the cool. I got pulled into this because I liked the person it presented to the world—the swaggering street hustler. What saved me was that I had basketball, a new love that also was crucially important to me. Lenny's younger brother, Rodney, was a student at an alternative school called The DOME Project, which had been created as a place to serve students who were struggling at my school, IS 44. The school was located in the basement of All Angels Church on 80th Street between Broadway and West End Avenue. It was just two blocks from our drug bazaar at 80th and Amsterdam. Rodney and Lenny told me a basketball team was being formed at The DOME Project, which was giving the players free sneakers and a real uniform. I didn't have to hear anymore; I was on my way there before Rodney had finished the words "free sneakers." But when I got there, I was informed that they had just given away the last spot on the team. Lenny was already in. I was out.

In the midst of my disappointment, I got curious about what was going on there. I saw a huge room filled with kids playing Connect Four, doing homework, getting tutoring assistance. The kids all seemed to be calling out to a guy named John.

"John, John, I need your help."

I was surprised when I saw who John was—a tall, white guy with a full beard. My mother was an avid reader with lots of books in the house—books that I would read, admittedly often looking for the sex scenes. One of the books I came across was *Helter Skelter*, the Vincent Bugliosi-Curt Gentry book about the crazy Charles Manson murders. I stared at the pictures of scary-looking

Manson inside that book for a long time. So, when I saw this John guy, my first thought was, *Oh shit, this is a cult!*

I got beyond my initial bizarre impressions of The DOME Project and really got to know John Simon after he had mercy on me and put me on the basketball team. He had a significant impact on the trajectory of my life. So many of the ways he motivated us and related to us were permanently filed into my long-term memory—to be revived more than a decade later. Before we got on the court to play basketball, John had the team sit in a circle and discuss books he had assigned us to read—texts like *Manchild in the Promised Land* by Claude Brown and *Great Expectations* by Charles Dickens, both about the struggles of boys outside the mainstream trying to make sense of their world. We would have to go around the circle and read out loud before we went on the court. This created the startling spectacle of me, Dave, and Lenny out on the corner getting high, drinking malt liquor, selling joints—all while arguing about the motivations of Sonny, the main character in Claude Brown's thinly disguised autobiographical account of his years growing up in Harlem in the 1940s and 1950s.

Though my friends would later tell me that I was one of John's favorite kids at The DOME Project, that wasn't the sense I had at the time. He didn't seem to pay any closer attention to me than he did the others. Actually, John once told me he most admired Dave, who had eight siblings and had the most obstacles to overcome. I was probably the kid who had anything close to a middle-class upbringing, mainly because of the Riverside Drive location where I lived. But there were two memorable and timely things he said to me that definitely changed my trajectory.

"You have potential, Shawn," he said to me one day. "You can really do some great things if you spend less of your time on the corner of 80th Street and more of your time down here at The DOME."

Yes, my dumb ass was still selling drugs two blocks away from The DOME, at a location my mentor and coach would have to pass every day to get to work. Though she wasn't aware of exactly what I was doing outside of our apartment, my mother probably said similar things to me about a half-million times. But that line from John proved the value of getting the right word from the right person at the right time. And we never really know where the word will come from and when it will come. We might not even be aware at the time of its impact. But hearing that from John let me know he saw something special in me, a spark of some sort, and that set me on a different path.

The second incident occurred on the side of a mountain in New Hampshire. Every summer, John would bring us camping in New Hampshire, near the New Hampton School, one of several New England prep schools that had given scholarships to several DOME students a few years earlier. Those students had done well enough in those unfamiliar circumstances that the schools were willing to take more students recommended by The DOME. Another school was Lawrence Academy in Groton, Massachusetts. One summer, when we were supposed to be dutiful campers, a few of us had escaped the campsite—or so we thought—to get high and mess around. John busted us and delivered a scathing lecture that still sits on my brain as a searing memory.

"You all want to go away to prep school, but right now the only one that's responsible enough to go to prep school is Dave."

I heard his words on the side of that moonlit mountain like a slap in the face. I wanted to be the chosen one. I didn't begrudge Dave, with whom I was always competitive, especially on the basketball court, but I needed to be in the special group too. *Fuck that!* I remember thinking. *I'm going too!*

At that moment, John had raised the competitive bar. Perhaps he even intended for his words to be a direct challenge to me. His plan certainly worked. I got serious on that mountain and became a different student. I ended my residency on the corner of 80th Street and took more interest in my studies.

The DOME is where my social activism first got piqued. I'm not going to say it was activated, because I was still an adolescent far more into self than the world around me. But I began to gain a more acute sense of injustice because of what happened to us with the DOME Garden. John decided that it would be a good idea to get these young city kids more in touch with the natural world and give something back to our community by creating a DOME Garden. We found a garbage-filled abandoned lot on 84th Street between Broadway and Amsterdam Avenue. The lot was actually owned by the Loews Theater, which was on Broadway between 84th and 83rd Streets. The theater gave us permission to convert this eyesore into a lovely garden, so we all dove into the project, clearing away the rubbish to create space for the natural wonders we were going to watch sprout up right there on the Upper West Side. But after we did the difficult work of clearing out the lot, the theater reneged on the deal. Somebody probably realized this property was potentially too valuable to hand it over to these Black teenagers. We were all outraged—so much that we organized a protest. We created signs and marched up and down the street in front of the Loews, letting the world know what they had done to us. The theater didn't budge; we were forced to start all over again on a city-owned lot on 84ᵗʰ Street between Amsterdam and Columbus, a much less valuable property. But I think we all began to realize that we had a voice and could force people to listen if we used it.

When I was 13, my mother decided that her only child would benefit from spending some time in her former realm—dance. Yes, she signed up a strapping 13-year-old boy for a dance class at a time when basketball was becoming my primary activity and when I was hyper-focused on my visions of what it meant to look and act like a man. It was me and a bunch of white kids on the Upper West Side filing into a dance studio on 88ᵗʰ Street between Broadway and West End wearing tight black leotards. I was terrified that one of my friends would see me and my life as I knew it would effectively be over. I didn't necessarily hate the class. It was creative dance, so anything we did was acceptable, kind of like writing poetry. I was in that class for a year and a half. Though it felt like torture at the time to slip on the leotards, I think that even that short stint with creative expression in body movement probably helped me down the line get in touch with my creative side and also enriched my ability to navigate within this predominantly white space. At some point, it got to be too much. I started cutting the class, leaving our apartment like I was headed to dance but instead veering off in the opposite direction once I got outside. I'm just grateful that social media and camera phones didn't exist back then—surely somebody would be approaching me with blackmail material featuring Shawn Dove in tights.

This issue of my manhood—that ever-present obsession in the childhood of almost every Black boy—came up again a few years later at a party in the Foster housing project on 112ᵗʰ Street (now known as King Towers). I was dancing in the project's big community center, jamming to the hit song that year, "Le Freak" by Chic. I noticed that there was a small crowd gathering around me and my dance partner. I'm thinking, *Damn, I really must be getting down.*

A guy I didn't know came up to me and whispered in my ear, "You know that's a dude you're dancing with, right?"

This was the late 1970s, a period when we weren't even close to our current levels of enlightenment and advocacy on LGBTQ issues. But though I cared about perceptions of my manhood, I wasn't infused with toxic levels of masculinity like a lot of my homeboys, who probably would have reacted violently in that situation. All I did was quietly slink away. I was embarrassed because apparently I was the only one who didn't know my dance partner was trans. I also was probably high at the time. But the stranger who spoke in my ear must have felt sorry for me and wanted me to know what everybody else knew. At another party, this time in Stone Gym connected to the hallowed Riverside Church, I was again confronted with the challenge of toxic masculinity when I stepped on a dude's foot. He was an older, hard guy. Since the party was crammed with bodies, I didn't even notice what I had done and continued dancing. But when I looked up he was staring at me, all menacingly, while he talked to his homeboy and pointed at me.

"Yeah, yeah, this motherfucker right here," he said. Now they were both glaring at me.

I could feel the chill race down my back. This was about to be a situation. But I intuitively had the presence of mind to check my ego, to diffuse.

"Oh, I stepped on your foot? Sorry, man!"

He let it go. I knew if I had kept dancing and tried to ignore him, he and his boy were itching to beat somebody up. The ability to set aside our egos and navigate such tense moments is a skill that we need to survive life in our neighborhoods—though I wonder whether young boys in my sons' generation, spending most of their time indoors in front of video screens, are nurturing such skills.

One day at IS 44, I was rushing down the stairs to exit the school building with a few of my friends. Suddenly, we were confronted by several older guys who had managed to get into the school. They blocked our way on the stairs, so we had to stop.

"I want your money!" one of them demanded, talking to our group.

I'm not even sure where the idea came from, but I had a ready response.

"Why you want to mug us?" I said. "Why don't you go to some white neighborhood and mug the white boys? We're all Black—why mug us?"

They all looked at each other, then they looked back at us.

"Okay," he said. They moved out of the way so we could continue down the stairs. I don't know where that came from, but it was some kind of innate adaptive leadership skill that was becoming apparent at the time.

At the end of my time at IS 44, I took the standardized test for high school admission, along with thousands of other New York City eighth-graders.

At the end of the process sat the shiny golden ticket—entry to one of the city's three elite, specialized high schools: Stuyvesant, Bronx Science, and Brooklyn Tech, which each had their own Hall of Fame list of notable graduates who for generations had been dominating the city landscape in many fields. But none of that was on my radar screen when I took the test. It was yet another exercise in filling in bubbles on a sheet, something every public school student for the last two generations quickly grows tired of.

Each of the three schools establishes a cut-off for entry, a minimum score students must reach to be offered admission. Because of the racial and socioeconomic bias embedded in these tests—similar to the infamous SAT—the numbers of Black and Latino students in these schools have been paltry to nearly nonexistent, a fact that hasn't changed in generations. Stuyvesant's cutoff score is highest, Bronx Science is second and Brooklyn Tech is third—meaning Tech always has the highest number of Black and Latin students of the three. I did well enough on the test to miss the Brooklyn Tech cutoff score by one point. The city had instituted a policy that any student who came within five points of the Brooklyn Tech cutoff could go to a summer academy before freshman year and be offered admission. If I had any hesitancy about going to the summer academy and Tech, my mother quickly dismissed it by telling me, simply, "You *are* going!"

She shipped me off that summer to stay with my grandparents in Crown Heights, which was much closer to Brooklyn Tech's Fort Green campus, and I did well enough at the summer academy to gain admission to Tech in the fall. The rest of my friends were going to the city's regular zoned high schools in Manhattan, like Brandeis, Martin Luther King, and Norman Thomas. At the time, I was blissfully unaware of the importance of my attending Brooklyn Tech—as evidenced by my embarrassingly lackluster performance when I got there. All too quickly at Tech, I found my "tribe"—the crew that joined me in getting high, cutting classes, and playing spades in the lunchroom for multiple periods. A big part of my problem, one that has plagued Black boys since the Brown decision sent us into hostile white environments for our schooling, is that I was trying to navigate two worlds that in many ways were polar opposites, with different value systems. I was leaving behind a friend group that put an ultimate value on cool, on pleasure over everything else, on going along with the crowd. I was joining a school environment that put the highest value on academic achievement. When I got to Tech, clearly the former value system was winning the battle—in a clear knockout. I gravitated toward a group of guys at Tech, all of them Black, who valued the same things I had valued back on the Upper West Side.

During my *Creative Cluster* days at IS 44, I was assigned to read *The Fountainhead*, Ayn Rand's iconic novel about individuality versus conformity that has had an enormous influence on generations of young scholars. The main character in the book is an architect, a profession that I decided would be cool to pursue. I declared in my mind that Shawn Dove was going to be an architect. I took a technical drawing class at Tech, getting ready to prepare myself for my glorious architecture career. But one day, I was sitting next to an Asian kid as we both pulled out our assignment and laid it on the drafting board. I glanced over at his and then I looked down at mine. My paper had fingerprints and smudges all over it, looking like an amateurish effort. His drawing looked smooth and professional, like a picture of a drawing. I made a quick and painful determination: *I'm not good enough to be an architect.* I concluded that this Asian kid possessed some kind of mysterious qualities that I just didn't have.

I truly wish I had the opportunity to go back 45 years in time and give young Shawn Dove a pep talk, telling him how ridiculous it was to judge the likelihood of his becoming an architect on one drawing in a beginner's technical drawing class. But even though I wasn't yet committing myself to academic excellence, I was putting in *some* effort at Tech. One night when I was sitting home alone trying to master algebra, I actually started to cry because I just couldn't quite understand the concept we were supposed to be learning. Clearly, I did care.

I also started to discover that maybe I wasn't as "street" as I thought. One day, I went to visit my homeboys Lenny and Dave at Martin Luther King High School, to watch a talent show they were holding at the school. I don't mean to imply that there weren't smart kids at MLK, because there were, but it was a zoned high school—meaning they had to try to educate whoever lived in the zone and walked through the doors—facing the difficult challenges that these schools faced in the 1970s and continue to face. Gangs. Poverty. Difficult home lives. Violence. Too many students knew that the education system was not designed for their success and just disengaged from school. While I had my tribe at Tech playing spades in the cafeteria and hiding in dark corners of the enormous building to smoke weed and cut class, at MLK they were playing dice in the hallways. For money. Even though it was located in the heart of the Upper

West Side's high-rent district, across the street from Lincoln Center, like so many public schools in the city the predominantly Black and Latin student population looked far different than the people walking the streets outside of the school, who were mostly white. (The school was closed in 2005 because of its many academic problems and divided up into seven separate high schools occupying different floors.) I was walking around in the school with Lenny when he introduced me to his boys.

"Yo. This my nigga Shawn," he said.

Of course, we were listening to comedians like Richard Pryor who constantly used that word back then, and we would sometimes use it when talking to each other, but something about hearing it at that moment didn't feel right to me. It was like a shift occurred in me; I felt really uncomfortable with that introduction. I think it might have been an awareness that I had stepped out of that space I had occupied with Lenny, Dave, and the others and had stepped into a new world at Tech—even though I still hadn't embraced the Tech ethos.

One of the things I believed was holding me back at Tech was the fact that I hadn't made any meaningful connection with any of the adults in the building. Tech was so massive at 6,000 students that I'm sure it was a challenge for the educators to manage that population, never mind establishing a meaningful connection with this Black kid who didn't appear to be very committed to his studies.

This brings me back to the study featured in "Schooling for Resilience" by Fergus, Noguera, and Martin. In order for Black and Brown boys to perform well academically, the researchers wrote, they need to have formed a bond with at least one adult in the school. I had nothing at Tech that looked like a bond.

I also was disappointed that I wasn't going to be able to further my basketball career at Tech. Though I knew I was good enough, there were so many kids trying out my freshman year that it was almost a joke. You got about five minutes to run up and down the court and make an impression. Unless you did something spectacular, like a 360-windmill dunk, you were not going to stand out. Along with dozens of other disappointed kids, I was sent home in a daze that day, crushed by the collapse of my high school basketball dreams. I'm sure that went far in increasing my disillusionment at Brooklyn Tech.

During my sophomore year, I told John Simon that I wanted to go away to school as some of the others at The DOME had done. He went to my mom and asked her if she would allow me to leave New York and spend my last two years of high school at Lawrence Academy in Massachusetts. When she gave the okay, I was told that I needed to really buckle down to prepare myself for the academic rigor I would face at Lawrence. I started going to The DOME for homework help to up my game. While I was chosen to attend Lawrence, my boy Dave would be heading to New Hampton School, which was considered more of a jock school and not as academically rigorous as Lawrence. I think the feeling was I was better prepared than Dave to handle the rigor at Lawrence.

In addition to the academic preparation Dave and I were getting at The Dome, there was also a serious effort made to prepare us emotionally and socially for the culture clash. Once a week, we would go to the fancy home of Martin Tandler, the multimillionaire owner of Tandler Textiles who was chairman of the board of The DOME Project. Tandler lived in the San Remo building on Central Park West and 74th Street—a building whose list of notable residents, past and present, reads like a roll call of names on the Hollywood Walk of Fame: Steven Spielberg, Glenn Close, Dustin Hoffman, Steve Martin, Bruce Willis, Demi Moore, Diane Keaton, Rita Hayworth, Tiger Woods, Bono. The building's matching spires were made famous in the 1980s by a scene in *Ghostbusters*. I'm sure the intent was to expose us to the kind of high-society wealth that we would be colliding with in New England. In my case, it surely helped. Tandler had an interesting background—a former radical with the Students for a Democratic Society (SDS) in the 1960s, Tandler got fired as a teacher when he got busted with marijuana. So, he went on to take over his father's textile company and proceeded to turn it into a multimillion-dollar enterprise. We learned how to move, how to talk, how to be, in this sort of company. Tandler had us read George Orwell's *Animal Farm*, his way of giving us some of the additional intellectual heft we soon would need.

Weekly outings at Tandler's were not my only exposure to a different world. My mother had been shipping me off every summer since I was a little boy to Dominican Camp in upstate Poughkeepsie, New York, and for one summer to a program called Fresh Air Fund, which was created way back in 1877 to provide "life-changing" summer experiences to children from so-called "underserved" communities in New York City. Not only did I learn how to swim at the summer camp, I also got exposed to a whole lot of white people—exposure that prepared me for when I moved onto the lush, spacious campus of Lawrence, which looked more like a college campus than a high school.

I experienced the culture clash right away, but it probably could have been a lot worse. I went from a fairly diverse school of 6,000 kids to a leafy campus with 300 students, only 10 of whom were Black. I quickly had to become fluent in the art of code-switching. I had never heard of The Doors, had never heard of lacrosse, had never played ultimate frisbee—though I got to be quite good at it—and thought a *regatta* was a kind of pasta. I got comfortable enough to enjoy many of the activities and traditions on campus, but every so often I would think to myself that it was a good thing my boys back in New York couldn't see me jamming to The Doors, The Eagles, and Van Halen.

The difference between Brooklyn Tech and Lawrence was like the difference between schooling and learning. Despite its lofty reputation, Tech never infused me with a quest for learning, or even with the thought of what I would do after high school. When I was skipping class and playing spades in the lunchroom at Tech, I wasn't thinking about college. But when I got to Lawrence, there was such a prevailing ethos and expectation that higher education was in each of our futures that I adopted it without even thinking. Whether you were at the top of the class or the bottom, you were going to college. I am forever grateful to The DOME Project because had I languished at Tech, I'm not certain I would even have finished high school.

Right away, I made a connection at Lawrence with a teacher who had a profound impact on me. Her name was Mrs. Carlson, and she taught a poetry class that I initially hesitated to take. *Poetry is for sissies,* I remember thinking. But none of my homeboys were around, so I felt freed up to experiment with poetry. Besides, this was 1978 and the Sugarhill Gang's "Rapper's Delight" had become a huge hit, exposing the world to this new music form called rap that had sprung up from the streets of the Bronx. That quickly elevated spoken word and lyricism in the minds of Black teenage boys like me. After one early assignment in her class, I went up to the front of the class and read my poetry aloud. When I was done, the classroom erupted in applause.

"Who are they applauding for?" I said, looking around.

"They're applauding for you!" Mrs. Carlson said.

That gave me a big jolt of confidence. Up until that point, I derived most of my confidence from my corner jump shot. Now I was beginning to see that I had competencies in areas other than basketball. I started writing even more, gaining confidence as I got positive reactions from my teachers and classmates.

It was nothing at Tech to get away with cutting classes, but at Lawrence, the teachers were eating with us in the dining hall. If you didn't show up for a teacher's class, they were going to stare you down at the dinner table and ask, "Hey, what happened to you?" There was no escaping them. I took a public speaking class with Mrs. Carlson and she had me memorize MLK's entire "I Have a Dream" speech, which I had to deliver in front of an audience. That was yet another event that hugely boosted my confidence. Up at the New Hampton School, Dave benefited greatly from the increased scrutiny from the teachers—they discovered he had dyslexia, which explained everything about the struggles he had experienced in school up to that point.

One of the most important aspects of a boy's life is his peer group. If you attach yourself to the wrong crowd, as I did with the "gapping" crew back in Manhattan, you can quickly find yourself doing a lot of dumb stuff you would never have considered on your own. Almost immediately after stepping foot on the Lawrence campus, I found myself drawn to a gangly, Black, preppy-looking kid in khakis and a cardigan sweater. His name was Clarence. He was from Columbus, Ohio, and in short order, he became the closest friend I've ever had in my life. From the beginning, we just seemed to *get* each other, in that mysterious chemistry that draws some people together while repelling others. We would jokingly trade barbs about who came from rougher urban streets, we would tease each other mercilessly, but it was clear from the start that Clarence and I loved each other.

Clarence and I were part of a sprinkling of Black kids at Lawrence, but I'm pleased to say there wasn't a great deal of racial tension on the campus. However, things didn't start out for me on the most encouraging note. Shortly after I got to Lawrence, I got into an intense argument with my roommate, a white guy from South Boston. We were both playing football—at Lawrence, every student was required to play a sport every season—and were vying for the same starting position at tight end. That added a surge of competitive tension in our room. During the argument, the dude called me a "flat-footed nigger." I think I almost blacked out; I was so mad. Others came into the room to separate us before we commenced breaking up the furniture. I don't know if he faced any kind of disciplinary action, but they did move him out of the room and replace him with another student.

There was another incident that I will now describe as racial, but at the time my dumb, clueless, "unwoke" ass didn't even realize it. To this day, I'm still embarrassed to recount this story, but I know I must. During my senior year, my second year at Lawrence, a white girl named Carolyn came bouncing up to me with another girl a couple of days before Halloween. They had a request.

"Shawn, will you be our pimp for the Halloween party?"

I've repeated that scene in my head a thousand times, scripting out all the responses I should have come up with to put these clueless, privileged white girls in their place. All the ways I should have thrown them out of my room and taught them a lesson about their racism and cultural insensitivity. The speeches I should have delivered in that situation so they would never repeat such a painfully tone-deaf request. But what did I really say in response to Carolyn and her friend?

"Okay."

That was it. I just nodded my head in agreement. At the party, with me outfitted in a "pimp" hat and flashy clothes, and Carolyn and her friend barely wearing any clothes, we strolled into the cafeteria as Shawn the pimp and his two hookers. The place went wild, with an eruption of screaming and hollering. We won first prize, but the residual shame of me partaking in such a horrific stunt like that took years to shake from my consciousness. Again, I just thank the Lord that we didn't have smartphones with cameras back then.

When I would board the Amtrak train to travel back to New York for holidays or for the summer, I would have to begin a mental transformation on the train to turn myself back into the street-smart dude who could hang on the corner with his boys. I still had my "cool" up in Groton—probably even more so as the tough Harlem guy on a campus of rich white kids—but it wasn't the same kind of cool I needed in New York. I had to get my swagger back, my better-not-fuck-with-me aura. It's a transformation that will be intimately familiar to any Black kid, especially Black young men, who has had to bridge two vastly different worlds as I did. It's the same transformation that led to the tragic death in 1985 of a 17-year-old kid named Edmund Perry, whose situation was eerily similar to my own.

In an environment where the recent high-profile killings of several Black men—and 66-year-old Black grandmother Eleanor Bumpurs—at the hands of police had ratcheted up racial tensions in the city, where many Black New Yorkers felt that Black boys were walking around with targets on their backs, Edmund Perry and his older brother, Jonah Perry, had been the beneficiaries of programs that provided them with scholarships to escape from Harlem. Perry had returned to his Harlem neighborhood a few weeks after graduating from the renowned Philip Exeter Academy in New Hampshire. He had a summer job at a Manhattan brokerage firm and was about to attend Stanford in the fall. His older brother, Jonah, 19, was a student at Cornell, after attending Westminster, a fancy prep school in Connecticut. They were both back in Harlem for the summer, hanging out with their boys.

Exactly what happened that led to Edmund's death was a matter of bitter dispute. The police said that Edmund and Jonah tried to rob a plainclothes officer near St. Luke's Hospital on 114th Street and Amsterdam Avenue, very close to where Edmund and Jonah lived with their mother, Veronica Perry, on 114th Street in the Morningside Heights neighborhood, adjacent to West Harlem. The officer, 24-year-old Lee Van Houten, claimed that when Edmund and Jonah grabbed him from behind and tackled him, he reached down and pulled his gun from his ankle holster, firing three times. He hit Edmund in the abdomen and Jonah ran off. While the Black community bitterly rejected the police version of events, asking why these two shining stars would try to rob someone, city officials said they had 23 witnesses backing up Van Houten's story. It was a case that vexed many, leading to a bestselling book, a TV movie, a *Law & Order* episode—and numerous newspaper and magazine profiles examining the challenges faced by Black boys and girls who had to navigate between elite prep-schools and their home neighborhoods.

In one of those profiles in the *Washington Post*, written by Juan Williams, Edmund's Exeter roommate, 18-year-old Malcolm Stephens from Bedford-Stuyvesant, said, "Maybe it seemed to some people he had a little bit of a chip on his shoulder." Stephens claimed that Perry had difficulty getting along with many faculty members, "But it was more like he was out of one world and in another he didn't belong in... He had a hard time dealing with the preppy types who ignored and were unsympathetic to the world he came from."

Just a few years earlier, I also had to figure out how to straddle these two worlds. With episodes like the "gapping" in Central Park in my past, I could easily have gotten caught up in the kind of situation that ended Edmund's life. I had actually met their mother, Veronica, a community activist and local school board member, in the years when I was bouncing around on Amsterdam Avenue before I went away to Lawrence. As I heard about Edmund's death, I deeply identified with his trials on a cellular level.

When it was time for me to start thinking about colleges, I got advice and counsel from many of the white people who had become vital parts of my life. The college advisor at Lawrence helped me create a list that included colleges like Syracuse, Pepperdine, and LSU—large public and private schools with diverse student bodies. But when I talked to John Simon on the dorm payphone one day, he told me to throw away that list. He wanted me to replace it with smaller elite liberal arts and Ivy League schools in the Northeast—places like Hamilton, where he had gone to school, Colgate, Brown, Haverford, and Wesleyan. Interestingly, it never crossed anyone's mind, including my own, to put any HBCUs on the list. But schools like Howard, Hampton, and Morehouse were not on the radar screens of these white Northeasterners. Wesleyan got even more traction because Mrs. Carlson's father had taught at the university for 30 years, and I was under the impression that she had dated the admissions director. I was getting a lesson in the value of social capital—and I didn't even realize it.

During that year, I made an important shift in my awareness of racial exclusion. I looked around campus and came to the realization that I was there so that the school could check its diversity box —in other words, I was a token in the quota slot. But along with that realization, I made the mature decision that it was useless to complain that I was there simply to represent a particular demographic. No, complaining wouldn't do much good. I decided I would take advantage of the opportunity. If they were going to let me go to Lawrence, I was going to exploit the experience for everything I could get out of it.

My relocation to Lawrence had little impact on my steadily growing abuse of alcohol and drugs. In fact, in many ways it got worse; the higher the expectations and the heavier the responsibilities I felt on my shoulders, the more I got high. I never knew what a bong was until I got to Lawrence, but I soon became an expert at hiding the odor from our bong hits. We would take hits and then blow the smoke into a moist towel. Next, we would strategically use a bunch of sprays and air fresheners. My substances of choice at the time were exclusively weed and beer. I would get the weed from kids on campus who were selling and sometimes I would bring some back with me from New York.

On one of my train rides back to New York, I found my way to the Amtrak bar car soon after we left Boston's South Street station and was giddy to discover the bartender didn't hesitate to serve beers to a 17-year-old—the drinking age was 18 at the time. I got so drunk that by the time we got to Penn

Station I was throwing up and in a seriously altered state. Somebody took me home—a trip I couldn't even recall—and when I walked into the apartment, I remembered my mother's two angry words.

"You're drunk!"

I decided to take my talents to Wesleyan University in Middletown, Connecticut—a small, 3,000-student liberal arts school that liked to call itself one of the "Little Ivies," along with Amherst and Williams Colleges—also known as "The Big Three." The student population was nearly identical to the kinds of students who attended Lawrence, so I experienced very little culture shock when I stepped onto the campus. Unfortunately, Wesleyan was also a place where I could really lean into drug use.

Chapter 5: Braving My Wilderness

Owning your story and loving yourself through the process is the bravest thing you will ever do.
  —Brene Brown, *The Gift of Imperfection*

It's a miracle that I managed to graduate from Wesleyan on time because I can probably count on two hands the number of days that I did not either drink, smoke, or snort.

When I traveled down to Middletown, Connecticut, from Massachusetts for the pre-freshman orientation, I immediately felt like I had found my new home. With just a little over 300 Black students in a student body of around 3,200 students, Wesleyan had an actual space, the Malcolm X House, a dorm for Black students to connect with each other and be immersed in fellowship without the interference of other groups. After coming from Brooklyn Tech and Lawrence, I was initially impressed that Wesleyan was concerned enough about the care and comfort of Black students that they had created a space for us. Yet, history and upper-class students would reveal that it was less about the university's care of Black students and more the result of the protests and demands of Black students who came before me.

I also was still harboring serious hoop dreams. Or maybe I should say hoop delusions. Going to Wesleyan would allow me to play college basketball. Yes, it was Division III ball, but it was still an opportunity to play at the next level. Besides, I thought Division III meant I would walk on the court and instantly become Julius Erving. I wasn't necessarily thinking I was close to NBA caliber, but I'm sure in the back of my mind I was thinking I still maybe had a shot at professional glory. I would soon discover how delusional I was; there were extremely talented players on Division III courts.

Even though I had been immersed in a college-going culture at Lawrence Academy, somehow the name Wesleyan hadn't pierced my consciousness until it came time to create college lists. I naively assumed that no one else had heard of Wesleyan either. But when I went into Tandler Textiles, the company owned by The DOME Project board chairman who also served as a mentor for my summer job, I was stunned by the reactions I got when I told them where I was going to college.

"Wow! Wesleyan?" they'd say, accompanied by arched eyebrows. Perhaps it was a combination of Wesleyan's prestige and their lowered expectations for a Black male teenager, but they were genuinely shocked. For the rest of the summer, I could tell many of them looked at me differently. Suddenly I had become a young Black man with an actual future.

Another fact of life at Wesleyan had me extremely excited about my matriculation—the 10/1 Black female/Black male ratio on campus. At Wesleyan, I began to cultivate the mystique and accompanying nickname the "Love Dove"—a nickname given to me by an upper-class teammate and native New Yorker, John Johnson. The combination of being a poet, a baller, and an activist gave me the extrinsic validation that at that time in my maturity level I was unable to derive intrinsically. I was the street-smart guy from Harlem—more accurately the Upper West Side at that point, but Riverside Drive didn't have quite the aura as saying "I'm from Harlem"—who also had the sensitive, seemingly soft side that wrote poetry and was in touch with his feelings. Because I had the hard side, I was able to cultivate the soft without compromising my masculinity—at least that's how I saw it in my 18-year-old mind. In all modesty, the attention I received from my female classmates was overwhelming for me. For the first couple of years, I was balancing two serious relationships—one with Allyson, a Black girl who was one of my colleagues on the staff of the Black poetry journal, *Expressions*; the other with Catalina, a Puerto Rican girl, who was also a gifted poet and contributor to *Expressions*. When Catalina did a semester abroad, I spent all my time with Allyson. When Allyson spent a semester doing a journalism internship, it was me and Catalina. The Malcolm X House and La Casa, the house for Latino students, were right across the street from each other, so my commute was short. I did the Malcolm X-La Casa shuffle. I really thought I was the living embodiment of what it meant to be a cool Black man, the Shaft image I became enamored with in the movie theaters of my youth.

While I was tentatively courting my passion for poetry at Lawrence, at Wesleyan I became a poetry enthusiast, organizing readings, editing the journal, delving deeply into my creative side. I also began to recognize something that others had already seen in me—leadership ability. That self-awareness joined together at Wesleyan with a growing activism activated by my outrage at the injustices I saw around me. It's a common phenomenon for Black students to become social justice activists when they hit a college campus and begin to have their eyes opened up.

One day during my freshman year, a senior named Kofi, a track star from Ghana who was deep into campus activism, walked up to me and pointed at my chest.

"You're going to be on the minority faculty search committee," he said.

It wasn't a request; it was a command. I dutifully obeyed because of Kofi's stature on campus and with the Black student body, and showed up at the next meeting—and was startled to discover I was in over my head. *Why am I here?* I remember thinking. I may have been high at the time, which certainly didn't help my comprehension of the proceedings.

We got word less than two months into my freshman year that the KKK was going to be holding a rally in Meriden, Connecticut, about 10 miles away from campus. We decided we needed to have a presence at the rally, to protest against the Klan's hatred. We got busy making up signs. I was anxious about how I would feel when I caught sight of those white robes. We gathered and organized in the Marcus Garvey Lounge of the Malcolm X House.

The Klan rally and our counter-protest got a lot of attention from the local news, which trained their cameras on these Black Wesleyan students, about 50 strong, coming together to show their strength. The whole thing was scary and thrilling. It was stunning to realize that these idiotic symbols of ignorance and hate were bold enough to stage a march in Connecticut in 1980. Not in Mississippi, but the heart of the supposed liberal Northeast.

Later that night, we all gathered around the television in the Malcolm X House to watch news coverage of the event. The screen filled with the image of our counter-protest as the reporter described the scene. We all cheered. When the camera zoomed in to show me and my sign, my head just about exploded. My sign was supposed to say, "The Klan Must Be Stopped." But somehow, in my haste and apparent nervousness to finish the sign, I had spelled "stopped" with one P instead of two. So, my sign actually said, "The Klan Must Be Stoped." The image of my sign lingered on the screen for what felt like forever—as the other students in the room burst into astonished laughter, at my expense, pointing at the screen. I was mortified. I was back to that kid on the Harlem street with the drying pee-stained sheet hanging on the fire escape. My sign was extra big and extra colorful, too. Clearly, I had spent far more time on the artfulness of it than on the words. To make matters even worse, I was on the verge of declaring my major—English. I could just imagine the white guys in the control room requesting that the camera stay on me extra long, to show this dumb-ass Black boy at this elite school who didn't know how to spell S-T-O-P-P-E-D.

In my embarrassment, it didn't occur to me to turn on my fellow students and ask, "Um, how the hell did y'all march right next to me for all that time and not one of the 50 of you recognize that *stopped* was spelled wrong?!" But unlike the embarrassment of my pee-stained sheets hanging from the fire escape on that Harlem street, I got over the incident quickly.

There's no doubt that my interest in social justice blossomed on the Wesleyan campus. Soon it began to show up more in my poetry, too. The Love Dove expanded his gaze beyond his own concerns—I started thinking about the state of the world beyond my sex life. I had written my first politically conscious poem in Mrs. Carlson's class before I left Lawrence, about my anger over the December 1979 police shooting of a Black man named Arthur McDuffie in the Liberty City neighborhood of Miami—a shooting that led to riots in 1980 when the police officers were acquitted. It was a potent discovery for me that I could use poetry as a method of releasing my anger and frustration.

At Wesleyan, I delved more deeply into using my poetry as a weapon to fight back. I can't overemphasize how important that discovery was for me as a young Black man trying to figure out his place in the world and coming to grips with the fact that I was not seen by many as deserving of a slice of the American dream. Over the past 400 years, much of American society has been constructed to silence Black men and make us internalize self-hatred. But the more Black boys can come upon tools to repel the imposed self-hatred and find constructive ways to reframe the images that America has drawn of us, the more agency we begin to feel in our own lives. That's what happened to me on the Wesleyan campus.

The famous image of the striking sanitation workers in Memphis holding up the signs in February 1968 that read "I Am a Man" is all about Black men finding their voice, dignity, and agency. Poetry gave me the voice that eludes far too many Black men. Our boys search for the voice in sports, or hip hop, or even in the kind of toxic masculinity resulting in violence toward women. As if a blow delivered to a woman's face would be telling the world, "I am a man." With poetry, I found an entirely new and cathartic place to show my manhood, my strength, my vulnerability, and my agency.

I have been thrilled to see the ways that Romero and Jamare have found their voices in their faith and music—and to use those voices not only for their own catharsis but to help other Black males who are struggling. They have come to that place far earlier than I did.

By 1982, my sophomore year, I was editor-in-chief of *Expressions*, the Black poetry magazine. I snuck a little bit of the Love Dove in one of our issues—in the photo montage on the cover, I included a picture of me kissing my girlfriend Allyson, who by that time was my serious and exclusive partner—several years later to become my wife. I was a *long* way from that clueless kid at Lawrence who showed up at the Halloween party as the pimp with two white girls on my arm.

During my early years at Wesleyan, I had the profound experience of sitting in the presence of one of my heroes, musician and activist Gil Scott-Heron, and absorbing the lessons he bestowed upon the student body after one of his shows on campus. The pilot light of my activism had been lit before Gil got to campus, but he turned me into a human torch. After his show, we gathered in the Marcus Garvey Lounge of the Malcolm X House and sat around in a circle, soaking up his every word. This was right on the heels of the release of "Angel Dust," one of Gil's biggest hits. I remember sitting there and thinking, *I want to be just like Gil Scott-Heron* (little did I know at the time how prophetic my words turned out to be, considering both of our allegiances to drugs at the time). It was the same feeling that washed over me when I was a little boy at Lel's in Harlem and sitting on the couch staring at a picture of Muhammad Ali wearing his white satin boxing shorts. I felt drawn in like if I stared at the postcard long enough I actually could draw strength from it. Gil was giving me strength in the Marcus Garvey Lounge.

While most artists come to a college campus, collect their checks, and cut out after their show, Gil felt like he needed to connect with us, fill us up. He had been a college professor before his music career took off, so I'm sure he felt at home around us. To me, he was larger than life—brilliant, artistic, fearless. These days, I often use the leadership mantra "bold as a lion yet humble as a lamb" and that's precisely the feeling I got from him. I didn't know at the time that he was also flawed, also extremely human—but that probably would have made me love him even more. Gil was joined that night by the legendary spoken word group, The Last Poets—a group that had a profound influence on Gil before he started his performing career. As you can imagine, I was in heaven.

There were a few white guys there in the lounge who had done their Gil research and knew he was deep into the ancient Chinese philosophy text, *I Ching: The Book of Changes*, which contains thousands of years of Chinese wisdom and is studied across the world. The white guys brought the book up to Gil. He talked about it and read a few of his favorite passages.

Gil validated me that night in the most profound way. I saw something in him that gave me strength, made me feel like I mattered. It's an extremely important experience for Black boys. We need people to tell us who we are before we know. The problem too many of us encounter is that there is so much trauma and toxicity in our lives that the tormentors significantly outweigh the mentors. We are being modeled unevenly. Too often our boys are hearing too much "You ain't shit and you ain't gonna be shit—just like your daddy wasn't shit." With enough of those words being poured into them, they have no choice but to manifest that, to prove it right. We have to find a way to pour more promise into them than peril. For me, even with all the promise I was getting, I couldn't concentrate on it enough to really absorb it all because I was too immature and distracted by the siren songs of sex and drugs.

I got validated in that same lounge a bit later by the celebrated poet Audre Lorde, who was famous for her poems that brilliantly evoked the rage that accompanies Blackness in America. After I said something to her during a group session, she paused and stared at me.

"There's something about you that reminds me of my son," she said, her voice filled with emotion. The room was packed with Black women who heard that; the Love Dove mystique got a serious boost that day.

Gil's music was truly the soundtrack to my years at Wesleyan—I played it in an endless loop. The man had me diving deep into serious hero worship. A few years later that hero-worship would lead me to an embarrassing scene when I wandered backstage after his show at the club SOB's (Sounds of Brazil) in the West Village of NYC. I somehow made it to his dressing room, stumbling drunk, holding up a picture of him at Wesleyan.

"Gil! You remember me?" I said to him.

He looked up, startled and more than a bit alarmed.

"Yo, brother," he said—more calmly than the situation probably called for. "I don't remember you. But man, you gotta go."

Like a lot of artists, I became convinced that my creative juices flowed even more forcefully when I was high. This led me down a spiral that got worse and worse at Wesleyan. It's a miracle that I made it through in four years because at times it felt like I was intent on self-destruction.

It was a gift that I had my writing because I injured my shoulder my junior year and my basketball career was suddenly imperiled. My career had been a lot of ups and downs to that point. While I was a key member of the Wesleyan freshman team that went undefeated, which gave me a certain cachet on campus, things kind of slid downhill after that. As I saw it, a big part of my problem was the varsity coach, an old-school gruff Irishman who all the Black players were convinced was racist. Coach had an affinity for Irish players who may have had sound fundamentals but were not as talented as many of the Black players. The coach *hated* the flashy swagger that city players brought onto campus; in response, he would try to bury all of us on the bench as much as he could get away with. He never used the word "nigger" when he was speaking to us, but he might as well have, considering his actions toward us. Eventually, his attitude chased most of us away—it got to the point where many of the best basketball players on campus were the brothers playing intramurals.

I had my flashes of brilliance on the varsity team, but it wasn't steady. I did get enough shine that I got a taste of what it must be like for elite athletes with the women that always seem to be buzzing around them. After one of the best games of my career—I got "Player of the Game" honors—when I was walking off the court, a beautiful girl from New York who I had been admiring for a long time walked up to me and planted a kiss on my lips. Out of the blue. With no warning. It was crazy.

During my junior year, I felt a sharp pain in my left shoulder and knew that something was seriously wrong. It turned out to be torn ligaments. I tried to keep playing, but my shoulder kept popping out of the socket, eventually requiring surgery. I now had surgical scars to prove my toughness on the court. I became so disillusioned with basketball that I decided to not even play my senior year. After being the primary source of my self-esteem and sense of my place in the world for most of my life, college basketball and I ended our relationship. Well, given I continued to play for many years after graduation, I should say we entered a new phase in our relationship. Fortunately, I had other things in my life at that point to fill me up—poetry, activism, writing. In fact, by then I was sports editor of the Wesleyan student newspaper, *The Argus*. I didn't need organized basketball anymore.

Academically I was a B student, but I could have done better if I applied myself. I was too busy getting high, playing sports, and having fun. When things got sticky for me academically, I leaned hard on my relationships to squeeze by. Clarence and I took a Latin American History class pass/fail one semester, so predictably we weren't serious enough about doing the work—until it was almost too late. When it came time for the final, we knew we were in serious danger of failing the class. We stayed up all night studying—mixing the books with weed and malt liquor. I was nervous as I sat in class watching Professor Whitman hand out the exam. Something came over me, a nudge that told me I needed to do a little more to push me over the top. I knew the professor liked me; I tried one last attempt to work that angle.

"Don't cry for me, Mrs. Whitman," I suddenly started singing, as she handed me the exam, "the truth is, we didn't study." It was a line from the play "Evita," which was crushing it on Broadway at the time. Professor Whitman burst into laughter, as did the rest of the class. I'm fairly certain her affection for me helped when it came time to put a check next to pass or fail for that class. She passed me, but I know if I had been taking it for a grade I would have failed.

Because I had dropped too many classes, it was looking somewhat dicey senior year whether I would have enough credits to graduate. I used relationships again by convincing one of my English professors to allow me to do a senior thesis project worth two credits, which would get me over the top. The project basically consisted of me compiling all my poetry together in one volume, with an accompanying narrative about the work. Over the years, I have come to discover that much of our world revolves around relationships—a lesson I'm sure most of my white classmates at Wesleyan learned long before they got to Middletown. It's a lesson that never reaches enough Black children, whose relationships with their schools and teachers are too often characterized by conflict, suspicion, and disaffection. This is especially true for Black boys, typically beginning around the fourth grade—as we saw with Jamare in Detroit.

There's no doubt that drugs occupied too much of my mind space at Wesleyan, literally and figuratively. Many other students were in the same place, so getting the drugs wasn't difficult at all. When I concluded that my creative juices flowed more freely while I was high—a conclusion believed by generations of creatives, particularly musicians—I was doomed, careening fast down the slippery slope.

You might wonder how I reconciled my campus activism and quest for social justice with my drug habit, but it wasn't really that difficult. I think many activists and leaders in the social justice realm reach for powerful diversions to escape the difficulty and stress of the work—whether it's drugs, sex, gambling, even the exhilaration from the limelight. I think that's why so many leaders get caught out there when some of their diversions are publicly revealed. When you're swimming in the deep waters, you don't always know you're in the process of drowning, like the lobster boiling in the pot. Richard Pryor had a hilarious cocaine bit in one of his stand-up specials: "I started off snorting little, tiny pinches, saying 'I know I ain't gonna get hooked. Not on no coke—you can't get hooked. My friends have been snorting 15 years; they ain't hooked!'"

To me, drug use was part of my social networking, connecting with others. In my junior year, I lived in a house off-campus with three seniors, all pre-med, who were the biggest potheads. Our place was known as the drug den. All the women knew if they wanted to get high, just come over to our crib. It was cathartic for me, but it also was an effective coping mechanism, a way to escape all the stress I was feeling in that predominantly white environment.

During the first semester of my senior year, Clarence came to me with an entrepreneurial proposal: Let's sell coke ourselves. It wasn't something that we needed to do to make money. It was not for basic survival or anything like that. We just thought it would be a cool way to make some extra money. In all honesty, it was quite thrilling. We already had connections—Clarence had some dude in Middletown who supplied him, and we had white boys on campus who could provide us with more supply. We went out and bought scales and opened up shop, selling out of the apartment we had in a high-rise building on the edge of campus—incidentally right next to a predominantly Black public housing complex. I was actually shocked when I first encountered a 'hood in Middletown—not something I expected to find in the cozy, little college towns of Connecticut. I didn't even see the irony of two Black Wesleyan boys at this elite school selling drugs in the shadow of the housing projects, but there it was.

Most of our clientele were wealthy white boys on campus, though we also had our share of Black, Latino, and Asian kids, too. Our biggest-selling item was little cellophane pouches of powder cocaine, in $50 and $100 increments. We would have lots of young women knocking on our door as well; it wasn't just guys. One of our celebrity customers was a member of a well-known political family. He came to our door a couple of times, though he more often would send his girlfriend to cop for him.

By the time we got around to the second semester when seniors start setting their sights on the rest of their lives, we decided to shut it down. There wasn't any specific incident that scared us away; we just thought it was time. We still had our own supply, and we were using it to get high, but we were no longer selling. The shop was closed. A little more than a week after we made that decision, the cops raided the rooms of the white boys on campus who were our primary supplier. It was big news, on the front page of the local *Middletown Press*—the sons of the wealthy elite turning out to be drug dealers. Middletown had the same class-based town-gown conflicts you'll find in most college towns, so I'm sure the *Press* and the locals were giddy about this scandal. But for me and Clarence, the news was terrifying. We were certain one of them, under the withering questioning of some hard-nosed detective, would turn on us and rat us out as one of their biggest customers. I had seen too many gangster movies, sending me on scary flights of fancy.

For weeks after the bust, I lived in terror that a rifle-wielding SWAT team would be busting down our door any minute. It was another case of divine intervention in my life—a guardian angel or higher force looking out for me. Because if we still had been dealing, I'm sure we would have gotten swept up in the case. The surveillance would have put the police on our trail. When I read that the guys had lawyered up—after their expulsion—I knew it would have transpired differently for me and Clarence. Our "lawyered up" would have consisted of the local public defender, offering us a plea bargain that would surely include jail time. I'm pretty sure none of my Wesleyan classmates who were busted saw the inside of a jail cell.

When we got close to graduation, I came face-to-face perhaps for the first time with cocaine's enormous downside. It happened the night of our senior dinner, an annual tradition among the Black students where we would give out awards and also use the occasion to roast particular students. The roasting could be pretty harsh, exposing clandestine activities and embarrassing experiences for students with creative humor. In retrospect, we were quite unforgiving and brutal with each other, all in the name of fun and celebration.

Even though I was on the dinner's planning committee, when the time came to leave for the dinner, we were just coming down from a cocaine high.

One of the worst parts of cocaine usage is the severity of the low you experience after being lifted by that euphoric high. We were both feeling awful.

"I'm not going," Clarence announced.

I wish I could say the same thing, but I knew I *had* to go, as one of the primary organizers. I also had to give some sort of speech at the event. Even though I was in the throes of addiction, I remained able to tend to my responsibilities—*kinda*. But as I made my way over to the dinner venue, I felt crazy. Really jittery and paranoid. One of my pre-med classmates came over to me, staring into my face.

"Shawn, are you alright?" he asked.

I nodded, but his question just made things worse. *I wasn't even that close to this guy; if he could tell something was wrong with me, I must look crazy!* I told myself. As I was sitting at my table, fidgeting and full of worry, I heard my name called. I was stunned. I had won an award for my campus activism, particularly for the role I played in organizing the publishing of *Expression* magazine. The moment I got up to walk to the stage, I snapped out of my paranoid state, like a light switch had been turned on. It felt like God was intervening once again, setting me straight before I embarrassed myself in front of my peers. Maybe the most embarrassing thing about that evening in retrospect was that there are now pictures of me that exist in the world accepting that award wearing a skinny, black, leather tie. Hey, it was the 1980s.

After I walked across the stage at Wesleyan to receive my diploma, with my mother beaming in the crowd, I went straight to corporate America. I accepted a full-time job with Tandler Textiles, traveling the country and working in the garment district selling textiles, for which I was quite generously compensated. I did that for four years—until it became clear to me that I was on the path to killing myself. I got married to my girlfriend, Allyson, who brought much joy into my life, but my drug use was accelerating. I could do okay during the week, but I would hit the alcohol and drugs hard on the weekend.

I would grow increasingly terrified as the work week moved toward Wednesday because that's when I felt all my inadequacies were on display for the whole company to see. Every Wednesday morning, during our weekly sales meetings, the sales force would sit in the boardroom and each of us give reports on what we had sold, what we hoped to sell, and what we had in the works. I had done a decent job of putting myself through a crash course in the history of textiles—the origins and uses of fabrics like tartan, madras, houndstooth, and gingham in the fashion industry. The Wednesday sales meeting was when my impostor syndrome would kick in real hard—this thought that I didn't belong there, I was in over my head, trying to fake it until I make it.

I had convinced Martin Tandler to create a sales trainee position and make me his first hire, the first Black salesperson in the company. But now that I was in the belly of the beast, I felt like I was drowning. I would try to use humor and storytelling to mask the truth—that I usually didn't have much to report. I was comparing myself to seasoned salespeople, some of whom were twice my age. I didn't find out until later that most of my colleagues would look forward to my presentations with great anticipation because they knew it was going to be entertaining and funny. I got embarrassed in the middle of the company Christmas party one year by Tandler himself because after I got a very big order from a rainwear designer named Larry Levine, I procrastinated and failed to go by Levine's office to officially take the order and close the deal. I didn't even understand then why I didn't close the deal, but I know now that it was a form of self-sabotage.

I was living way too fast. Doing cocaine at parties with my co-workers and then going back to the Upper West Side and getting high with my crew from The DOME Project. It was the epitome of the double life that so many Black men live, especially those who lift themselves out of the hood and ascend to corporate America. Promise and peril.

Chapter 6: Stepping into My Destiny

The world all around me was falling down
And when it crumbled I saw higher ground
Something happened inside of me
I stepped into my true identity.

—Michael Bernard Beckwith, *Life Visioning*

Two years into my four-year tenure at Tandler, which lasted from 1984 to 1988, I took the first monumental step on a new path—a step I still couldn't see ahead of me. In 1986, I was invited to join the board of directors of The DOME Project. I was a living, breathing testament to the groundbreaking work of The DOME—at least that's what I'm sure they all saw when they looked at me. I was just 24 years old, still trying to figure out the world. It was surreal to be in this decision-making capacity for a program that I first encountered as an adolescent in middle school.

Around this time, I also got inspired to pair two of my loves—poetry and basketball. Ever since Mrs. Carlson at Lawrence had introduced me to poetry, I had been harboring a need to explore my creative impulses. By now I recognized it was an important part of who I was. If I had stayed at Brooklyn Tech, had remained in the city for high school, I likely would never have made this discovery. It was the dawning of my realization of how crucial it is for Black boys to have creative outlets—something that still isn't manifested in most of the schools Black boys attend in America. I created a youth publication called *Poetry In Motion*, which featured young people writing about their love of basketball. The book came out in 1988. It was my first foray into the publishing world, though certainly not my last.

At the time, I was the gleaming poster child for Black male success—a young Black man who had emerged from a less-than-ideal childhood, the son of a struggling single mom, graduated from a prestigious university, married to an ambitious journalist, living in a fancy condo in a well-heeled Upper West Side condo and now firmly ensconced in the corporate world as an $80,000-a-year salesman in the glamorous fashion industry. But my success story obscured a darker truth. Black men, driven by the survival instinct, often become masters of deception, presenting a smooth public face that we can use to hide trauma and uncertainty behind the façade. I was struggling with a drug addiction that was starting to swallow me whole and plagued by not only the impostor syndrome but also by what I now recognize as survivor's guilt—what was so special about me that I had "made it" and now had so many opportunities flowing my way?

At The DOME, my old mentor, John Simon, had been replaced by another white male, Tom Pendleton, who informed the board that he was going to resign. The board appointed me chair of the search committee for a new executive director. One night while I was sitting in my condo reading through a stack of resumes, I had a revelation. I thought about my office mate at the textiles firm, a Jewish guy named Steve who appeared to be doing quite well for himself. But I knew that Steve was not truly happy as he would regularly express his discontent. He'd complain about maintaining an expensive lifestyle with a condo in Manhattan and a house in the Hamptons, wishing he had made different choices with his life now that he was almost 50. Was that what my future looked like? Would I look back with regret 25 years down the line, torturing some young office mate with my wistful I-coulda-been-a-contender stories? That was a terrifying thought to me. I knew that this textile business was not my true North, was not what I was put here to do. I was hit with a thought.

Shawn, you should apply for the executive director job. Throw your hat in the ring, Shawn! You can do this job.

In retrospect, I don't know if it was the voice of God beaming down—or my inner voice telling me that this was a way for me to save myself from the catastrophic ending I was careening toward. Maybe it was both. The next day I went to the board and declared that I wanted the job. My announcement was warmly received around the boardroom. I think there were two factors at play— the board had grown tired of the search and they loved the idea of someone who grew up in the organization coming back to lead it. I would be the first Black person to lead the organization after two white males. The optics of it all were ideal; it was a true feel-good story.

I walked into The DOME Project as a uniquely young and clueless executive director. That first year was packed with promise but teeming with peril. It quickly dawned on me that I was taking over an organization filled with staff members who still saw me as little Shawn, the kid running around the building with the bushy afro. Now I was their boss, struggling to gain their respect while they felt like they would be able to easily sway me to act on behalf of their personal agendas and the directions they believed I should take the organization. It was a situation fraught with emotional hazards at every turn.

Things really got hairy when I went to my first board meeting as executive director. I was so young and lacking in self-awareness that it hadn't even occurred to me that Martin Tandler, my boss at Tandler Textiles who was not happy—to say the least—with my resignation, was still going to be my boss at The DOME as chairman of the board. The board meetings quickly devolved into what felt to me like personal attacks. Martin was relentless in his criticism of me. In my mind, he was the jilted mentor, the jilted white savior, who felt like he had gone out on a limb to make me his first Black salesman—and I had unceremoniously left him and the company for a hot new thing.

It was hard enough that I had no idea what I was doing. I had naively assumed that because I managed a sales account at Tandler selling millions of dollars of textiles, I would be able to run a million-dollar not-for-profit organization. Man, was I painfully wrong. And it felt like Martin let me know it every chance he got. If the board members were savvier and thinking more clearly, they would have come right out and asked me during my interview, "What real experience do you have to run this organization?"

In the back of my mind, I thought I was saving myself by going to The Dome, but it didn't take long for me to realize I had made my situation worse. I had left my job at a company with a culture where my drug and alcohol use were socially acceptable. But now I was a 24-year-old child prodigy, in a sense, going to a place where the pressure I felt to be a role model and an example for young people was extreme. I simply brought my addiction with me. I had thought being in a leadership role, being a visible role model, would make me stop, but I didn't realize at the time that I had a disease. I made matters worse by hiring one of my old DOME Project buddies on my staff; he was also my connect—the guy who procured my drugs for me. He had already done two prison stints for drugs and was on his way to a third. That was self-sabotage at work—me subconsciously looking for ways to sabotage my success because a part of me didn't feel like I deserved it. I have seen this aspirational gravity at play in the lives of successful Black men all around me for the past 30 years—and I still grapple with it myself.

The ridiculousness of my audaciousness—or perhaps desperation is the right word—came to a head one day when I went up to Washington Heights to cop cocaine. It's where I went for coke when I embarked on my own. I was at the train station waiting to go back downtown when I ran into one of the youths from The Dome, a Dominican kid who lived in the Heights.

"Hey, Mr. Dove! What are you doing up here?" he asked, excited to see me in his neighborhood.

I couldn't tell him that I was up there to buy drugs. I can't remember what I said to him, but I know having to think up a lie felt absurd. I was what is called a "functional" addict, able to be productive during the week and fool everybody around me, but then turn into a weekend warrior after five on Fridays. However, the weekends started to creep into weekdays. One Thursday I stayed up all night with Lenny getting high. When I showed up for work on Friday morning, Lenny looked at me and smiled.

"Wow, you're a trooper now!" he said. "You really know how to do this—stay up all night and still come into work."

But it felt strange to be congratulated for something that I wasn't at all proud of. I think if anybody looked at me that Friday morning, they'd be able to see that I was hurting. I was losing my sense of self-awareness, my ability to follow social protocols. I went on a trip to Jamaica with my old buddy Clarence and I was really keen on bringing my coke with me. I went through security at Kennedy Airport and got on the plane. I went into the airplane bathroom and was appalled when I looked in the mirror. My nose was caked with cocaine.

How the hell did they let me through security, with coke not only in my bag but on my nose? I asked myself. Before I was even at the point in my life to acknowledge it at the time, in retrospect it was clearly only through the grace of God that I avoided being arrested.

I had a ton of responsibilities and felt a ton of pressure in my role as the new executive director of The DOME Project. We had a subcontract with a nonprofit named Rheedlen Center for Children Services, which had been founded by a guy named Richard Murphy, to manage its Attendance Improvement Dropout Prevention (AIDP) program. Funded by the NYC Board of Education, AIDP included home visits and case management, under the notion that if an elementary student was truant from school, then there was something bigger going on at home than just a kid playing hooky. I was drawn to and loved the hands-on aspect of working at the Dome with young people and their parents, though mostly just the moms were present or engaged. Management, fundraising, proposal writing, and the administrative stuff, I hated all of that, what felt like drudgery and not playing to my strengths. This was a social awareness lesson that would be repeated over my career.

I came into The Dome Project thinking that doing this important community work would somehow help me with my addiction. But in actuality, the stress and guilt of living this double life made it so much worse. I was supposed to be a leader, going out and making speeches, talking about uplifting our people, but in private I was a completely different person, shamefully using narcotics to numb a pain I wasn't even aware that I had.

That year at The Dome, from the fall of 1988 to the fall of 1989, brought me to my knees. It got so bad that I started to devise a plan to take my life. I figured that was my only way out. I would jump on the tracks at 34th Street at Penn Station, on the Uptown local track where the C and the E train stopped. I would scramble down onto the tracks and grab the third rail. I had it all planned out. My mind was racing as I stood on the platform, headed back up to my Towers on the Park condo in Harlem. I was coming down hard from a cocaine binge. The depression was so deep, so encompassing, that I literally felt like I was suffocating, as if an enormous weight were pressing down on me.

I fought against myself for many moments, my depression versus my survival instinct. Finally, the C train came, and I stepped into the car. Though I made it home that day, I was terribly rattled. I knew some type of serious intervention was vital. I had been selected that year as one of 10 executive directors to go through a professional development program at Columbia University's Institute for Not For Profit Management. As God saw fit, one of the executive directors with whom I bonded was a guy named Jim Little, who ran a therapeutic addiction treatment community called Veritas—a name that means "truth" in Latin.

I decided to stop running from the truth of my addiction and asked for help. I had dinner with Jim at Dock's Seafood Restaurant on Broadway and 89th Street. As I sat across from him, I gave myself a pep talk. *Come on, Shawn, you can do this.*

I took a deep breath.

"Jim, I think I have a problem. I want to come to Veritas."

Veritas was an intensive program that extended over 18 months. It wasn't one of those quick 28-day celebrity rehab programs. I had to travel to a facility in upstate New York—and I had to go on welfare for the first time because it was a state-funded program. That was the only way I could qualify. I left behind everything I knew—my wife, my job, my friends and family—and moved into

Veritas. When I got there, I already had an aura surrounding me. I was "Jim Little's colleague." The residents there couldn't figure me out. I felt my embarrassment and shame like a blanket weighing down on top of me. No matter which way I turned, how much I slept, it was always there.

My presence provided an interesting lift to the other residents. In some small way, it was almost like what happens when a cop goes to prison. I could see it on their faces when they looked at me: *You might have this fancy education and all these credentials, but you a junkie too, motherfucker! You might have been doing the rich man's drugs instead of smoking crack and shooting dope, but you an addict just like us.*

Interestingly, though it was humbling and shameful, being there was also a huge relief. For so long I had been desperately trying to hold it together while crying out for help. I realized through serious self-reflection that I had even decided to marry Allyson, even though I was really in love with another woman at the time, because I felt that marrying my upwardly mobile Wesleyan sweetheart was the right, responsible, life-stabilizing thing to do. I had concluded these superficial external things would somehow come along and save me from self-destruction. But the only thing that could really save me was admitting that I needed help. When I got clean, my goal became living my authentic self, not hiding anymore from painful truths. That was the only way I was going to stay clean.

I made important discoveries about myself at Veritas—how I had been running for so long, using drugs as a way to flee my light. I was truly a living embodiment of that Marianne Williamson poem, from her 1992 bestselling book, *A Return to Love: Reflections on the Principles of a Course in Miracles* (a quote often mistakenly attributed to Nelson Mandela):

> *Our deepest fear is not that we are inadequate. Our deepest fear is that we are powerful beyond measure. It is our light, not our darkness, that most frightens us. We ask ourselves, who am I to be brilliant, gorgeous, talented, fabulous? Actually, who are you not to be? You are a child of God. Your playing small doesn't serve the world.* [2]

---

2   Marianne Williamson (1992), A Return to Love (HarperCollins: New York). Page 190.

I recently discovered that I am still carrying a crucible from that difficult time. In the back of my head for a long time, I was operating with the philosophy that the higher up I go, the further I will fall when the inevitable failure comes. And my behavior sometimes correlated to such a fear, putting measures in place to stall my rise. I also recently came to realize that I still carried much-unresolved trauma, stretching back to incidents from my childhood—such as my abduction when the guy stole my fur coat. I tried to shrug it off when I was young, but elements of that terrifying day certainly stuck with me. I had memories that remained prominent for years. A vivid one was when a girl —who was my "girlfriend" from kindergarten to fourth grade—announced to the class, loudly, when we returned to school, "I don't know who would want to kidnap you, Shawn—you ain't worth anything!"

Many of the adults with whom I interacted who were doing the difficult community and youth work were dealing with unresolved trauma from their childhoods, the baggage they have been lugging around with them for decades. I had my own formula for fighting the pain of trauma—self-sabotaging behavior.

Veritas during those years held its annual fundraiser at Birdland, the famous jazz club that had temporarily moved uptown in 1986 to Broadway and 105th Street (where it stayed for a decade before moving back to midtown). As a resident of Veritas, there I was inside Birdland in March 1990, helping to set up for the fundraiser. Exactly a year earlier, I had attended the fundraiser as a benefactor in my role as executive director of The DOME Project. Now I was back at the same spot, setting up chairs with the other recovering addicts. I heard a knock on the window and looked out to see a familiar face waving to me and gesturing for me to come outside. It was Richard Murphy, executive director of the nonprofit Rheedlen, who was a popular figure in the nonprofit world, gleaming at me through his glasses and over his ever-present bowtie and his big heart. I was so ashamed of my current status that I didn't want to go outside. But finally, I relented. There had been all kinds of crazy rumors swirling about why I had left The DOME. One of them had me leaving because I was dying of AIDS—clearly a sign of the times in 1989.

Murphy greeted me with a big smile and a warm hug. It was evident he was pleased to see me. He told me that he understood I was going through a difficult period.

"You were doing a fantastic job," he said. "Nobody knew that you were struggling. It wasn't an obvious thing that you were struggling with addiction until you resigned."

He looked at me closely. "The field still needs you," he said. "Young people still need you."

Most importantly, he told me that if I wanted a job, there would be one waiting for me at Rheedlen, the organization he had founded in 1970 in Harlem to serve children and families struggling in poverty (the name came from a combination of two of his aunts' names).

In a brief shining moment, that happenstance meeting changed my life. I had no idea what I was going to do after I left Veritas. I was in a state of such emotional and spiritual shock that I was numbed. But I knew what I didn't want to do—go back into youth development. However, after the street corner conversation with Murphy, which recast my time at The DOME in a new light, I began to consider that perhaps such work was my true calling, my North Star. Maybe it's what I was born to do. Murphy and the affirming memories of my many relationships with young people helped to rekindle the pilot light for me—that flickering flame that still exists in us even during the valley moments of our lives. That period also solidified for me an approach that eventually would become a crucial part of CBMA's mission—tending to the mental health, healing, and well-being of Black men, grappling with the unresolved trauma that many of us spend most of our adult lives fighting off and trying to ignore.

I took Murphy up on his offer; I joined Rheedlen in the human resources department, a placeholder position until we figured out where I fit in. I had an office in a school building, the Sojourner Truth School between 118th Street and 117th Street on Malcolm X Blvd (formerly Lenox Avenue). In a full-circle moment for me, it was a block away from the spot where I looked out the window of Lel's apartment and saw the Woolworth's store being torched during the Harlem riots after King's assassination. Murphy pulled me aside one day and told me he was leaving his position as executive director of Rheedlen to take a job in the administration of newly elected Mayor David Dinkins, the city's first Black mayor, as commissioner of youth services. A man named Geoffrey Canada was replacing Murphy as executive director of Rheedlen, moving up from his current job running an afterschool program at Booker T. Washington High School on 107th Street and Columbus Avenue. I didn't know Geoff very well, but since he was going to be my new boss I had an interview of sorts with him as we walked along 107th Street between Broadway and Columbus. I don't remember any details of what was said, but by the time we hit Columbus Avenue, two blocks later, he had informed me I would be taking over for him running the afterschool program at Booker T. Washington.

It wasn't an easy job— many of the staff were Geoff's proteges and his karate students (he had been a Black Belt karate instructor for many years). I was the new dude stepping into Sensei Geoff's shoes. A year into my tenure, I had lunch with him at Birdland, and I was doing some unfiltered, and probably unwise, complaining about the afterschool program and staff.

"Well, you know, some folks got complaints about you, too," he said. I was taken aback, but it made sense. Geoff looked at me closely. He told me about an opportunity on the horizon that might suit me—Richard Murphy, as youth services commissioner, had gotten approval and funding from Mayor Dinkins for an idea to keep schools open all night and on the weekends to serve as community centers, which he was calling "Beacon Schools." In many ways the idea was modeled after the program I already operated at Booker T. Washington Junior High. Geoff told me Rheedlen was submitting a proposal to operate one of the Beacons. If Rheedlen was chosen, he wanted me to operate the Beacon along with a current Rheedlen program director named Joe Stewart, who was the director of the evening and night programs at Booker T.

That conversation turned out to be a pivotal moment in my life. Joe and I helped to write Rheedlen's proposal for the Beacon School and were elated when Rheedlen did indeed get one of the first ten Beacon School contracts. I moved to this new job and became a key figure in an influential community service model that sowed the seeds of the revolutionary Harlem Children's Zone project that elevated Geoffrey Canada into iconic status in the field of youth development and education. The lessons I learned over the next decade in many ways became the foundation for my eventual leadership of the Campaign for Black Male Achievement.

When we toured schools in Harlem to decide where the Beacon would be located, I was moved by what I saw at PS 194, the school on West 144th Street also known as Countee Cullen School, named after the Harlem Renaissance poet. It was next to the Drew Hamilton projects and I could just feel despair in the air. This was 1991, in the midst of the raging crack epidemic that crippled Black communities across the country. If there was a place that needed hope, a beacon, this was surely it. I was excited and terrified at the same time. I knew it was an amazing opportunity, but there was also tremendous pressure to make sure this project worked.

As executive director of Rheedlen and my boss, Geoff Canada also became something else to me—my friend and mentor, a brilliant and inspirational leader who taught me so many things. Countee Cullen is where I really began to cut my teeth as a social entrepreneur, which I might also describe as an intrapreneur, devising and experimenting with creative programming that I envisioned moving the needle with Black children and families. I knew that the Beacon School concept was forward-looking and important, but I had no idea at the time how ground-breaking and influential it would be on a national level.

Chapter 7: A Beacon of Light

For we must be one thing or the other, an asset or liability, the sinew
in your wing to help you soar, or the chain to bind you to earth.
　　—Countee Cullen

The Beacon at Countee Cullen was an ideal opportunity for me to exercise my artistic and creative impulses on an array of programs and projects and see what stuck to the wall. We introduced a youth newspaper called *Harlem Overheard* to draw young people into writing, journalism, photography, and graphic design; a fitness center to focus the community on the importance of health and exercise; a youth enterprise that sold items such as t-shirts designed and printed by young people; an inspirational choir for those whose gifts were in the music and singing realm; a Kwanzaa speakers series that brought in Black luminaries such as Nikki Giovanni, John Henrik Clark, Benilde Little, KRS-1, and Susan L. Taylor, in addition to celebrities such as Bo Jackson, Wesley Snipes, and Isaac Hayes, and political figures like Mayor Dinkins, Attorney General Janet Reno, and Treasury Secretary Robert Rubin.

To my utter joy, we hosted a Gil Scott-Heron concert in the school auditorium. Gil lived just a few blocks away from the Countee Cullen Community Center and I would occasionally bump into him on 145th Street. One day I asked him if he would perform at the center. I sat in the front row; it felt like it was just me and him in the auditorium as I listened to the best of Gil Scott-Heron. We also brought in Jack Travis, one of the leading Black architects of the time, to work with the young people and create a design for a corner newsstand, which unfortunately never got built. We created a magnet for Black beauty and Black excellence. It was incredibly invigorating work, which taught me so many useful lessons about how to engage and uplift our children and community.

Joe Stewart, my co-director, and I traveled around the country spreading the word about the magic and impact of the Beacon School concept. Early on, I saw one of the most valuable lessons from the Beacon was the power of relationships. You can sit there and design the most intricate and sophisticated programming for young people, but if you don't tend to the relationships in the building it all will fall apart. I'm talking about *all* the relationships in the building, not just the one between the director and everybody else. We brought in professionals to work with and mentor the young people. Well-known journalists and authors Nick Chiles and Denene Millner served as the editorial directors of *Harlem Overheard* while they were still newspaper reporters in New York City, well before they started their prolific book-writing careers. When such high-level professionals interact with kids, it opens their minds about the possibilities for their lives, expands their conception of where this might all lead for them. I still hear from former students at Countee Cullen, people whose names I don't even remember, reaching out to me on holidays like Father's Day, telling me that they saw me as a father figure and thanking me for the influence I had over their lives. These notes are deeply affecting because it's not hard for me to think back to my own childhood and remember how important it was for me to be pulled into the orbit of adults like John Simon from The DOME and Mrs. Carlson at Lawrence Academy. What it comes down to is the importance of loving on our young people, who too often don't have enough sources of love and concern in their lives. An abundance of love can overcome all manner of deficits. It's no coincidence that the hashtag for CBMA is #LoveLearnLead. That's what I believe tapping into the potential of our children is all about.

One of the most powerful lessons I learned in my decade at Countee Cullen is that everyone has a gift. Over and over again, I stumbled into encounters and experiences that hammered that revelation home to me. There was a young man named Galvin Ferguson who worked security for the Beacon after school while he attended nearby City College. He lived in the Drew Hamilton housing projects right next to the school. Whenever I saw him sitting in different spots at the school, controlling the flow of afterschool program traffic and ensuring safety in the school building, he would be holding a sketch pad. One day my curiosity was triggered.

"What are you drawing?" I asked him.

He turned the sketch pad toward me and flipped through the pages. I was amazed at the artful whimsical cartoon characters I saw.

"We got this newspaper that we're doing in the storefront across the street," I said. "Do you want to come start a comic strip?"

He nodded excitedly and grinned. "Yes!"

The strip was called "G-Man" and it was brilliant, depicting the struggles of a young Black boy in Harlem. I didn't follow the ins and outs of the plots as closely as I should have, so it wasn't until years later that I discovered the G in the title was referring not to Galvin but to God, as he was a devout Jehovah's Witness. I went back and read through a bunch of the comics and realized that this young man had cleverly infused them with Biblical principles without hitting the reader over the head. Clearly, the Biblical elements were disguised so well that the publisher of the paper, one Shawn Dove, didn't even see them.

As an off-shoot of the paper and the strip, Galvin helped us launch Harlem Overheard Publishing Enterprises (HOPE), through which we started designing, printing, and selling T-shirts. These activities had a multiplying effect on young men like Galvin, gave them a sense of self and certain confidence that could serve them well in many diverse settings.

Another young man, Gary Lyles, who also worked security for us, was an outgoing, gregarious sort. Gary wasn't very good at working security because he was often so busy singing and socializing at the front desk and talking about music that people were constantly slipping by him without signing in. One day I challenged Gary.

"You love music and singing so much, we should start an inspirational choir," I said to him.

Gary, or G-Lyles as he called himself, loved the idea and ran with it, bringing together other young people in the neighborhood who could hold a note to form the Countee Cullen Inspirational Youth Choir. By no means do I fancy myself as some kind of gifted songwriter, but I was so inspired by the work that I penned a song called "Keep on Keepin' On, Weather the Storm." It was the mantra for the youth newspaper after we got off to a rocky start that jeopardized its existence and, I thought, encapsulated that message we were trying to get across to the young people, about how to handle adversity. I showed the song to Gary one day and promptly forgot about it. But he took that song, massaged it, expanded upon it, and debuted it with the choir at an event where former *Essence* editor-in-chief Susan L. Taylor had come up to speak to our young people.

I'll never forget the majesty of that night, where I heard the choir pour so much life into a song I had created, in front of a packed auditorium listening to the most gracious and beautiful Susan Taylor. It was that night when Susan said, "The essence of success is that you have to show up fit, focused, organized, disciplined, and with a plan." It was one of those moments when, though there were over 600 people in the auditorium that night, I felt she was speaking directly to me. Her words would come to serve as one of my mission fuel mantras to this day.

It's noteworthy that in both examples the guys were working security. It shows how keen we were on seeking out the gifts of our young people, no matter what they might have been doing at the time. Over the years I have been consistently awed by the talent I have seen in our young people. They have residing inside of them what I called the G-Spot—the genius spot, the gold spot, the God spot if you will. It's a spark of divinity, a magical essence that too often gets covered up, or bulldozed into nonexistence or, worse, never even discovered, especially in our boys. I discovered my own G-Spot through poetry and developed it with writing and public speaking. That idea stays with me always, that the more opportunities we can create for young people that contain the possibility they will dig down and tap into their G-Spot, the higher is the probability that they can use it to save themselves.

There's a quote from the Gnostic scripture, the Gospel of St. Thomas, which was presented to me by Rashid Shabazz, a program officer and dear friend during the early days of CBMA:

"If you bring forth what is within you, what you bring forth will save you. If you do not bring forth what is within you, what you do not bring forth will destroy you."

This resonates so strongly with me because it has definitely been at work throughout my life and the lives of so many Black men I see around me. I was thinking about the quote when I was in Detroit for an event and I came across a news story about two young Black men who had robbed a man at a gas station and shot him in the face, for no apparent reason. The faces of the young men were vividly clear on the surveillance cameras at the station, so their faces were plastered all over the news. It wouldn't take long for them to be located, cuffed, and buried under the jail. I wondered what the gifts these young men possessed were, what were their G-Spots that had not been acknowledged and nurtured? What was inside of them that was not brought forth, thus destroying them? How did we fail to tap into their gifts?

When I think about the lives of young men like Jamare in Detroit and Romero in Oakland, I pray that the discovery and nurturing of their G-Spots—music with Jamare and spirituality with Romero—will be enough to get them through the pain and trauma they have experienced and deliver them safely into a prosperous adulthood. There is a thriving not-for-profit industrial complex in this country that has been built to "fix" Black boys, but too often these programs fail to sufficiently tap into Black boys' gifts and assets, instead seeing them as broken and dysfunctional.

Trabian Shorters, founder of BMe Community, a national network of cross-sector Black leaders, has done important work with elevating an asset-based narrative for and about Black people—one that focuses first on our aspirations and gifts as a people before our problems and deficits. This is a mindset shift that must be spread across the nation and a strategy to counter the historical anti-Blackness we still face in this country.

I don't mean to imply that it's easy to unearth the gifts and to clear away enough of the emotional and traumatic clutter so that our boys will be able to focus on their gifts. I have many examples to illustrate just how difficult this work can be. Most profound is the case of a young man named Victor. Victor was one of the many children who grew up in Harlem in the heart of the crack epidemic—a child who was largely on his own, navigating the streets of Harlem because his family and community were being devastated by drug addiction. He was filled with anger, but he was also desperate for connection. I developed a mentoring relationship with him as I got to know him better. He became comfortable enough with me that he revealed to me his love of writing. I encouraged him to start writing his thoughts and poetry in a journal. We sat down and read James Allen's famous small book, "As a Man Thinketh," which deals with the influence that our thoughts have over the kind of person we become and conditions we create for ourselves. I introduced him to Les Brown, the motivational speaker, and we listened to Gil Scott-Heron, just a couple of the inspirational Black men in my life at the time to whom I wanted to expose him.

When Victor showed me the pages of his journal, I was taken aback by the beautiful way he expressed himself on paper. There was a poignancy and raw power to his words that was deeply affecting. I was so inspired that I decided to publish a book of his poetry, which we called *Armed and Dangerous*. The premise was that this young Black man was armed with a pen instead of a gun, turning on its head the notion of why he was to be feared. We became quite the duo, traveling to various events to talk about the impact of the Beacon School and the effect it could have on young men like him.

In many ways, Victor was the kind of gifted young man in the youth development and community-building space that Romero and Jamare have become. Like so many others, Victor also revealed the peril as well as the promise. While he was being seen as a prominent example of the success of the Beacon, Victor still wasn't removed from the life of the streets. He likely looked similar to the way I looked to John Simon at The DOME, when I would leave the program and go sell drugs just two blocks away. Victor was still hanging out with his crew, including a sect of the Bloods, selling drugs and engaged I'm sure in all kinds of perilous activities. One day the managing editor of *Harlem Overheard*, our youth newspaper, came to me and said Victor was coming into the storefront on 144th Street, where the newspaper was located, and harassing her. I told Victor that he was banned from the storefront, which was seen by many young people as a safe haven even more intimate and special than the Beacon School across the street. Victor was extremely upset by the ban. In a fit of rage, he swept his arm across my desk in my office and knocked everything onto the floor, including my computer.

As he was storming out of the office, he loudly pronounced, "I'm going to get my dogs!"

In my naïve mind, my first thought was, *Oh shit, he's going to get his pit bulls!*

I thought I was street smart, but I guess I wasn't up on the current lingo at the time. What he meant, of course, was that he was going to get his boys. He didn't come back that night, but Victor made things very uncomfortable for us going forward. He lived on the block and he now saw me and the entire program as his nemesis. For him, it was all personal and emotional. He was modeling himself as a street organizer, the 144th Street version of Tupac, his idol.

Victor and I eventually reconciled, as he got older and more mature. No doubt a life-changing event for him was when one of his best friends, Mark, got shot in the head while they were playing dice on the corner of 144th Street one night. Somebody rolled up on Mark and ended his life. Mark was also close to Salahadeen, another young man who lived in the Drew housing projects and who started hanging out at Countee Cullen and spending time in the *Harlem Overheard* storefront. I think both Victor and Salahadeen realized that either one of them could have suffered Mark's fate.

Salahadeen dove headfirst into the activities at the storefront. He had a gift for art, especially graffiti—his tag was all over the neighborhood—and I saw him becoming increasingly interested in the graphic design that was being used in the newspaper. I would see him at a computer when everybody had vacated the storefront. Only later did I find out he actually taught himself the graphic design programs that he would use to start designing the newspaper pages himself. Salahadeen eventually became the creative director of *Harlem Overheard* and went on to a thriving career in both the arts and in youth services, a Beacon success story. I can still see Salahadeen's beaming smile the day our first Special Hip Hop edition of the paper was released, with his first-ever cover design for the newspaper. While I was disappointed by the immaturity Victor showed when he turned on me, I realized that the two years I spent working closely with him likely kept him alive. He discovered a new identity and a sense of belonging that was equally affirming—and safer—than his gang. Victor and Salahadeen took it hard when Mark was killed. It added yet another layer to the unresolved trauma that so many of us carry around, a version of PTSD that can often destroy us if it is not recognized and reconciled.

The incident with Victor generated a critical lesson that emerged from those years—the power of ownership and giving folks agency. One of the most striking aspects of the Beacon School was that it brought people from the surrounding neighborhood into the school building and created an invaluable sense of community that could be a crucial tool in making the area safer for all residents. Rheedlen was an outside organization running a program inside the school, so we had to learn how to work inside the constraints of a public-school environment. We also had to learn the hard way that when it came to a school building, there were adults who had deep emotional connections to the place, vital memories that in many ways made them the people they became. During one of our weekday nights, we had the school open for what we called Open Gym Night. One of our staff members, Andre, who taught karate to young people, had grown up in the community and knew it well. On Open Gym Night, Andre called me over with a serious look on his face.

"You see that dude over there?" he said, surreptitiously nodding toward a guy who was standing on the court. "He's one of the biggest drug dealers in the neighborhood."

Then he turned toward another guy, a bit older than the first. "He's a hit man."

He looked at me. "Something could go down here at any moment," he said, watching my face.

Andre wasn't trying to tell me that we needed to eject these fellows from the gym; his purpose was to shed some light for me on the elements that we were entertaining in our little Beacon School innovation. This was the essence of hands-on, direct services. We made subtle changes to the way we structured the evenings after that, allowing us to keep these more hardened adults away from the children who also liked to play in the gym. But our change brought us headfirst into a major crisis.

It happened on a Thursday night, which was the weekend night when I was in charge. Joe Stewart and I worked late shift on alternative nights at the Countee Cullen Community Center, with him opening the school on Saturdays and me on Sundays for operations. On this particular Thursday night, the gym was supposed to be reserved for the young people to play, which sometimes included games against staff—when I had to prove that I indeed could play the game. But on this particular Thursday, there were a bunch of grown men playing ball. I walked over to them.

"Hey guys, this is not your night," I said, trying to sound authoritative but not confrontational.

My statement was received like a long, loud screech on a vinyl record.

A few of them glared at me. "Fuck you, man—we ain't leaving!" one of them said. They went back to playing ball, purposely ignoring me.

"This is not your night. You got to leave," I repeated, still not raising my voice. I'm not a small guy and I don't normally even think in terms of being physically threatened, but at that moment I was getting pretty uncomfortable.

The same dude, apparently the ornery ringleader, turned to me with a snarl.

"We went to this school! Fuck you, man. We ain't leaving!"

I abruptly turned around and went up to my office. I called my boss, Geoff Canada, on the phone.

"I think we got a problem up in here," I said. "We've lost control of the gym."

I explained to him that I wasn't talking about kids; these were hardened adults, grown men who were acting like they were out in the yard.

"If you think it's a problem, then call the police," he said. Geoff grew up in the hardscrabble South Bronx, as he chronicled in his groundbreaking book, *Fist Stick Knife Gun*, so he knew exactly what I was dealing with. I did as he suggested and put in a call to the local precinct.

I decided I would give them one more chance to leave on their own before the reinforcements arrived. I walked back to the gym and engaged with them again, repeating that they needed to leave.

They told me once again they had gone to PS 194 when they were little.

"Who's in charge of this place anyway?" the ringleader asked with a scowl on his face. I was tempted to say, "Joe Stewart is in charge—and he'll be here tomorrow at 9!" but of course I could do no such thing.

"I'm in charge," I said.

"And who the fuck are you?" he said.

Just then, the door opened, and several police officers walked in. All of their eyes widened when they saw the police.

"Oh, you called the cops on us?" they said, incredulous.

They started moving toward the exit before the police reached us. But as they were leaving, the ringleader said over his shoulder, out of earshot of the police, "Alright nigga, we gonna be waiting for you outside!"

I felt a chill slide down my back when I heard his words. I watched them walk out, with a few of them throwing angry glares in my direction. I went back to my office, my mind racing. At that moment, I felt my life was in danger. The police couldn't really protect me—especially since I was supposed to be the authority figure in charge of the space. Also, while calling the police was a last resort, it only added fuel to an already fiery situation. I grew up in the Bronx and in Harlem, but it was apparent to me that night there were levels to the real street life of this Harlem neighborhood.

Had I ever shot anyone?

No.

Had I ever killed anyone?

No.

Had I ever held anyone up at gunpoint?

No.

My first home visit as co-director of the Countee Cullen Community Center informed me quite forcefully that I was spared from a degree of poverty and trauma that was happening in the lives of many of the young people and their families who participated in our programs. I went into a tenement apartment to find a young man who hadn't been showing up to school. The level of poverty and intensity of the chaos I saw in the apartment was heartbreaking. *Shawn, don't you ever say again that you are hard or that you grew up hard.* I knew this was what many of the young people walking through the doors of Countee Cullen dealt with when they went home.

These guys who were in the gym were a different kind of hard. When I called the cops, I was thinking about safety, not about the potentiality of creating a police brutality incident by bringing the cops into an encounter with a group of Black males. I was thinking about immediate relief, about regaining control of the school building. When I went up to my office, I parted the blinds and looked out the window. I could see the group of guys waiting for me on the corner next to the school.

Damn! How am I going to get out of here?

In the midst of my angst, I was rescued by Jackie Bradley, our lead community organizer who grew up in the neighborhood, when he interceded by going to the corner and negotiating a truce. It was a potent example of a term in community building called "the power of positive deviance," which was coined by researchers in a 2010 book of the same name. Basically, the idea is that often the solutions to incredibly intractable problems lie in the hands, heads, and hearts of community residents who are often not engaged in social change solutions brought on by outside entities. This is how one of the authors, Oxford University professor Richard Pascale, described the concept in a 2010 interview with Harvard Business Review:

> *In almost every impossible situation in companies or in societies, there's usually a couple people who against all odds are succeeding when everyone else is struggling. And these outliers, in effect, are deviant in a positive direction. That is, they are somehow out-performing the norm, and, by the way, with the same resources as everyone else. And I said it's deceptively simple because getting a community, and that's the crucial part of this, to actually discover the wisdom in their own midst, the people just like me who work with me every day or who live with me in the same community who are just somehow doing better against impossible odds, turns out to be tricky.*

For example, in the book, they discuss how villagers in Vietnam where malnutrition was running rampant discovered a solution by investigating how the children in some families were not malnourished, although the families had access to the same amount of food as everyone else. It turns out that these mothers were feeding their children several small meals during the day instead of one larger meal. It was as simple as that.

At the Countee Cullen Community Center, one of the strategies we employed was hiring folks in the community to work with us. Jackie knew the neighborhood well because his father had run a youth program for many years. Jackie had a relationship with the guys who were waiting for me on the corner; they had known each other for years. Jackie went down to the corner and talked to them, negotiating a momentary truce. He arranged a meeting to take place at the school the next day. Positive deviance at work.

Geoff came uptown for the meeting. We allowed the neighborhood guys to express their grievances. In addition to stating that they deserved to be able to use the gym when they wanted, they also complained that we hadn't hired any of them to work at the school. Of course, as I said, we actually *had* hired people like Jackie and Andre the karate instructor. But these guys meant that we hadn't hired any of the more hardened neighborhood types. As a compromise, we got them to concede to certain nights they would use the gym and we agreed to hire a couple of them to work security for us. Importantly, on the nights they used the gym they would manage it and regulate the traffic. In other words, they would take responsibility for everything that went down in the gym. We had had difficulty figuring out how to regulate who could enter the gym. We required people to hand over ID cards to get in, but this didn't sit well with some of the guys in the neighborhood. One guy named Johan terrorized the front desk on a regular basis, once even knocking over the ID machine. There were more than a few occasions when I had to admit I was a bit afraid, wondering if I would be able to retain control. By this time, I was nearly 30, many years removed from real street life.

It was in this environment that I learned something about ownership and agency. After we had negotiated the truce with the older brothers, I walked into the gym on their first night in charge to see if I could get to know them better. One of their leaders was named Mark. I looked at the large blackboard at the front of the gym and saw that he had written in giant letters: THIS IS MARK'S HOUSE.

It dawned on me that what folks want most of all is a sense of belonging. They want a place where they feel like they are somebody, like that theme song from the show *Cheers*.

Sometimes you want to go
Where everybody knows your name
And they're always glad you came

For those guys who grew up in Harlem and went to PS 194, they needed to know that if somebody was opening up the gym at night to the surrounding community, they should be welcomed back with a red-carpet entrance, because they were the ones who mattered most. As we know, that's often the thinking behind turf battles between gangs that can result in violence and bloodshed. These guys didn't own their homes, they didn't have property, but they did feel ownership over the elementary school they attended in the neighborhood. It belonged to them, not to some random dude from a community-based organization proclaiming that he's in charge.

"Okay, okay, I get it," I said to myself when I read that blackboard. "I understand now."

We employed the idea of ownership all the time at the Beacon. We were constantly printing up T-shirts for the young people that they could wear to tell the world they were down with Countee Cullen. And they wore them proudly, treasuring the sense of belonging the shirts provided. It wasn't hard for me to remember that incredible pride I would feel when I was younger, and I got the T-shirt showing I had played in the Rucker basketball tournament. It's why we always will have gangs, fraternities, country clubs. Humans—and most animal species, too—desperately need to feel membership in a tribe. I think one of the ways we fail our Black boys is we don't give them enough positive options for tribe membership. As a result, they become attached to negativity—horrifically, prison has become an alternative rite of passage for too many Black males that gives them the feeling of membership and belonging.

Illustrating how influential the Beacon School concept was in the youth development field, the *New York Times* wrote laudatory words about Richard Murphy and the Beacons in his obituary that ran on February 15, 2013. The *Times* credited Murphy with being a pioneering giant in the field who created the community school concept that eventually expanded to cities across the country, including Chicago, Denver, Minneapolis, Philadelphia, and San Francisco.

"The idea, Mr. Murphy said, was to create dozens of 'small universes' in which young people could learn, dream, and grow and, in the process, stay out of trouble," the *Times* wrote.

The paper quoted Murphy as saying in 1990, "You can have a policeman on 178th Street and a policewoman on 179th Street and you can sweep kids off the streets, but unless you give them something to do, they'll simply go to 180th Street. You have to give kids something to do."

The Harlem Children's Zone's success was about taking the seeds of Rheedlen's initial programming and growing it into a coordinated anti-poverty strategy. Geoff conceived the idea of creating wrap-around services for an entire 100-block community and it became a globally famous phenomenon. The program was so revered that President Barack Obama would earmark more than $100 million in grants for its replication through his Promise Neighborhoods initiative.

Murphy's Valentine's Day passing in 2013 was painful for me. When Geoff informed me that Murphy was on his deathbed, I rushed to the hospital to say goodbye. In typical Murphy fashion, he was much more interested in talking about me than about him.

He told me, "You have so much more in you. You have barely scratched the surface."

I wanted to talk more, but he knew I had an Open Society Foundations board meeting I had to attend. Up to the last minute, he was offering key advice.

"Positioning in the room is everything," he said about my board meeting. "You gotta get there early."

Profoundly, several days after Murphy's moving funeral service, I got a package from Amazon delivered to my home. It was from Murphy, ordered just a few days before he passed away. I tore open the package. Inside was an illustrated copy of Maya Angelou's children's poem, "Life Doesn't Frighten Me." The poem ends:

> *If I'm afraid at all*
> *It's only in my dreams.*
> *I've got a magic charm*
> *That I keep up my sleeve*
> *I can walk the ocean floor*
> *And never have to breathe.*
> *Life doesn't frighten me at all*
> *Not at all*
> *Not at all.*
> *Life doesn't frighten me at all.*

My next stop was at another Harlem Children's Zone (HCZ) initiative called Truce (The Renaissance University for Community Education), an after-school program on 117th Street for high school students, focusing on media and the arts—a natural transition for me after starting endeavors like the youth newspaper. It was here that I began to zero in on the importance of health and wellness for Black people.

If you walk down 125th Street in Harlem, one of the things you quickly notice is how much obesity you see, in addition to the clear social, emotional health challenges so many in the community are struggling with. I felt a calling to do something about it, so we made a presentation to the HCZ board of directors and created the Truce Health and Fitness Center. We purchased exercise equipment, treadmills, stationary bikes, and we opened it to the public, allowing community residents to come in and exercise. That's what I loved about HCZ—the freedom to be creative, to be a social intrapreneur.

Initially, I cut a deal to be a consultant to HCZ while I launched a publishing enterprise, producing inspirational *PocketMagicBooks* written by myself and others that I felt would be useful to the community. I ran into some difficulty when I went to buy a house with my second wife, Desere, and discovered that I needed a stable salary to get a mortgage. I took a job at the National Guild of the Community School of the Arts to lead an initiative called Creative Communities. I oversaw a partnership with 20 cities across the country to bring community schools of the arts to young people in public housing communities—stretching from Los Angeles to Pawtucket, Maine. Not only did it give me a chance to emphasize and nurture the importance of the arts in the lives of young people, but it tapped into one of my greatest strengths, bringing together disparate populations to build community and effectuate change.

I left that job after three years to become vice president of a national non-profit called MENTOR/National Mentoring Partnership, where I was responsible for the leadership and management of The Mentoring Partnership of New York (MPNY). The focus was on bringing mentors into the lives of young people, in many ways responding to the worsening crisis of father absence in the country. But a huge part of that job was fundraising. I think a big factor in them hiring me was they thought they were getting a Geoff Canada clone, that I would come in and convince a lot of people to write a lot of big checks.

A major segment of the model was partnering with law firms, accounting firms, financial services firms. It's fascinating to look back on who were some of our biggest partners—firms like Bear Stearns and Lehman Brothers that were shuttered a few years later during the financial meltdown. Part of the revenue-generating model was to create workplace mentoring programs with these firms. At the end of the year, we held an annual event called Back To The Bull, where we raised a bunch of Wall Street money. It was my first significant exposure to these high-net-worth folks, working with managing directors at firms who were writing $50,000 checks on the spot. We held quarterly meetings bringing together dozens of mentoring organizations that were under our umbrella. When I asked them what were the biggest challenges they were facing and how we could be most supportive, the first three things they would mention were funding, funding, funding. But then they would say the lack of Black and Latino male mentors. That was pivotal because it prompted me to start applying an explicit focus for the first time to Black and Latino males.

Overwhelmingly, the mentors we recruited were white, disproportionately white women, who were signing up at the firms. I knew we needed to extend beyond these corporate firms, expanding our community and faith-based mentoring programs, if we were going to reach Black and Latino males. I started something we called the Male Mentoring Project. We held assemblies with the purpose of recruiting Black men. Mentoring organizations would come and set up tables, there would be art, there would be inspirational speakers, mentors, and mentees telling stories—all things I later would employ in my leadership of the Campaign for Black Male Achievement.

It was interesting to trace the evolution of the word *mentoring*, which didn't even really exist in the 1970s when I was at The DOME and connecting with men like Ed Scott, Omar Vargas, and John Simon. I had seen the power of mentoring in both positive and negative ways. In my childhood, Squeaky, an older guy was doing sex education classes on the corner of 80th Street and Amsterdam Avenue, telling us clueless adolescents about a woman's anatomy in language and using descriptions that even now almost makes me blush. That too was a form of mentoring. But I was beginning to start publicly talking intentionally for the first time about the plight and the crisis of Black males. It was the first time in the history of the organization that we were going to venues and places where we would reach Black and Latino potential mentors.

In the 1980s and 1990s, writers and educators like Dr. Jawanza Kunjufu began publishing books that focused on Black boys, such as *Countering the Conspiracy to Destroy Black Boys*, whose first volume was released in 1985 (the fourth volume came in 1995), and Haki Madhubuti published *Black Men: Obsolete, Single, Dangerous?: The African American Family in Transition* (1990). Those books didn't really make it into the mainstream philanthropic community, where it wasn't considered acceptable to talk openly about specific populations like Black boys.

In March 2006, the *New York Times* published a story by reporter Eric Eckholm that abruptly changed this narrative. Above the fold in the upper left corner, the headline read "Plight Deepens for Black Men, Studies Warn." The first three graphs of the story went on to paint a horrific picture of the dangers Black men faced:

> BALTIMORE - Black men in the United States face a far more dire situation than is portrayed by common employment and education statistics, a flurry of new scholarly studies warn, and it has worsened in recent years even as an economic boom and a welfare overhaul have brought gains to Black women and other groups.
>
> Focusing more closely than ever on the life patterns of young Black men, the new studies, by experts at Columbia, Princeton, Harvard, and other institutions, show that the huge pool of poorly educated Black men is becoming ever more disconnected from the mainstream society, and to a far greater degree than comparable white or Hispanic men.
>
> Especially in the country's inner cities, the studies show, finishing high school is the exception, legal work is scarcer than ever, and prison is almost routine, with incarceration rates climbing for Blacks even as urban crime rates have declined.

While the story didn't really recount much that the Black community didn't already know and see on a daily basis, the account was received in the corridors of philanthropy like a hungry, roaring lion. It made the case quite clearly: As the American economy was booming, Black men were being left far behind. This was before the advent of social media, but that story achieved the email version of going viral, as it was shared in countless circles across the country.

When I left HCZ, many people were shocked because, as I began to hear, I was Geoff Canada's protégé and many assumed I was the heir apparent to eventually take over HCZ. Before I took the job at MENTOR, I had lunch with Geoff and brought this up.

"When I left, folks were saying to me that I was a successor to you," I said. "But *you* never said that to me."

"You know what, Shawn," he said. "You didn't know whether you wanted to be a publisher, a youth development professional... You never knew what you wanted. I wasn't going to turn my agency over to somebody who didn't know what they wanted. And as a matter of fact, as you are looking to take this next job, I still don't think you know what you want."

Perhaps he was right. I probably didn't *really* find out what I wanted until a few years later, when Open Society Foundations (OSF) crashed onto my radar screen. Since Open Society's founder, billionaire George Soros, first funded scholarships for Black university students in South Africa in 1979 during apartheid, he had been engaged in very progressive, risk-taking philanthropy endeavors.

After the *New York Times* article hit, OSF engaged in intense internal debates about how they were going to respond. One side said, if they were going to consider themselves pioneers in making investments in marginalized communities and helping them become actors and owners in their own change, why weren't they on the front end of this crisis with Black men and boys in America? The other side retorted, well, we are—look at our criminal justice fund, trying to make a difference in the inequities in that vital area.

Soros was born in Hungary in 1930 and managed to survive the Nazi occupation of Hungary that resulted in the murder of a half million Hungarian Jews. His family secured false identity papers and concealed their backgrounds—and helped many others do the same. Once he launched a hedge fund many decades later and became one of the most successful investors in the history of the United States, Soros first began his philanthropy in Eastern Europe with re-entry and criminal justice as one of his focuses.

Soros had several compelling African American leaders on the Open Society board pushing the question of what to do about Black males—not only Geoff Canada but Harvard Law professor and activist Lani Guinier, Equal Justice Initiative founder Bryan Stevenson, and now NAACP Legal Defense and Education Fund president Sherrilyn Ifill. There's a saying in the field among Black folks that "philanthropy is not going to fund the revolution," but OSF was being pushed to do more. The foundation came up with the idea of funding a three-year campaign originally called the Campaign to Promote Opportunities for African American Men and Boys—yeah, a real mouthful.

In January 2008, I began to get emails from friends and mentors in my network, telling me I should apply for the job of running this new campaign. At the time I had moved into another position—director of youth ministries at First Baptist Church of Lincoln Gardens in Somerset, New Jersey, working with its brilliant pastor, Rev. DeForest "Buster" Soaries, to create programming for young people. I was underwhelmed about the OSF job—I was happy to be back working hands-on with young people and had grown somewhat disillusioned with philanthropy.

One day, I was driving down Route 27 in New Jersey after dropping my kids off at school when Geoff called.

"Shawn, I don't know where you are in your career—whether you want to be a publisher, whether you want to be a preacher, or what," he said, starting in on what had become a familiar theme with him about my zigzagging passions. "But Open Society Institute is launching this campaign for Black men and boys and I think you should throw your hat in the ring."

He shared that not only was he on the OSI board of directors, he also was on the hiring committee for this new position. Even if he hadn't been on the hiring committee, it certainly would have gotten my attention to receive such a call from him. After applying, I underwent the most rigorous interview process I've ever been involved in. The turning point was when I went before the committee for my third interview. I asked Michael Prince, the graphic designer at *Harlem Overheard* and also for *Pocket Magic Books*, to create a beautiful brochure that outlined my vision for the campaign. I called it "Catalyst." In the brochure prototype I depicted my vision for the work, which included building the capacity and infrastructure of organizations leading the work, creating a "Mega Fund" to support the work, the regular convening of leaders "from the block, the ballot, and the boardroom," along with additional approaches to the work that over the next dozen years would eventually materialize.

Despite this tremendous opportunity to work for Black men and boys across the country, I was harshly reminded how we as Black men have to take shit—racism and oppression—and suppress it. That morning, while on my way to Kinko's picking up the prototype brochure that convinced Open Society to hire me, I may have made an illegal turn or something. The police stopped me. I didn't even realize I was driving with an expired registration. The officer took me to the police precinct. Literally, they took a mug shot. So, you know when you go online and you see those ads, Does so-and-so have an arrest record? This was the morning of my interview to lead a national Campaign for Black Male Achievement. It was an embarrassing and humiliating experience. We rarely get the benefit of the doubt in police-involved scenarios like this. We are not afforded the luxury of receiving warnings without enforcement.

I could have lost my chance for the CBMA job because of this encounter with the police. I can't blame it on the police, necessarily, because I was driving with an expired registration. Sometimes our own irresponsibility comes into play with putting us in positions of vulnerability with law enforcement. That broken taillight that we promise ourselves we'll fix next week, that illegal turn at the wrong place and time with a patrol car in the vicinity puts us in more precarious scenarios with the police.

As we got near the end of the hiring process—at least what I prayed was the end—I received an interesting call from one of the women on the hiring committee.

"I just want to ask you a question," she said. "I know that you are working right now as the director of youth ministries at the church. Part of this work and part of OSF is really embracing the LGBT community. How do you feel about that?"

I understood right away what was happening. They wanted to make sure I wasn't some rabidly ultra-conservative Christian. Luckily, in one of the editions of a newsmagazine I had created called *Proud Poppa*, which featured African American men as loving and caring fathers, we profiled a gay Black man who was lifting up "same gender loving" communities for Black men. I quickly pointed out that profile and said that the magazine was dedicated to elevating these communities, not derogating them. With that response, they were reassured they could bring me into this ultra-progressive culture, and I wouldn't react with revulsion.

After they called and notified me that I had gotten the job, I began to hear through the Black grapevine that there were many Black folks in philanthropy who had their designated candidates they were hoping got the job. I was a glitch in the matrix. The whisper campaign went into high gear: *Who is Shawn Dove, and how did he get this job?* I tried to ignore the whispers, but they led me to experience another severe case of impostor syndrome. *Hmmm, maybe I didn't deserve this job.*

When I began to hear the elation and see the celebration in my network, I realized how big a deal this was. It reminded me of when I was young and told the folks at Tandler Textiles that I would be attending Wesleyan. I learned that I was starting out with a budget of $5 million, which I would be able to use to bring about change on behalf of Black men and boys. At the time, that sounded like a great deal of money to me.

But after I walked in the doors of OSF on May 12, 2008, and then officially launched the campaign on June 12, 2008, I started to get the calls. People I had worked with over the years, congratulating me and happening to mention the wonderful things they were now doing that could be made even more fabulous with a little more funding.

"Shawn, you don't remember me—we went to day camp together..."

We launched the Campaign for Black Male Achievement on June 12th—by June 13th, I realized that $5 million was not going to be enough money.

Hmmm, I thought after yet another call. *I think we're going to need a bigger boat.*

Chapter 8: CBMA Takes the Field

He who is not courageous enough to take risks will accomplish nothing in life.

—Muhammad Ali

I have to admit, my first few months working for Open Society Foundations were a bit rocky. Impostor syndrome was crippling my ability to be instinctive and creative. I felt uncomfortable with the overwhelmingly white culture. This is an experience with which generations of Black men and women can identify—getting the job is one thing, but then you have to figure out how to *do* the job without going crazy. All while fighting off the ever-present suspicion that you don't belong.

I remember walking through the corridors of OSF's Manhattan offices in those early months and thinking, *I just don't fit in.* There was a forced intellectual air to the philanthropic world that I found off-putting and a bit intimidating. At one of the meetings, somebody asked me, "Shawn, what's your theory of change?"

What the hell is a theory of change? was my first thought. I can't even remember what I came up with, but I was unsettled by the question. (For the record, a "theory of change" is a framework for understanding what types of activities or interventions will yield the long-term goal you are trying to achieve.) I began to question whether OSF had indeed made the right decision in hiring me. It got so bad that I was ready to leave during the second year, having concluded that philanthropy was not a good fit for me.

One of my mentors is Reverend Alfonso Wyatt, a New York City legend in the faith and youth development community who has been invaluable to me over the years in providing me with the spiritual support and guidance I often need. Since he was one of my references for the OSF job, they spoke to him about me during the grueling interview process. Alfonso told them that I was a "social entrepreneur."

"With Shawn, you're not getting a professional philanthropist. He's going to need room to create."

To be honest, I think he saw that in me more than I saw it in myself at the time. But that was one of my trademarks in the other jobs I had up to that point. The question I faced was, how could I bring that creativity and social entrepreneurship to a job and campaign that was firmly entrenched inside a fairly rigid philanthropic organization and culture?

One of the smartest things I did in 2009, almost a year into my role as campaign manager, was to hire a program officer named Rashid Shabazz. Rashid came with advanced degrees from both Yale and Columbia—and he was the perfect match for my creative, hands-on approach. We would brainstorm together, coming up with ideas that we were certain could start moving the needle. I began to think of us as philanthropy's Buck and The Preacher, the duo played by Sidney Portier and Harry Belafonte in the early 70's film that exposed my eyes for the first time to Black men as heroes in a western film.

Rashid knew I was having all kinds of reservations, so one day he popped into my office and made a pronouncement.

"I got two tickets. I'm going, and you're going, too," he said. He was talking about a retreat called "Taking Care" in San Francisco being hosted by the Association of Black Foundation Executives (ABFE), in partnership with a group called the Bay Area Blacks in Philanthropy. Before we left, I told myself this event would be one of the last ones I attended as the head of CBMA. But in a sharing circle of Black folks at Cavallo Point, a serene retreat facility literally located under the Golden Gate Bridge, I discovered my leadership voice for this season of my life and deep sense of purpose for the CBMA work ahead of me. We had an amazing facilitator named Estrus Tucker from the Center for Courage and Renewal. He incorporated wellness, poetry, reflection, and collaboration over two-and-a-half days, and I emerged with a clearer vision and more focused mission for the challenging work in front of me. During that retreat, I began to see the immense power of bringing together folks from around the country with a sense of belonging and movement building. It became a key part of my approach at CBMA—and I would reach out to Estrus on many occasions over the years to recreate his magic at CBMA convenings.

One day as I sat and probed the origins of my feelings of impostor syndrome, I had a revelation. Actually, it was more like a conversation with God. On one hand, I was asking myself how I could be the right person to lead a national movement, considering that I wasn't too far removed from many of the

Black male disparities and challenges we were trying to alleviate. But then a voice came into my head.

This is why I chose you for this position. This is why you are the ideal person to lead this movement.

It was a vital change in perspective for me. After that, I approached the job with humility but also with a sense of curiosity and growing confidence. I would see folks in important philanthropic positions strutting around like it was their money they were giving away. I saw them as a cautionary tale for me. In my first week at OSF, someone told me that I would now have to remove my direct services hat that I had worn for many years—OSF was instead about policy advocacy and systemic and structural change. In other words, they viewed problems from 30,000 feet, instead of getting their hands dirty by working directly with programs to help provide services. But that didn't sound quite right to me—or at least *for* me. I instinctively shot back, "No, it's a both-and. It's not an either-or." I pulled back after I made that statement, thinking perhaps that was a bit too much impudence for my first week on the job. But it soon became apparent that I was going to be a lot different than many of my colleagues in the building.

During my crisis of confidence at the start of my tenure with Open Society Foundation, I had a breakthrough when I decided to start playing to my strengths. One of my biggest strengths was communication. Stretching back to the literary magazine and poetry slams at Wesleyan, I had always been drawn to the power of words to bring about change. I decided that I was going to gather a group of leaders in the Black male achievement space and do a podcast. I didn't ask for permission from my supervisors, choosing to embody the adage that it's easier to ask for forgiveness than to ask for permission. I did coordinate the podcast taping with the OSF communications department, who seemed energized by the clandestine attempt to infuse strategic communications into my role. While we were recording in an OSF conference room, in the back of my mind I was expecting one of the executives to burst into the room, point a finger at me, and angrily accuse me of insubordination for doing something that OSF program managers didn't customarily do. But my fears were unfounded. I grew accustomed to eyebrows being raised in the OSF offices because Rashid and I once again stepped outside the box and did something disruptive.

One of the earliest indications that I was now operating on a much grander scale was the change in the power dynamics I observed when I was out in the field. All of a sudden, my jokes got funnier, I got more charismatic, everything I said became more interesting. When I walked into a room, my head was surrounded by a halo of OSF dollar signs—the possibility of a cash infusion that just might save their program from collapse.

When we developed our strategy in the first six months, we decided we would direct our dollars into three areas. The first was educational equity, with an emphasis on innovative strategies to enhance Black male achievement and reducing suspensions for Black boys. We were one of the seed funders for the Oakland school system's trailblazing Office of African American Male Achievement, which was the first district-wide office created in an American public school system specifically to lift achievement among Black boys. For our second strategic focal area, strengthening family structures, we funded Columbia University researcher Dr. Ron Mincy's work on using the earned income tax credit as a way to improve the economic and social mobility of Black men and boys. We supported groups that focused on single moms raising Black boys, groups that worked with Black men returning to the community from prison, and a researcher looking into establishing a living wage for Black men. Our third focus was investing in strategies that advanced living-wage work opportunities for Black men. One of our early investments in this space was to help seed the start-up of the Los Angeles Black Worker Center, led by Lola Smallwood Cuevas.

The first grants we issued showed what we viewed as our priorities at the time. One of the grantees was the Center for Urban Families, a groundbreaking program founded by Joseph Jones that waded into one of the most distressed communities of Baltimore and pulled in men and women on the streets who had dropped off the grid, many of them formerly incarcerated men. Jones, a recovering addict who also spent some time in prison, was a galvanizing force for change in Baltimore. He epitomized the work of Black Male Achievement, reimagining the possibilities of what Black men could do with their lives when given opportunity and hope. Jones was already on the board of Open Society Institute-Baltimore, so he was a familiar entity inside the foundation.

Another grant went to the 21st Century Foundation, a now-defunct Black-led foundation that was doing transformational work with Black men and boys focusing on community revitalization. There were national organizations issuing grants in these areas already, so we weren't the first by any means. The Ford Foundation was doing some work in the arena, as were a sprinkling of others. But when we stepped in, we were much more hands-on than the philanthropic community was used to—leading to a bit of friction and resentment in some quarters. *Who do these guys think they are?* I brought all the community building and community organizing skills from my previous jobs, combined them with Rashid's strategic communications background, and we began to create a new mold.

In our field, most folks would hand over the money and get out of the way. But we wanted to stay involved. Inside the OSF offices, there was a move to begin hiring program directors who had done work in the field, so we joined a number of folks who were entering philanthropy for the first time and were more hands-on—what we called "philanthropoids." We also began to weave strategic communications and storytelling into everything we did, understanding that the messaging around Black boys needed radical restructuring, moving from a typically deficit-based narrative to one that was asset-based, building on the many strengths that Black men and boys brought to their families and communities

I would sometimes have to catch myself in meetings with potential grantees. I'd get so excited about their project that I would start saying, "Yeah, we could do this..." or "We should do that..." I would have to pull back and tell myself, *Shawn, this isn't your project! They're coming to you for the money.*

Because of my background and my belief that we needed to bring spirituality into the work, we created an atmosphere at our convenings that was deeply moving and also a bit surprising for the participants. At the end of a two-day strategic planning convening in December 2008, Sherrilyn Ifill closed with a spiritual devotional. I could see people looking around in surprise, thinking the same thing: *Wow, we can say the word God up in here?* We weren't trying to turn our sessions into denominational church gatherings, but I always felt it was important to call on a higher power when bringing together leaders in our field to engage in truly challenging racial justice work. It's always been a vital part of our culture, a dramatically important source of strength for the Black community. Our gatherings would always take on a revival-like atmosphere. For people doing the difficult and vital work in our community, being surrounded by kindred spirits whose commitment matches your own is a spiritual, life-changing, emotional experience all by itself. At one of our convenings, I heard somebody joke, "I ain't never been with an organization where people be crying so much."

From the beginning, we've been modeling male vulnerability in a different kind of way.

There was a pivotal moment that occurred halfway through the three-year campaign, that dramatically changed the trajectory of CBMA. We were on the agenda of a February 2010 OSF board meeting to provide an update on where we were with our strategy. I invited several of our grantees to the meeting, including Joe Jones of the Center for Urban Families, to dive more deeply into how we were assisting their organizations. George Soros was taken with the presentation and started talking about the importance of mentoring. We had created a flyer to summarize our work, a strategy I brought from my publishing and strategic communications background—something that program officers in foundations customarily didn't do. I know the inclusion of that document, which was closer to a public relations effort, raised some eyebrows in the room. But I wasn't interested in doing things by the book.

During the meeting, Soros said, "I like this." He looked around the room and stated, "I can go deep with the Campaign for Black Male Achievement." He paused and continued. "You know what? I can go as deep with the Campaign for Black Male Achievement as I'm going now with my Special Fund for Poverty Alleviation."

That Special Fund for Poverty Alleviation had been created to respond to the Great Recession, the ravages of which were still devastating the country in early 2010. The special fund had a budget of $250 million over four years. Was he really saying what it sounded like he was saying—that he was about to make the Campaign for Black Male Achievement one of the cornerstones of the entire organization and seeding it with a quarter billion dollars? People in the room didn't fall out of their chairs exactly, but I think I saw spirits falling out of chairs. Up to that point, we were a time-limited little three-year campaign, one that would allow the foundation to check the Black Male Achievement box. In one sentence Soros had upended the dynamic and transformed the fortunes of Black male achievement in the U.S. He went on to pronounce that the term limits were being lifted from CBMA and he wanted me to think about how to scale it up into something much larger.

That was the exciting aspect of working for a living donor. In an instant, your portfolio in a board meeting can either soar to the next level as it did with CBMA, or it can go south in a heartbeat and you suddenly find yourself packing your stuff and thinking, *Oh, damn, I gotta go look for another job.*

After the meeting, there was a great deal of chatter and hand-wringing about his pronouncement. One of the program directors who led an initiative examining democracy and power started throwing around the term "fund equity"—implying that a big CBMA increase was somehow unfair. I thought to myself, *Oh, you want to talk about fund equity now, but it wasn't a problem for you when your budget was $10 million a year and mine was less than $5 million a year!*

A white woman who worked in the foundation's Baltimore office groused, "I don't know if this Black Male Achievement framework is going to go over in Baltimore." Because Baltimore was predominantly Black. Mind you, we had already been working in Baltimore on Black male achievement for a year and a half at that point. Her statement didn't even make sense.

This was my moment of disillusionment at OSF and with white philanthropy. I had thought I was working in this bastion of progressivism, a risk-taking, left-leaning philanthropic organization that was committed to transformative work. But the response to Soros' proclamation made me realize that no matter where I was, the issues of race and gender were still the same. When I talked about it with people who were close to me, they essentially said, *Shawn, where did you think you were? What made you think this place would be different?* I had to accept that there was a ceiling with white liberal progressiveness when it came to Black people. That's how philanthropy works. We'll give you project funding for your next grant request, but we're not going to invest in you in a way that will bring about long-term sustainable growth and transformation. Activists have long said that philanthropy is not going to fund the revolution. I saw that term come to life right before my eyes.

But while I had to fight the disillusionment with the response of my white peers, I was extremely excited about what had just happened. Soros had essentially tripled our budget, from under $5 million to $15 million a year. We were charged with creating a plan to scale up. It was a seismic moment in the nation and in the movement. Not only was one of the largest foundations in the country making an explicit commitment to Black men and boys, but the announcement of the commitment was like an earthquake jolting the other foundations in the country—even ones that weren't doing work in this area. Suddenly the Campaign wasn't some flash-in-the-pan but a real institutional entity. It began to give cover to other foundations to make commitments to Black men and boys. Overnight, CBMA had power.

It was transformational for us to talk specifically about *Black* males. Foundations like the Robert Wood Johnson Foundation, the California Endowment, and the Ford Foundation were putting money into the work, but their strategies revolved around a broader boys and men *of color* lens. That's an entirely different strategy in tone and substance from focusing solely on Black men and boys. We were unapologetic in our name and our approach.

Rashid and I spent a lot of effort on the plan to scale up. When it was time to send in our grant requests, I felt a great deal of trepidation. Usually, if you had 10 potential grants to present, that was a lot. I had 22 grants on my list that I wanted OSF to fund. Approximately 19 of the grants were to Black-led organizations—including many grassroots groups that would have never cracked the Open Society code if not for us advocating for them. My finger was literally trembling as it hovered above the SEND button. I didn't know how such an ambitious list would be received by my colleagues.

In the end, all the grants wound up going through, which opened the eyes of a lot of organizations in the community who were used to getting the cold shoulder from white philanthropy.

It's one thing to launch a national campaign, but no matter how grand your plans are, you must acknowledge that change happens on the local level, one person at a time. That was the thinking behind one of our most important early approaches, to identify a regional approach to our investments. We decided to pour our energies and resources primarily into specific cities so that our efforts could be concentrated rather than scattershot to more easily quantify the change we were bringing about. Our regional cities were Philadelphia and Baltimore in the Northeast, Chicago and Milwaukee in the Midwest, and New Orleans and Jackson, MS in the South. As the campaign evolved, we realized the importance of investing in hometown heroes and local leaders and launched a place-based strategy called *Promise of Place*. It was crucial for us to start exploring what it looked like on a city level to be winning around Black Male Achievement. Promise of Place in my mind personifies the lead mantra for CBMA: There is no cavalry coming to save the day in Black communities. We are the iconic leaders we have been waiting for; curators of the change we're seeking to see.

When I travel to a city like Baltimore, I am consistently inspired by the number of talented folks I encounter in the Black community. But then I see the division, folks scrambling around for limited resources and not collaborating, and I begin to understand the things that are preventing us from winning. After Freddie Gray was murdered by Baltimore police officers in April 2015 a few days after he was handcuffed in the back of a police van and Baltimore exploded in rage, a significant amount of dollars and resources poured into the city from the state and federal governments and from philanthropy. But four years later, homicides in the city were at an all-time high. I watched it all transpire from up close. Promise of Place is really about how to magnify promise in our cities in the midst of constant peril.

Partly in response to the frustrations we were feeling, in 2015 we created our first Promise of Place report, which scored and rated cities based on their engagement with Black males. We wanted to quantify what cities were doing on behalf of Black men and boys, but we had to figure out the best way to do that. What should we measure? How do we quantify engagement? We were very clear that our scan was not about outcomes. It wasn't about impact, because there is no city in America that's winning when it comes to sustaining positive life outcomes for Black men and boys. We felt that in order to get to impact and outcomes, we first had to begin with engagement.

The BMA City Index scored 50 cities that are home to more than 5.5 million Black men and boys, representing more than 30 percent of all Black men and boys in the United States. Based on a total of 100 points, the cities were scored using five indicators to determine their level of engagement and committed action on behalf of Black men and boys. The five key indicators measure:

- Demographics around race and gender (10 points)
- City-led commitment to supporting and addressing individual and systemic challenges facing Black men and boys (30 points)
- Number of local organizations and leaders that are members of the CBMA national network (20 points)
- Local presence of national programs, initiatives, and organizations supporting Black men and boys (20 points)
- Targeted philanthropic funding focused on Black men and boys (20 points)

In the last ranking that came out in 2019, the top five cities were Detroit, Washington, DC, Oakland, New Orleans, and Boston.

Because of CBMA's credibility in the field, groups that were not on the list were calling in, asking, "What about us?" The ranking brought out state rivalries—Memphis was upset that Chattanooga was a few points ahead of them. Since part of the scoring was around funding, our rankings couldn't be up to the minute because we had to use public 990 tax forms to assess foundation support, and 990s are about 18 months behind. Cities were protesting, telling us they had poured millions into Black male initiatives and should have gotten higher scores. I thought the angst and the competition were healthy and exactly what we were looking to come out of the rankings.

Around the idea of the importance of place, we started to do Promise of Place convenings, bringing together cohorts of about a dozen or so cities to share best practices. The cohorts included young people, folks from nonprofits, philanthropy, and governments—really elevating the sectors we need to advance the work. I have always felt that CBMA exists at the intersection of field building and movement building. The Promise of Place convenings are about field building, assessing the structures, systems, and strategies that are going to drive change. In 2019, we pushed all of our POP efforts to one city, Detroit. We asked ourselves, *What does it look like to operationalize Promise of Place in one place?* Eighty percent of the attendees were from Detroit, where we also opened up a CBMA Promise of Place office. The gatherings were an effort to get people in the field out of their silos and to start collaborating and cooperating.

As the role of CBMA evolved, I saw that one of our most important functions was as a catalytic force in the field. That means our presence accelerates the pace of change, pushes forward the nation's agenda on behalf of Black males much faster than it would have proceeded otherwise. One of the most dramatic examples of that is our annual event called Rumble Young Man, Rumble. This is the essence of CBMA's movement building, convening all the elements of our work together at the Muhammad Ali Center in Louisville for three days of inspiration, uplift, transformation, and healing. The essence of the Rumble is what I've been creating since my days at Wesleyan as editor of the poetry magazine, where I created spaces that enabled people to read their poetry for the first time in public, building their cultural and social capital and creating a sense of belonging to a community—what meant the most to me was witnessing the gleam in their eyes and the disbelieving smile that spread across their faces.

The spark of the idea for Rumble came from my deep love and admiration for Muhammad Ali—my first hero. I wanted to create a space where we all could come together and feel the purpose and power of this great man's life and his spirit. The leaders from my generation, men like David Banks, founder of the Eagle Academies, understood exactly what drew me to the Ali Center. But the younger generation, who grew up on Mike Tyson, had to be educated. The Rumble provided me with the motivation to travel to Louisville and have my spirit renewed.

Louisville's Mayor, Greg Fischer, said he first became aware of CBMA after his city experienced a triple homicide in May 2012 and he extended an offer to various entities in Louisville to come together to talk about solutions.

"The next day, I just put out an open invitation that evening for people to come to my office and about a hundred people showed up from all walks of life," Fischer said. "Nobody blamed anybody. They didn't blame the preachers, the drug dealers, the police, or whoever, they just said, 'What can I do to help?'"

In response, Fischer launched the city's Office for Safe and Healthy Neighborhoods, which led him to become aware of CBMA and the Rumble.

"I always try to seek out national best practices and practitioners, people that have any type of work embedded in their mind, in their heart, in their life," Fischer said. "It was immediately apparent to me that Shawn Dove was that person, with the kind of spirit and enthusiasm and conviction that he carries. And, of course, with his deep love for Muhammad Ali, we had a common cause with that."

Fischer said it hasn't been lost on him how few white people he comes across who are involved in this work on behalf of Black males.

"I guess I bring my whiteness to this, which is a weird thing. Issues around race are so bizarre to me. Skin color is such a demarcation point for people on how they approach things, how they're included or excluded, or what have you. So, I'm like, look, if I'm welcome in what you all are doing, I want to learn and I want our city to be a model for how we can approach this work about empowering more young men and boys of color. Let's learn from each other and let's be motivated by each other."

Fischer added that while the Rumble is invigorating and enjoyable, he always comes back to the same question that I'm constantly asking myself: *Are we making a difference here?*

"We're going through that right now here in Louisville," he said. "We have all these wonderful initiatives going on, but I'm not happy with our systems change. I mean changing all of these systems that are in place that are still producing disparate outcomes for communities of color and low-income communities. We got to be realistic about where we're at and the outcomes we get as a society since many of these systems are 400-year-old systems... But what I say is, this work is about the fight for the soul of our country. Do we believe that every life matters? And if it does, as a mayor you got to be getting to work on this."

The first Rumble took place in 2011. It was evident from the start that Rumble wasn't really a conference or convening, it was more like a revival. People flocked to Louisville without airs or pretense—they came because they needed the connection, the inspiration, and the healing that they found there. During the first Rumble, Emma Jordan Simpson, who at the time was executive director of the Children's Defense Fund of New York and is Executive Pastor of Concord Baptist Church in Brooklyn, came up to me and whispered in my ear, "You are leading in a pastoral way. Are you doing that intentionally?" She didn't wait for an answer; she just dropped that gem and floated on. Emma's question has resonated with me ever since that first Rumble—a question I believe is at the heart of my loving and leading Black men and boys.

There are several scenes over the years that stand out for me as representing the ethos of Rumble. A few years ago, during the closing intergenerational session, Willie Hamilton, founder and president of an organization in Omaha called Black Men United, stood up in a room of 200 leaders and told the story of his daddy hunger. He was one of the leaders who hadn't gotten a grant from CBMA but came to Rumble because being a member of CBMA gave him a certain validation in his city. Rumble provided leaders in the Black male achievement movement with love, safety, and belonging in a vulnerable, healing space. A dignified man in his late 50s, Hamilton broke down and sobbed about the father wound in his heart, one that had been aching for decades. The community became a living cocoon around him, and he had a healing moment.

During another closing session at a Rumble, Susan L. Taylor, founder of National CARES Mentoring Movement and former *Essence* editor-in-chief, had joined with Rev. Dr. Alfonso Wyatt to lead a discussion and the subject of depression came up. They asked, "How many of us are dealing with depression?" Half the room raised their hands.

"How many have thought about suicide?" they asked. A quarter of the room raised their hands.

It was a riveting confirmation of what we already knew—that so much of our leadership was in just as much pain and in just as much need to resolve trauma as the young men we were seeking to support. I was so inspired that I announced right then that whether we got it funded or not, we were going to launch the BMA Health and Healing Strategies.

"How are we going to do this work if the cavalry is ailing?" I said.

We did get funding for the initiative. I soon began to see this as one of our most important undertakings. Dr. Phyllis Hubbard, who oversees the initiative, has become a national leader in the space. I met her in 2009 and on a personal level she's been working on me for the last decade to apply the healing strategies to my own life and take better care of myself. And she's not the only one. A couple of years ago, a brother named Terry Boykin, who runs a California group called Street Positive that does a lot of work with gangs on issues of masculinity, came up to me at a Rumble and whispered in my ear, "This is wonderful, this is beautiful—another great Rumble. How you doing with your health?" When he said it, for some reason it triggered something in me. But it still took two more years for me to take concrete action. Phyllis would corner people and have them record messages to me—including my twin teenage sons, Caleb and Cameron—about the importance of my health. In 2019 the message finally seeped into my stubborn cerebral cortex and I began to take action, focusing on diet and exercise.

This is an area that we may sometimes try to take lightly, but I have heard more than one leader say that if we work ourselves to an early grave, there'll be a nice memorial service for you—and then folks are just going to keep it moving. We have to be more intentional about our health and welfare, setting up 401(k) plans, planning for proper retirement. So many of us devote our entire lives to this work, this movement, and wind up broke. I've had 70-year-old Black men on the phone with me, crying as they tell me they can't retire, and they haven't paid themselves in more than a month because they had to pay consultants and meet payroll.

At our Promise of Place convening in Detroit in October 2019, I missed the group photo because I was getting reflexology on my feet. I have had many challenges over the years with my troubled feet. I'm a little bit sensitive about how they look. Anybody who knows me well is probably laughing when they read this, thinking that the word "sensitive" is the world's biggest understatement. I was so stressed out that I was actually letting somebody mess with my feet. The massages and reflexology at our convenings have become so effective and commonplace that other organizations have taken up the practice. It's a path that I never would have planned or expected for CBMA, but it falls in line with one of our mission mantras—there is no logic model for love.

During the 2019 Rumble, one of the young leaders, an activist and artist from Chicago who had participated in a number of our gatherings, let go at a morning spirituality circle and revealed that she had been holding onto childhood molestation. We use those circles to get vulnerable and support each other; this young lady felt safe enough in that space to unburden herself and to feel the powerful and moving support of everyone in the room. It was all part of the healing journey and more evidence that we cannot heal in isolation. We cannot heal without community. CBMA had grown into the place where we created that space.

Ron Walker, founder and executive director of a vital organization called Coalition of Schools Educating Boys of Color (COSEBOC), which was one of our early grantees, can recall the resistance he witnessed when we first introduced the concept of mental healing at one of our convenings.

"Nobody brought up mental health, wellness, self-care, healing-centered approaches in a unified way until CBMA started to make that a real important and critical aspect of the programs and the convenings that they gave," Walker said. "I remember when we were in California someplace, and it was the first kind of introduction to Dr. Phyllis and this whole notion, and brothers were saying, 'I don't want to do that. I don't want to do that. It's taking us out of the mission. Why should we do that?' Now, it's become standard operating procedure that someway, somehow, someplace, we will build wellness into the agenda of our convenings."

Walker said the focus on self-care challenged Black male notions of masculinity in a very healthy way.

"You had to cross a threshold with brothers who said, 'It's not masculine, I ain't doing that. It's too touchy-feely.' Now, it is integrated into how we build—at least I'll speak for COSEBOC—how we do our thing, the speakers we bring in, the topics and workshops we have. There's always a strand around healing."

Why is that important?

"At the end of the day, as a leader, I—and any other of these leaders—can't do our work without being in touch with ourselves," he said. "It's important because if we are walking around wounded and stuck in a mindset that it's too macho or too touchy-feely, then we can't be fully of service to those wounded young men, women, and other people that we know carry trauma each and every day. So, it's being a model for the work we do with others that are in pain and trust me, people who are leading these organizations, people who are participating, are carrying a lot of wounds. So, I think it gives us an opportunity to decloak and really say, 'You know what? In order for me to be my full self, to do the work of healing others, I got to be healed myself.'"

Regina Jackson, CEO of the East Oakland Youth Development Center, said one of the most important aspects of the convenings has been something she calls "cascading mentoring."

"It's so empowering, the seed-planting of the elder men to the younger men, in a thoughtful, sensitive, emotionally intelligent way, to reach out and hold their hand and say, 'I'm here for you, and that this is not just about you finding your way, it's about *us* finding *our* way.'"

From day one, it's been clear to us that we needed to work to change the narrative surrounding Black males in the U.S. We knew it was crucial to create a narrative that sees Black men and boys as assets to our communities and for us to support leaders across the country who were engaged in this work. It was to that end that we launched something in 2010 that we called "Black Male Reimagined," an initiative to affirm accurate portrayals of Black people in the mainstream media and encourage influencers in media and entertainment to help transform how our men and boys are portrayed in popular culture. To be sure, this includes the way we portray and talk about Black males inside of the Black community. The initiative was the baby of my deputy Rashid Shabazz, who had a background in community organizing and strategic communications, but who also was raised around activists in the Nation of Islam who have been working for many decades to change the Black male narrative. Rashid crafted a campaign with Alexis McGill Johnson, executive director and co-founder of the Perception Institute, an anti-bias research group, and currently president of Planned Parenthood, that brought together prominent activists, artists, filmmakers, writers, storytellers—anybody whose work touched on the image of Black males—to begin reframing the narrative of what it means to be a Black male in America. With folks like Spike Lee, Thomas Burrell, and Steve Stoute in attendance, the first convening in 2010 was a rousing success.

"No one had ever done anything like that before," Rashid recalled. "Bringing together philanthropists, activists, industry insiders, and centering the event around the conversation of what it means to be a Black man. Reframing the conversation around assets."

"It was a legacy piece for me at CBMA," added Rashid, who is now serving as the founding executive director of Critical Minded, a grantmaking and advocacy initiative that supports an ecosystem of cultural critics of color, "to the degree that it has now created a shift in philanthropy to invest heavily in culture and narrative in a way that people feel confident about. Before, people saw it as a second thought, 'Oh, communication, narrative, culture change, those are cool, but what about policy, what about the education platform?'"

Anthony Smith, Executive Director of Cities United, a national movement working with cities to create comprehensive violence prevention plans to eliminate homicides and shootings of young Black men and boys, said that shift to asset framing that CBMA brought about has been an immense contribution to the field of Black Male Achievement.

"CBMA came in with an asset frame, with a love for Black boys, telling them that you are valuable," Smith said. "Saying to boys that we already see promise in you and we already have love for you—that feels different when you're not coming at it from that you're-an-issue-and-a-problem perspective. Telling boys, we're going to celebrate you. We're going to love on you. We're going to create space for you. And we're going to highlight who you are, the way we see you, and not the way that the world sees you... CBMA has always been able to celebrate individuals by pushing the system to think different."

Tonya Allen, president and CEO of the Skillman Foundation in Detroit, said the conversation before CBMA was how we can "fix" our boys, or "save" our men.

"It was about looking at these individuals and saying something is wrong with them," said Allen, who has served as chair of the CBMA board.

Allen believes changing the narrative has been one of CBMA's greatest accomplishments.

Another narrative desperately in need of shifting is around Black males and financial stability. It was at a conference in Omaha in September 2014 when my antenna became tuned to the idea of Black male equity. I heard finance experts George Fraser, Randall Pinkett, and Dr. Pamela Jolly break down finance, ownership, and wealth-building issues in a way that really opened my eyes. Jolly talked about the key to wealth being ownership and that Black people were the only people in America that were assets before we were able to own assets. I told myself that this was what the field of Black Male Achievement needed to focus on next: equity and ownership. It aligned perfectly with my plan to transition the Campaign into the Corporation for Black Male Achievement.

In 2017, we finally came together and said, *Okay, what are we going to do?* We decided to create the Black Male Equity Initiative in Detroit, where we formed a cohort of Black men—we started with 25 and ended with 20—who for an entire year engaged in quarterly, intensive, all-day retreats and then bi-weekly video calls with the purpose of establishing wealth portfolios. They had to develop budgets, determine their personal wealth, describe their story around money, their family history around money, and how it impacts them. It was painful, probing stuff. We did a group "genealogy reveal" sharing our results from AfricanAncestry.com. The ultimate goal was to pool their dollars together and invest in properties in Detroit. The Black Realtors Association of Detroit was one of our partners. As of this printing, we hadn't made the purchase yet, but I believe the education component was even more important than the actual acquisition.

The way Dr. Jolly teaches it touches a chord inside of Black men, delving into how we must break the psychological chains of slavery. As I talked to her, I shared that sometimes it feels like we almost need CPR as Black men to be resuscitated and really see ourselves as owners. The trust aspect was really deep—how we can get together and talk about surface stuff like sports all day, but when we had to write down our personal budgets, the vulnerabilities quickly rose to the surface. It forced me to look at my own relationship with managing money. A pivotal moment was when I said out loud during our first meeting in the Skillman Foundation boardroom that this isn't about anybody being the "bigger nigga"—a word I rarely use—but is about us coming together and building. In the post-session interviews, folks said that when they heard those words from me, it broke down the barriers and built trust.

I sometimes underestimate the effect I can have on people when I show up in a space. Ray Winans who runs a hospital-based violence prevention program in Detroit and is now purchasing and remodeling properties in the city, once confessed to me that when he happened to be in New York to make a presentation for CBMA, he saw me sitting at a table signing checks.

"It did something to me," he said. "I saw that it was possible for me."

I actually don't remember the scene, but he brings it up all the time—a catalytic moment for him. It was a classic example of spreading Black male equity outward.

Dr. Jolly told me that the way CBMA deployed our resources—the largest amount of money ever directed toward Black Male Achievement—was like a private equity entity, which was a radical departure from the way we customarily have operated in the Black community.

"What I mean by that is that in the Black community, we're often given debt, all day long, and we have to repay it. Well, in the philanthropic world, what debt looks like is a grant where you don't get to do what you want to do, you have to do what they tell you to do. Shawn was given equity. He wasn't told what to do. In my mind, Shawn has been operating as a corporation burdened under a campaign."

According to Jolly, the difference between debt and equity in the philanthropic world is crucial for people to understand.

"CBMA has deployed equity investments into Black organizations that would not have otherwise been funded," she said. "When I went to my first Rumble, a grown Black man walked up to me and broke down in tears and said, 'I knew I had what it took to take care of our young boys, but I've never had the resources. And if Shawn hadn't given me those resources, I wouldn't have been able to see what was possible.' That's what equity does."

Jolly said equity expands vision. She noted that CBMA allowed Black men to expand their vision about what's possible when they're not strapped for cash.

"My father, God rest his soul, has amazing quotes, but two of the quotes really come to mind," Jolly said. "The first one is, 'A man can only see as far as he can afford.' Shawn took the blinders off. He took the blinders off of what was possible by investing in what needs to come to fruition in our community.

"The other quote my father said is, 'A man can't value what he does not understand.' And if you really listen to Shawn, he understands what Black men don't understand yet, and have suffered through, and he wants them to start to value themselves first before they can do this great monumental visual work that everyone's expecting Black achievement to do. He's done that work with these men. He built up the men who will become the institutional owners of achievement for Black men."

As always, I find Dr. Jolly's words to be incredibly uplifting and extremely humbling.

After we had been firmly established as a major philanthropic force, in 2012 there were a couple of pivotal moments that substantially directed the arc of CBMA's growth. One of them was when we decided to partner with the Foundation Center to produce a groundbreaking report called "Where Do We Go From Here? Philanthropic Support for Black Men and Boys," which analyzed the level of philanthropic support around the nation for Black males. It was an important endeavor, for the first time chronicling the actual dollars being targeted to this population, getting past all the talk, and looking at who was taking action. I purposely didn't tell the directors inside OSF that we were working on this report, so its publication was greeted with some consternation in the building. I knew had I gone asking for permission from the OSF bureaucracy, I likely would have gotten a decisive "No"—bureaucracies tend to abhor change and deviation. When the report came out, it was generally well-received inside the walls of OSF, but I got the sense that I was beginning to get the reputation of being hard to manage. This would come back in later years to work for me and also against me.

The other tipping point came later in October 2012, when we gathered leaders and movers in the field for an event we called the Black Male Achievement Impact and Innovation Forum. It was a two-day conference at the Grand Central Hyatt in midtown Manhattan that brought together more than 200 leaders from across different sectors to share best practices. Mike Bloomberg and George Soros were there, so we had billionaires in stereo. It was the biggest gathering in the field up to that moment, like our version of the Million Man March, the Black Male Achievement Grammys, Oscars, Coachella all rolled into one.

At one point in the midst of the event, Trista Harris, at the time the president of the Headwaters Foundation for Justice, came up to me and said, "Shawn, I want to thank you. We have been trying to elevate this issue in philanthropy. But thanks to you and CBMA, we have brought over 200 people here to talk about this issue, to elevate it. Do you realize how important that is?" When she said "we," I knew she was talking about the conscious Black folks in philanthropy. To be honest, at the time I did not realize how important or unusual it was. But if this was the narration of the CBMA movie, that was a definite inflection point, when the protagonist begins to get the first taste of success and starts to believe in himself.

Pedro Noguera, one of the researchers behind the book *Schooling for Resilience: Improving the Life Trajectory of Black and Latino Boys*, which I referenced in Chapter 6, was one of our speakers, as well as *Ebony* editor-in-chief Kierna Mayo and other luminaries. When I addressed the audience, for the second time I said aloud something I had been thinking for a couple of years: "We don't need a Campaign for Black Male Achievement; what we need is a Corporation for Black Male Achievement." My vision at the time for the Corporation for Black Male Achievement was the creation of an endowed philanthropic social enterprise that would serve as the catalyst for funding and building the infrastructure of a nascent and fragile field of Black male achievement.

That event was a seminal moment that gave us significant momentum. We clearly had started to draw the attention of OSF leadership. After that convening, the new director of U.S. Programs for OSF called me into his office. "You've been talking a lot about this spin-off," he said. "Let's see what this is about."

While Open Society Foundations had a history of spinning off its "best programs," I was quite sure his interest in spinning CBMA off into a separate foundation was less about advancing and building up the movement and more about, "How do we get this guy out of the Open Society Foundation? He's getting too much of the boss man's attention." That was the opening salvo in what became a process that ultimately took many years to see to fruition.

Months later, I stepped into one of the most pivotal moments in my leadership in the Black male achievement movement.

Chapter 9: The President is Looking for You

I am asking you to believe not in my ability to bring about change – but in yours.

—President Barack Obama

In 2013, after a Florida jury acquitted George Zimmerman for the killing of Trayvon Martin, the Black community was rocked by shock and broiling anger. On a brutally hot July day in the New York metropolitan area, with the afternoon temperature inching toward 100 degrees, I was having my own moments of frustration, trying to figure out how an organization dedicated to the upliftment of Black boys could respond in a meaningful, proactive way. I was driving along Route 22 in central New Jersey on my way home when I got a curious text from *Ebony* editor-in-chief, Kierna Mayo.

"The president is looking for you."

Six words that to me were incomprehensible. *Which president? The president of what?* Since I was driving, I didn't bother to ask her what she was talking about. But when I reached the house and turned on CNN, I quickly figured it out. President Obama had given a speech from the White House at 1:33 p.m., responding to the Zimmerman verdict. I sat down and watched the excerpts that kept playing on the news. It was one of those momentous occasions when the nation's first Black president dared to speak frankly to his country about race, Black men and boys and their perilous history in this nation.

> *"You know, when Trayvon Martin was first shot, I said that this could have been my son. Another way of saying that is Trayvon Martin could have been me 35 years ago. And when you think about why, in the African American community at least, there's a lot of pain around what happened here, I think it's important to recognize that the African American community is looking at this issue through a set of experiences and a history that doesn't go away.*

> *"There are very few African American men in this country who haven't had the experience of being followed when they were shopping in*

a department store. That includes me. There are very few African American men who haven't had the experience of walking across the street and hearing the locks click on the doors of cars. That happens to me—at least before I was a senator. There are very few African Americans who haven't had the experience of getting on an elevator and a woman clutching her purse nervously and holding her breath until she had a chance to get off. That happens often."

Then the president went on to lay out preliminary plans that felt like he was speaking to me directly—just like I felt hearing Susan L. Taylor's comments in a packed Harlem elementary school auditorium some 16 years earlier.

"Now, the question for me at least, and I think for a lot of folks, is where do we take this? How do we learn some lessons from this and move in a positive direction?

"We need to spend some time in thinking about how do we bolster and reinforce our African American boys. And this is something that Michelle and I talk a lot about. There are a lot of kids out there who need help who are getting a lot of negative reinforcement. And is there more that we can do to give them the sense that their country cares about them and values them and is willing to invest in them?

"I'm not naïve about the prospects of some grand, new federal program. I'm not sure that that's what we're talking about here. But I do recognize that as President, I've got some convening power, and there are a lot of good programs that are being done across the country on this front. And for us to be able to gather together business leaders and local elected officials and clergy and celebrities and athletes and figure out how are we doing a better job helping young African American men feel that they're a full part of this society and that they've got pathways and avenues to succeed—I think that would be a pretty good outcome from what was obviously a tragic situation. And we're going to spend some time working on that and thinking about that."

My mind immediately went into overload. *Had the president of the United States basically just spoken about committing the resources of the world's richest economy to address the issues that I spent every hour of every day obsessing over? What did this mean for the work and future of CBMA?*

I ran to my computer and fired off an email to George Soros's assistant, Kim, whom I knew would forward it to Soros. I said in the email that in the aftermath of the president's speech, we should make a bold investment of a hundred million dollars to launch the Corporation for Black Male Achievement. Little did I know that Kim not only forwarded emails to Soros, but she also sent them to another guy who was very close to Soros, kind of like his consigliere. It didn't take long for the consigliere to call me and inform me that I was no longer allowed to send direct emails to Mr. Soros. I had gotten busted trying to make an end-run around the bureaucracy.

The next day I got a phone call from Joshua DuBois, who was the White House Director of Faith-based and Neighborhood Initiatives. He had an urgent message for me and Rashid—we needed to help him come up with a plan to follow up the president's speech. I decided that we wouldn't mention any of this to the OSF leadership. I didn't want them to step in and squash it or try to take it over. Three days after the speech, Rashid and I found ourselves in the East Room of the White House, meeting with Joshua and a few folks on his team to talk about our next steps.

Even though I had been warned not to reach out to Soros directly, I did it anyway by calling Kim and asking her if I could get to Soros. I wanted to ask him directly to invest $100 million in the Corporation for Black Male Achievement.

"Well, you know, he spends most of his summers in the Hamptons," she said. "Are you willing to come out to the Hamptons?"

My eyes lit up. That scenario was even better. His Manhattan office was right down the block from OSF's offices. I could just see myself getting busted again ducking into the office to meet with him. But now I could conceivably drive out to the famous playground of New York's wealthy in Long Island and have some privacy while we met.

That week was our third annual Rumble Young Man Rumble gathering in Louisville, one of CBMA's highlights of the year. While in Louisville, I was trying to concentrate on the Rumble proceedings, but my mind was racing—oscillating between my boldness and my fear. I think this is probably a psychological dichotomy that hamstrings many Black men while trying to navigate white power structures. I saw myself driving out to the Hamptons and meeting with Soros, telling him, "This is what needs to be done."

But I also knew he was going to push it back to the president of the foundation and U.S. Programs, who would have looked at me with widened eyes and asked, "Wait, you went to George after we told you not to?"

I would have won the battle but lost the war—and maybe also my job. While I was at Rumble I was losing sleep, one-minute feeling bad and bold, the next moment thinking about job security. The proverbial angel on one shoulder and the devil on the other.

Go ahead, Shawn, you can do it!

Nah, Shawn, you can't do it!

On the last day of Rumble, I got a call from the OSF executives, informing me that Valerie Jarrett, President Obama's longtime advisor, had reached out to OSF and said they wanted to meet at the White House to figure out how philanthropy could partner with them to respond to the president's speech. The Open Society Foundations president, Chris Stone, wanted me to come with him. I greeted that request with a huge sense of relief—it got me out of my dilemma. I couldn't be out in the Hamptons asking Soros for a hundred million for the Corporation for Black Male Achievement while the president of his foundation was meeting at the White House at the same time.

That White House meeting with Jarrett was an eye-opening experience for me. I had sent OSF a leadership memo about spinning off into the independent Corporation for Black Male Achievement, but their response was clear disinterest. However, sitting in the White House, after listing all that he had done in the past on behalf of criminal justice reform, Chris then pivoted and asked Jarrett, "Would the President be interested in partnering with us to create something like a Corporation for Black Male Achievement?"

Now I was the one with my spirit falling out of my chair. Maybe he was getting the impression that Jarrett wasn't feeling him or something, so he went for broke and grabbed my idea. He didn't even give me attribution, like "Oh, Shawn has had this idea." I wanted to poke him and ask, "You do know I'm sitting next to you and I can hear you, right?" His idea immediately piqued her interest; she wanted to talk more about it.

In many ways, those were the opening chords in the president's groundbreaking My Brother's Keeper Initiative. We began having planning meetings with White House officials. In September 2013, I found myself sitting across from President Obama in the Roosevelt Room of the White House. When I first walked into the room, accompanied by a bunch of foundation presidents, I spotted my name tag and saw that I had been placed directly across from Obama's chair. *Oh shit!* I said to myself. As we sat down, Darren Walker, who had just taken over as head of the Ford Foundation and who was seated next to me, leaned over and said, "You know this should be called the Shawn Dove meeting, right?"

Somebody took a picture of me gesticulating in the president's direction while I was talking. I don't remember what I was saying during that moment, but I certainly appear to be animated. I can't recall why I was wearing my glasses that day instead of contacts. Obama had two fingers on his temple as he listened to me, looking like a contemplative Malcolm X. The narrative is that was the moment when we convinced him to launch My Brother's Keeper. I'm not so sure of that, but I'll take it.

In February 2014, President Obama officially announced the My Brother's Keeper program. That day was fascinating to me in many respects. When I got to the White House that morning and showed my ID to the security guard, he saw the North Plainfield, NJ, address on my license and remarked, "Hey, I'm from Scotch Plains, New Jersey." I had a short conversation with this white man from New Jersey that would soon prove to be very important. Later, as we were leaving the meeting, I was asked to participate in the press conference outside in the Rose Garden announcing the president's plans to create something on behalf of Black boys. I went out and stood near NYC Mayor Michael Bloomberg as he spoke. It was an incredible and surreal moment for everybody involved. When it was over, some folks scattered, others milled around networking. But I realized I had left my coat and briefcase behind in the White House, so I went in search of the coatroom.

I realized after a few minutes that I was lost inside the basement of the White House, wandering around looking suspicious as hell. It was an eerie feeling. *How are they letting me walk around this hallowed space unattended? Is this how they protecting Obama? Good thing I wasn't a terrorist!* In the middle of my ruminations, a Secret Service agent suddenly appeared in my face.

"What are you doing?" he asked.

"I was just part of the press conference," I said, trying to remain calm. "I was trying to find the coatroom."

There was no other person anywhere in sight. My story must have sounded quite suspect, a stranger wandering through the White House all alone.

"Come upstairs with me," he said curtly. As I walked with him, he got on his radio and asked somebody about me. I kept looking around for a familiar face, maybe somebody from the White House staff who could vouch for me. *Damn, where did everybody go?*

We came upon more security. I breathed a sigh of relief when I saw who it was—the white guy from New Jersey.

"I saw this guy," he said, nodding toward me. "He's legit."

I had a quick flashback to the movie *Sankofa* when the Black model visits the slave castle in Ghana on a glamorous photoshoot and finds herself transported back to the time of the slave trade, where she then becomes an enslaved woman in the American South. I came for My Brother's Keeper and had wandered into a much different and potentially harrowing scenario.

There was another scene a couple of years later when I was having trouble gaining access to an official My Brother's Keeper event. I got held up on the line while they checked my credentials. I heard a voice pipe up from behind me.

"You better let him in!" It was Nkechi Taifa, who at the time was a program director for Open Society Institute – DC's Justice Roundtable and the author of her memoir, *Black Power, Black Lawyer: My Audacious Quest for Justice.*

"There would be no My Brother's Keeper if it wasn't for Shawn Dove," she said, to my profound embarrassment.

As we continued to try to push OSF to spin us off, I heard from the executives that they wanted to see what Obama's program was going to look like before they gave the go-ahead. I couldn't take it anymore, all the limbo. At a meeting with the leadership, I said, "I don't know what Obama is going to do, but this is how we got here, and if I can't spin off the Campaign for Black Male Achievement, then we're spinning off the Institute for Black Male Achievement."

In other words, I was going to do it whether they blessed it or not. I would just change the name if I had to. When those words came out of my mouth, the voice on one side of my head said, *Oh shit, you heard what he just said?* And the fearful voice said, *No, no, don't say that!* I could see them exchange looks around the table. They didn't verbalize it, but the looks said, *Damn, he's serious about this!* So, they finally agreed to do it. We got the thumbs up to spin-off. But I knew the real reason was they were more interested in getting me out. Most mornings I had to meditate on how I was going to show up to work—somewhere along the continuum between *Django Unchained* at one end and *The Butler* at the other. I knew that I likely showed up too often on the *Django* end of the spectrum.

One of the directors told Geoff Canada, who was our board advisor, "Oh, Shawn can be a little prickly."

When Geoff told me that, I was upset. *Prickly? What does that even mean?* It was not a word I had ever heard used to describe a Black man; we didn't grow up calling each other prickly. But I understood what was going on. The way I led could be difficult to manage inside a structured institution like OSF.

During a process like this one, as we were negotiating with OSF, it's really important to have both an inside and an outside game. We were able to leverage relationships with allies inside the organization, but we were also able to benefit from our relationships with people like Alberto Ibargüen, president and CEO of the Knight Foundation, and Tonya Allen, then the president and CEO of the Skillman Foundation (who later became my board chair) to lean on OSF and say, "Y'all need to do right by CBMA."

I realized that it is difficult for Black leaders within philanthropic institutions to break barriers around Black liberation. You're always trying to calibrate the level of Blackness you can bring to the table. When we delved into the negotiations over how much money OSF would invest in the spin-off as I sought to break away, the first number they slid across the table was $2.5 million over three years. *What? How is that setting us up for success?* I wanted to express the full extent of my outrage over the lightness of the number, but I remained calm. We settled on $10 million over five years. I originally was seeking $100 million—but five years into the spinoff I realized that $100 million would have crushed us. I was not prepared to manage that much money. I would have spent too much far too fast.

OSF was very supportive during the transition. The legal team was helpful with all the logistics; the facilities management team helped us look for space. It became very surreal. The president of OSF's U.S. programs gave me great advice during a couple of mentoring sessions. He said there would be days when you feel like you are the master of the universe, the world's greatest social entrepreneur, and there will be days when you feel like you don't know what the hell you're doing.

He was certainly right about that.

It wasn't until a few months after we were comfortably ensconced in our new space that I sat back and marveled. *Oh wow, we actually did this? How many Black men could say they have cut this kind of deal for a Black-led organization?*

The entire process had begun in December 2011, when I said out loud for the first time that I had a vision of spinning off into an independent entity. We started the planning in spring 2013; most of 2014 we spent negotiating and planning some more. I had a dicey moment when I let out my frustration in the wrong damn place. I thought I was texting my wife, Desere, and I said: "They f**king driving me crazy up in here. I don't know if I'm going to spin off or if I'm spinning out of here!"

Turns out, I had posted that on Twitter, not in a private text to my wife. Moving too fast, not paying close enough attention. I rushed to delete it. Luckily, I didn't have nearly as many followers then.

On Martin Luther King, Jr. Day in 2015, we bought out a movie theater in Detroit and had our official launch event, screening *Selma* and holding a panel discussion with Detroit leaders and young people.

The next five years of CBMA were equal parts spin-off and startup. I had to transition from a grant-maker to a grantee, seeking funding at the same time as I was giving it away. But when we published our 2018 impact report, entitled "CBMA Turns 10: A Decade of Risk, Urgency, and Momentum," I was proud to publicize our 10-year numbers. We had leveraged more than $320 million in national and local funds for Black Male Achievement. We had built a BMA network of more than 5,700 members and 2,765 organizations.

But despite the numbers, it's so abundantly clear that our work isn't even close to being done. I continued to grapple with the paradox of promise and peril for Black men and boys in America. Fortunately, we are witnessing more visible championing of Black men and boys who are demonstrating their brilliant contributions to this country. Yet, the peril persists for our boys and men, particularly in the face of police brutality and increasing community gun violence. Any organization has to evolve, as needs change and the landscape you operate in constantly reshapes itself. Amidst our evolution, I had to dig down and ask myself what kind of organization I wanted CBMA to become.

The spring of 2020 accelerated my ruminations about the evolution of CBMA when in the wake of COVID-19 and organizational challenges with resources we chose to sunset operations of the Campaign at the end of 2020. We made the announcement on May 1st. Twenty-four days later, George Floyd was brutally murdered by Derek Chauvin and the Minneapolis Police Department for the world to witness, which set off global protests and rumblings about a racial reckoning in America.

What is our future going to look like? What role are we going to serve in this movement over the next decade? What role am I going to take as I move into my retirement years? And most fatefully, what does the future look like for Black men and boys in America?

Chapter 10: Jamare and the Lyricist Society

"I think all Black boys need an outlet, but everybody don't have an outlet. It keeps you from messing up. It helps you relieve stress or something you can use to vent or when you feel down. That's what I get out of music."

—Jamare Winston

A lot of educators try to structure their classrooms and instructional approaches with their students in mind, even as they're working with repressive state-mandated curricula. *Would my kids like this? How do I tailor this to my students?* These days, that thinking even has a fancy name in education circles—student-centered learning.

I don't think I've ever run into an educator who instinctively puts students at the center of everything he does more than Quan Neloms in Detroit. A decade ago, Neloms looked around at the school where he was teaching, Frederick Douglass Academy for Young Men, an all-Black all-boys school, and felt like the extracurricular offerings were missing something.

"I noticed that they had a band at that time, and you had students who were interested in art and music and things like that, but it wasn't band they were interested in," Neloms recalls. "It was hip hop, rap, and stuff like that. So, it just started off really as a hobby club, where I got together some of the guys who weren't into being in the band or chorus or anything, and I said, 'Well, let's see what you guys can do as far as rap.' It was very interesting. We recorded, put some things out, and the darndest thing happened. All these people, including kids at the school, were listening to it. And I thought, okay, well this can maybe be a teaching tool."

That's where Neloms' genius and ability to connect with kids took over. In the message and history of hip hop, he saw an opening to bring in a vast array of lessons in English, history, psychology, race relations, sociology, economics. Almost every subject that high school students are tasked with learning could in some way be woven into lessons around this thing called hip hop. Neloms gave the students two main directives—no profanity and you have to talk about something. They responded with stunning recordings featuring brilliant lyrics and wordplay. They were showing skills that many of them would never have presented in English class. Neloms appropriately named his group Lyricist Society. The students hit up a wide range of topics with their songs—ranging from personal issues and demons they were tackling in their lives to historical events like the '67 Detroit rebellion. In recent years they added a video element to the work. Students who aren't interested in performing learn about the vast array of related skills needed in the industry, such as audio engineering and videography.

"As my skill set grew, we started adding more things to it," Neloms says. "So, they started doing things like documentaries, public service announcements, music videos, and things like that."

They even won a local Emmy Award for video production, beating out a well-funded white suburban school. Neloms had found a powerful way to give Black boys a voice and a platform—two things that American society rarely gives them without a leather ball or the specter of violence somehow involved.

"We talk about student voice a lot, but I think with Black boys, especially in education, they don't necessarily have a chance to have a voice," Neloms says. "And hip hop is one of those art forms where you're forced to listen to what people are saying. So that's a wonderful marriage with the boys at Douglass, that they get a chance to talk about something that's important to them, and people are listening."

The first time I became aware of Quan Neloms and Lyricist Society in 2016, I immediately knew that this was a program and a philosophy that CBMA needed to be investing in. It was so potent and scalable—I could easily imagine similar programs in high schools across America, using hip hop to stimulate a generation of talented writers and music industry professionals. We provided funding to help Neloms expand his program, which is now in four Detroit schools. Neloms also became a CBMA Fellow in 2017, a program we created in partnership with the American Express Foundation, to invest in developing his leadership and his vision on a personal level.

Detroit was an exceedingly important city for CBMA—hell, for America as a whole. Personally, I have a great deal of emotional energy invested in seeing Detroit make it, return to a semblance of its former glory. As I discussed in Chapter 8, it was one of our Promise of Place cities, where we were trying to direct resources and investments to scale up the local impact of our dollars. We even opened a Promise of Place office in Detroit to really dig in there. Coming from New York City and Harlem, I can appreciate the love and pride Detroit residents seem to have for their city. They might complain about it all day long, but they won't let any outsiders get away with speaking ill of the Motor City. Clearly, there's a great deal of trauma flowing through the city's streets, but whenever I'm there, I sense the devotion and commitment to bring about change. There is an enormous confluence of energy and passion in the philanthropic sector—entities like the Robert F. Smith's Fund 2 Fund Foundation, Steve Ballmer's The Ballmer Group, the Skillman Foundation, the Kresge Foundation, and many other local and national philanthropies. One of CBMA's roles was to serve as a connector, bringing together organizations that tended to work in isolated silos, so that we might maximize everyone's efforts. I want Detroit to be one of those places that we can point to in a decade and be able to identify a substantive transformation. It is already an incubator of innovation, but we need that innovation to start dramatically transforming lives in large numbers. Right now, there is no city that we can really point to and say, "This is what winning looks like for Black men and boys." Detroit could be one of those places where we see a positive path for Black boys from cradle to career.

Jamare Winston is a fabulous example of the talent in Detroit, but his future is certainly not assured. All of the people pouring into his life must remain vigilant, make sure we see his talents translate into adult success. I had already seen up close Quan Neloms' work at Frederick Douglass before I met Jamare for the first time. When I went to the media lab in the building where the Lyricist Society students spend a great deal of time, the energy in the space reminded me of my days in high school writing for a student paper called *New Youth Connections*. It felt like a safe haven for these young men. I saw in them a sense of pride in their creativity, their maturity. I went into another room and saw a program at the school called the Dream Kings, which educator William Malcolm turned into a fraternity of sorts, requiring young men to apply for membership and have their applications adjudged by current members. Again, the power of belonging. He transformed the classroom into a mini-Black history museum, with images of icons like Marcus Garvey and Harriet Tubman. The room even has a throne where the young men can sit while they wear their special Dream Kings jackets, bringing to life the idea that these young men were kings—kings with dreams and aspirations for their life. Inside Frederick Douglass Academy, Jamare was a key member of both groups.

One of the first things I noticed about Jamare was his beaming smile. It was a smile that drew you in, made you want to get to know this ebullient, charming young man. He sat on a youth panel at the Rumble we held in Detroit in 2018 and he was so eloquent and self-assured. I heard him recite a poem and was really taken with his self-confidence and self-awareness. When you look at him and talk to him, you get no sense of the challenges he has been through in his life. It's a similar quality I see in so many Black boys, where their charming exterior masks or hides pain and trauma. It's like a coping skill that's been coded into our DNA, our cellular memory, over the last 400 years. Through centuries of being labeled a threat, a monster, a sexually rapacious predator, we had to develop ways to survive by putting the white world at ease. There's a remarkable spark of resiliency and creativity I see whenever I'm in the presence of Black men and boys. It's a divinity that America has actively been trying to snuff out for centuries, but it survives. Often, it thrives.

But the charm we employ that is a manifestation of the fear we carry inside can also manifest in another exterior we show the world—the scowling, angry Black male. It's a decision we make, which one we choose to employ. But they both come from the same place—a knowledge that we are constantly judged, attacked, not accepted. It's like a strategy that has evolved into a protective mechanism, almost like the fight or flight reflex. Either I'm going to repel you with my thug persona or disarm you with my charisma. Both have the same intent—survival. But we also must know when to use them. The thug won't be effective in school or corporate America; the smile and charm can be mistaken for weakness in the streets. Speaking from experience, I know trying to navigate the world and balance these two personas is emotionally exhausting.

Jamare says he saw right away in Lyricist Society an outlet for his interest in music. He had an uncle who was in Neloms' group, so Jamare started poking around when he was still in eighth grade. He says he was always drawn to music, to lyrics, but he didn't recognize it as an important outlet for him until Neloms invited him to join.

"I used to play around with music when I was younger, but I never really noticed how big it was in my life," Jamare says. "It's an outlet. I think all Black boys need an outlet, but everybody don't have an outlet. It keeps you from messing up. It helps you relieve stress or something you can use to vent or when you feel down. That's what I get out of music."

Music plays a big role in what Jamare sees as his future. He says he wants to be a recording artist. But he also can see himself as an audio engineer—and a detective, a psychologist, a motivational speaker. He's still got quite a few paths beckoning to him.

"The psychologist ties in with music," he says. "I can do music therapy. And I want to be a motivational speaker because people say that when I talk to them, they can feel my energy and how when I say things, I'm all about positivity. They all feed off each other."

Neloms says Jamare was probably the strongest ninth grader in the Lyricist Society when he started out. Neloms actually had Jamare as a student in one of his ninth-grade classes, which helped them grow even closer. Whenever he brought the students on trips, he made sure Jamare was in the group. Over the next two years, he came to rely so much on Jamare that he was practically like a staff member, helping when Neloms would do presentations to middle schoolers.

"Jamare is very helpful," Neloms says. "He's very good with kids. I imagine that comes from him really having to take care of his own siblings. Any type of opportunities, whether it was a conference, or camp, or any type of field trip, whatever that might be, I'll always make sure I tap Jamare to go. Because he was such a phenomenal wordsmith, any time you needed a young person to speak, or I needed an ambassador for anything, I would let Jamare take it on. So, he took on a leadership role. He's so gracious that when we do events, people will call up and specifically ask for him."

Neloms says he could tell at times that Jamare was grappling with demons like most Black boys, that he was hiding pain below the surface. He would look at Jamare in the morning sometimes and be able to tell that it was going to be a challenging day.

"Sometimes that pain would come out, and he would explode on an individual. Not all the time, but sometimes that would happen. I've seen him get in fights. I've seen him shut down. I've seen him maybe get a little testy with words with adults and things like that. It didn't happen a lot, but I did see it and I could tell when the day wasn't going as well. But since then, I've seen that he's grown a lot. He got that together through just wanting to be in school and having me and other people like William Malcolm of the Dream Kings really taking him under our wings."

Neloms was struck by Jamare's willingness to dive into most everything the school had to offer, from yoga to wrestling. His personality and work ethic led Neloms and others to recommend him for jobs in the community. In 2018, he had an internship with a local radio station.

"Jamare built up his community himself, which is very unusual," Neloms says. "He would see things and think, 'I need to be a part of this.' To his credit, he knew that he needed a strong tribe. If it wasn't there, he was going to go out and get it. He's worried now that he won't be a part of these things because he transferred to another school outside of Detroit. I told him, 'Young man, the relationships you established transcend the actual school building.' Those relationships will always be intact. He has a strong backing that will stay committed to him, wherever he is."

Jamare says the approach Neloms takes, using music history to pound home lessons about the problems with narratives that are too often employed by hip hop artists, has been extremely illuminating. These are lessons and perspectives these young men are unlikely to get anywhere else. Neloms, who spent many years as a history teacher, connects the music to the portrayals of Black men in popular media, going all the way back to minstrel shows.

"At one point, minstrel was the most popular form of entertainment in the *world*, right? Not only the United States but in the world," Neloms says. "They portrayed Black people in a very stereotypical way and, as you know, the first minstrel characters were white people in blackface. And then came Black people who still had to put on blackface; you had to wear a mask, behave in a way that was stereotypical. I find it very interesting that the first Black man to become a millionaire in Hollywood was Stepin Fetchit. I think the same thing is happening now—Black entertainment portraying Black people in a very stereotypical way."

Neloms teaches his students about Stepin Fetchit, but he also presents them with Paul Robeson, one of Fetchit's contemporaries, a fiercely proud Black man who used his celebrity status to bring attention to the plight of Black people in America—and who was ostracized in the industry because of his activism.

"He's the first Colin Kaepernick. The first Muhammad Ali. You also have the Harlem Renaissance, which was trying to combat all that negative imagery you saw in popular media at the time. And so, what I try to tell my students is that they have an opportunity to be like Paul Robeson, to be like artists during the Harlem Renaissance, and change how people view not just hip hop but how they view young Black men."

Neloms says he isn't telling his charges they have to be sweet and corny. They just have to say something meaningful.

"It's just been a blessing when they've gotten opportunities—like the song that they did about the '67 Rebellion was actually picked up by NPR. They got recognized and did radio interviews and stuff like that. They see that, hey, you can get people's attention by not doing the regular things that they are singing about in hip hop today. They start believing me. That's why we started doing the music videos. If you can see it, that makes the song sound ten times better, especially if it's done well. I just try to put them in a position where they can see that they can help change the narrative about themselves *and* their city by using their words. The response from the public and from people outside the school has really uplifted the program, uplifted the students involved."

When they won an Emmy for the music video for a song called "Peace," Neloms says it was overwhelming to watch his boys go up on stage at the black-tie event and give an acceptance speech. He has sent students on to college, where they are diving into careers in areas such as sound engineering, videography, broadcast engineering.

On a fall afternoon, Neloms brings a new group of middle schoolers through the early stages of the Lyricist Society lessons at an afterschool program. Called GOAL (Get On And Learn), the program has buses loop around to area public schools and bring students to the Northwest Activity Center for afterschool enrichment. The mayor's office hired Lyricist Society to do sessions with youngsters in the program. GOAL is part of the longstanding informal network of programs across the nation that cities like Detroit—and Oakland and New York—must create to supplement what doesn't happen in schools. Since integration splintered the Black community, we have never been able to rely on white schools to give our young people all the tools they need to make it through the American gauntlet of oppression. Neloms is joined at the center by Michael Siebert, a 25-year-old former Lyricist Society member who has come back to assist Neloms in running the program.

Neloms starts from scratch, first offering $1 to any middle schooler who can tell him what "lyricist" means. Out of two dozen or so students in the room, a few of them reach their hands toward the ceiling. A young lady smiles broadly when Neloms hands her the dollar bill for giving the correct answer. He tells them the Lyricist Society classes aren't intended to change what music they listen to—but they will be learning about the history of hip hop, and why it was created, they will learn how to think critically about music and media, and they will have the opportunity to create music "with a message" and shoot accompanying videos.

Neloms scans the room.

"What are you listening to?" he asks them. As they start naming the hot artists and songs of the minute, Neloms and Siebert make a list on the whiteboard. It's clear where this is headed, but the students don't know it yet. He will soon ask them to categorize songs by the ones that have a negative message and a positive message. But before they go there, Neloms shows them a video featuring minstrels in blackface, cavorting on-screen in mocking, painful imitations of Black stereotypes. The students watch, wide-eyed. Many of them are seeing these images for the first time. The loud, rambunctious temperature in the room, which necessarily comes with dozens of middle schoolers, cools considerably. Neloms has them where he wants them, with their minds wide open, receptive to the messages he will slowly feed them.

Countering narratives is a strong theme that runs through all the Lyricist Society's work. I believe that we must find innovative ways to become masters of our media, so I am a huge fan of what Neloms is doing in Detroit. And just as I brought together many aspects of my past experiences in developing the CBMA model, Neloms did the same thing with Lyricist Society. As a teen, his life was transformed by a program called Project ADAPT (Awareness Development And Pride Teamwork) in Detroit's Northwest Activities Center, the same center where he works with the GOAL students. It was run by a larger-than-life woman named Yvonne C. Rush—known to the community as Mama Rush—who was committed to getting her youngsters to see as much of the world as possible. Her motto was: "You have to move from ghetto to global." She did exhaustive fundraising so she could bring her students to the opera, the theater, to cultural events in Detroit, to other cities around the country.

"By the time I was 17 years old, I had heard Michael Eric Dyson, Na'im Akbar, Maulana Karenga, Cornel West, Jawanza Kunjufu, all these heavyweights," Neloms says. "Going out of town, being exposed to these different things, it definitely changes your outlook on life. It made me more goal oriented. I know I didn't come in as the best student, but it made you have a goal, and, secondly, it showed you that there was life outside of your community, your school, your city. Like Frederick Douglass said, when you learn how to read, it ruins you for being a slave. Well, I say when you learned that there was something outside the city, it ruins you for being captive to whatever was going on in your city."

Neloms brought Mama Rush's lessons with him when he became an educator, committing himself to show as much of the world as he can to young people in his care. Neloms, who also raps himself on some of his projects, can be heard paying tribute to Mama Rush on a powerful rap song he produced called "In Demand," featuring Black male teachers from Detroit dropping verses about the impact of Black male educators in the classroom. When Neloms raps "Mama Rush was the blueprint," he is testifying about the forces that made him.

Early in his career, Neloms had an experience that brought home for him the importance of influences on young people. While he was working in a program with young Black boys, trying to get them to see the light, many of them were going back to their neighborhoods and being drawn in by an older guy who was teaching them how to steal cars.

"Kids are going to get poured in one way or the other," Neloms says. "I saw this up close and personal. My kids had both influences, positive and negative, competing with one another."

In the cases of several young men, Neloms did not prevail. They ended up smashing into another car when they were driving a stolen car. A pregnant woman was in the other car, and she ended up miscarrying. The boys were swept away to prison.

"When the two sides are competing, the positive influence has got to be glaring almost, to the point where that negative influence can't even hold a candle up to it," he says. "That's what I try to be. I want my kids to be like, 'Yo, this is dope! I want to be here and not over there.'"

After teaching for 16 years at the middle and high school level, Neloms in 2019 moved to a K-8 elementary school to be a counselor. He has two boys of his own at home—ages 10 and 8—so all his work is incredibly personal to him.

Jamare's departure from Frederick Douglass Academy to the school in the suburbs reminds me of the path I took from Brooklyn Tech to Lawrence Academy, also when I was a high school junior. Like I did, he will have to navigate a predominantly white world without losing himself and the lessons he learned in Detroit. I believe Jamare has the self-awareness and emotional intelligence to be able to survive the transition. I've learned that when we're talking about the peril facing Black boys, we're not just talking about them dodging bullets and gang membership in dangerous neighborhoods. We're also talking about the perils of existing in all-white spaces.

Recently, I was traveling with a gentleman who runs a charter school in Brooklyn, who told me a story about one of the students graduating from his school to attend one of the top private schools in Manhattan. Less than two months into the school year, he was joking around with his classmates about water guns. Somehow the conversation prompted one of his classmates to go home and tell his parents that this Black boy was planning to shoot up the school. By the time the boy's mother got to the school, the police had already taken him down to the precinct and had him handcuffed to a desk for hours. Alarmed, the boy's mother actually withdrew him from that school. But just as I carried around the unresolved trauma from my kidnapping incident, I'm sure this boy will carry the residue from this trauma for many years. In other words, the peril can also come when we are in environments where we are not loved and considered.

I had a revealing conversation with a young man who joined us at one of the CBMA retreats. He was 23 and had graduated from Bard after growing up in the Manhattanville projects in Harlem. He shared that no matter where he is, what kind of space he's in, his default response is to scan the room and determine whether he is physically safe. He looks around for the exits, a remnant of his childhood in the projects. Only now is he recognizing that as the residue of trauma.

While Jamare has removed himself from the dangers of Detroit streets, I pray that he will not find too much peril in all-white Gibraltar. My wish for him is that his beaming smile and ebullient charm will bring him to a fabulous place, to be a leader among his people. His promise, his future, is the reason that so many of us lie awake at night, hoping and praying that the ancestors continue to watch over him, that the angels continue to smile down upon him.

Chapter 11: Romero and Oakland's African American Male Achievement

> *"He [Romero] has a life force energy, man. Just someone that you knew that if given the continued support and just the right space, so to speak, he would thrive completely."*

—Chris Chatmon

I will never forget the moment I saw Romero for the first time. It was at our fifth annual Rumble Young Man Rumble event in Louisville in December 2015. Always one of the highlights of the year for me, Rumble featured a stunning collection of inspiring leaders and talented young men basking in the mutual love and exhilaration and leaving everyone—including myself—with a much-needed injection of what I like to call "mission fuel" to do it again next year.

One of the culminating events was bringing together the flyweights, the youth participants, and the heavyweights, the mentors and leaders of the field, for an intergenerational session, where we talked about healing, tell stories, and share what's on our hearts—a perfect distillation of the CBMA tagline, *love, learn, lead.* I watched a slim, handsome, young kid take the mic with an unmistakable aura of confidence, like this was something he did every day. Unprompted, Romero launched into a mini sermon. He quoted scripture; he talked about the power, the promise, the encouragement in that room of more than 200 Rumblers ranging from high schoolers to elders. I stared at him, stunned.

Where did he get this from?

I didn't know anything about him, except that he had made it to Louisville as part of Chris Chatmon's contingent from Oakland. Clearly, this young man was anointed. But it also was important for me to note that Romero was connected to a community of Black men and women who love him and who work hard to infuse young men like him with focus and pride. In Oakland, they call them "kings," which was one of the first places I heard use that word to refer to young Black boys. While I'm tempted to use terms of exceptionalism in describing Romero, I know that all our young men have these gifts. Some are more skilled than others at displaying them for the world to see. Romero was an annual fixture at the Rumble for several years. I saw him up close at the CBMA offices several years ago, when the young men from Oakland were rehearsing a presentation they would be doing at a convening of the Coalition of Schools Educating Boys of Color (COSEBOC) in New York City. They would be sharing their creed and their stories with an audience of more than 500 educators and activists.

In this setting, I saw Romero surrounded by a whole group of Romeros—boys whose many gifts were obvious. There was such a vibrant sense of community, love, and potential in that room. But at the same time, as I watched them, I couldn't fight off a sneaking sense of dread. I knew that any of those young men's futures could be snuffed out in a moment—either by police violence or by the suffocation of their dreams at the hands of their perilous environments.

The manifestation of their promise and potential was far from inevitable, far from a guaranteed victory at the end of a clear and shiny path. I couldn't help but wonder how differently the thoughts of white adults would flow in a gathering of talented white boys. There would be a sense of expectancy, a vague acknowledgment that perhaps some of them would fail to realize their potential—but the worry quotient would be dramatically lower, almost nonexistent.

Romero's life took a crucial turn one day in 2013 when he was sitting in math class in seventh grade at Frick Middle School. A counselor came into the classroom and gestured for Romero to follow him.

"I'm like, did I do something wrong?" he recalls. "Because the way he was talking to me felt like I was in trouble."

Romero wasn't in trouble at all. In fact, he was being led to a sanctuary created in the midst of the Oakland school district, specifically for young men like him—a classroom under the auspices of the Office of African American Male Achievement. One of the office's early emissaries was a caring, engaging Black man named Keith Muhammad. When Romero was led into Muhammad's classroom, it was the first time he had ever had a Black male teacher. The class Romero walked into was called "Manhood Development," which is an essential part of the program developed by the Office of African American Male Achievement (AAMA). Romero was mesmerized.

From the beginning, Romero sensed something different in the class. For the first time in his life, he was part of a program intended to change the way schools see Black boys, as opposed to trying to make Black boys see school differently.

"It wasn't your typical school lesson like your math class or your English class. It was actually lessons that Black men need to be taught, Black boys need to be taught, every single day," Romero says. "Because especially living in a world like this with all the corrupted systems, and our crazy government, it's like, you have to know what it's like to be a Black man in America, because if you're not, then it's like living a blind life."

Romero was astounded to find a whole network of Black men like Muhammad and Chris Chatmon who became father figures—stand-ins for his own missing father. These men have been an immense help to him.

CBMA was first approached in 2009 by Oakland Superintendent Tony Smith about helping the district improve outcomes for Black boys. Smith said that while he and the district were receiving accolades for the performance of their students, he had dissected the data and saw that Black boys were being suspended and dropping out at much higher rates than the rest of the Oakland school population. He was getting all this praise in Oakland as a school reformer, but he felt like his efforts wouldn't be adequate if he didn't address this glaring issue. It was a stunningly progressive request from the head of an American public school system, especially a white man, who was approaching this work with sensitivity, empathy, and acute perception. But it was emblematic of Oakland. After all, this was the school system that made national headlines and caused a huge stir in the 1990s when it announced that it was studying the impact of students using non-standard Black English—also known as Ebonics—in the classroom. Oakland wasn't even one of our core Promise of Place cities at the time, but it soon became one. We made an initial investment of a million dollars in Oakland as a seed investor in the Office of African American Male Achievement.

Smith hired Chris Chatmon to run the office. Chatmon was perfectly positioned for such a role as the principal of an alternative high school in San Francisco and the education chair for the Bay Area chapter of 100 Black Men— with whom he had been trying to open a school for Black boys in Oakland. I found Oakland to be a fascinating place. With its eclectic artistic ethos, its history of rebellious militancy, and its Afrocentric orientation, it was the quintessence of "wokeness" among American cities. But at the same time, there was a great deal of suspicion and distrust that flowed through Oakland's streets, especially of government institutions. That wasn't hard to understand, considering how the government took down the Black Panthers and used Cointelpro, a counter-intelligence program conducted by the Federal Bureau of Investigation, to target Black activists in the late 1960s and 70s. That distrust sometimes made it hard to get collaboration on the ground in Oakland.

AAMA is a riveting case study—a program designed to upend an enduring American narrative: the nation's public schools are set up to benefit everyone equally, and failure in that system lies at the feet of the failed. AAMA began with the opposite contention, that public schools are designed to destroy Black boys—thoroughly proven by the available evidence—and to bring about their success requires a reconstruction of the system and re-education of its primary actors. Chatmon embarked on transformation using an "outside and inside game": build a dedicated cadre of community activists on the outside and focus on identifying the policies, procedures, and practices on the inside that led to poor academic outcomes for Black boys.

"The question was, what are you guys going to do differently to improve education outcomes for Black boys, as well as, simultaneously, deal with the system and the structure and the condition, and ultimately the culture that was fueling and feeding the school-to-prison pipeline?" Chatmon says.

Chatmon approached the task with a revolutionary idea—treat Black boys with love. In the 2019 book, *We Dare Say Love: Supporting Achievement in the Educational Life of Black Boys* (Columbia Teachers Press), which chronicles the impact of AAMA in Oakland, Jarvis R. Givens and Na'ilah Suad Nasir explore the subversive nature of this thinking:

"It has become difficult to comprehend a sincere relationship between public schools and Black male students (or all Black children for that matter) that is predicated on love. The American school, with few exceptions, is too often the place where Black students come to know they are despised, feared, and deemed to be of little to no human value in the world. In this context, the gamble of love is high stakes. Yet those who care deeply for Black children, as an extension of ourselves, recognize that insisting on love anyhow is of the first order." [3]

3   Jarvis R. Givens and Na'ilah Suad Nasir (2019), We Dare Say Love: Supporting Achievement in the Educational Life of Black Boys (Teachers College Press, New York). Page 2

Chatmon implemented a game plan that included creating an Afrocentric curriculum that would engage Black boys, establishing specific "manhood development" classes to gingerly nurture Black boys, using data to elucidate and dramatize the crisis for all the doubters in and out of the system. And perhaps most crucial of all, recruiting as many Black male teachers as possible.

"Many of our kings hadn't ever had a Black male teacher," Chatmon says, shaking his head. "In our listening campaign back in 2010 in the first few weeks, there were three things that had over an 80 percent response rate. One of them was, we need Black male teachers. This is from children, kings, from kindergarten through 12th grade. There are Black men on their campuses, but typically they were classified as staff, attendance clerks, school security officers, school resource officers. But the vast majority weren't teachers."

Chatmon went far outside of the traditional teacher pipeline that fed public schools, which had proven woefully inadequate over the decades in attracting Black males. Chatmon and his team went to brothers who were coaching, working in afterschool programs, even brothers who were working in the community.

"There were a lot of brothers that you may not see as 'teachers,' but they are teachers in a non-traditional sense," he says. "So, we helped them kind of navigate and get into the system."

There was pushback from the teachers' union, so they found a new path to state certification, through something called Career Technical Education. AAMA was able to increase the numbers of Black male teachers in the system by 25 percent—and to keep them there with a remarkable retention rate of 93 percent.

Success was a challenge to the status quo, a denunciation of the well-worn narrative that Black boys can't make it. Success was an indictment of decades of school inertia that had destroyed generations of Black boys.

AAMA was such a radical change from the status quo that Chatmon often felt like he was stepping through the corridors of power with a target on his back. There was plenty of resistance. Superintendent Smith left two years after AAMA was created, and the Oakland school system was taken over by a series of leaders who weren't exactly enthusiastic about the mission of AAMA.

"Systems of oppression self-correct. Let me be clear," Chatmon says as he leans forward in his chair, intense as always. "The more you actually eliminate achievement gaps or innovate and dismantle the institution, the more that system will try to purge you. So, I have gone through my highest of highs in these ten years and some of the lowest points of my life in leading in this position. And a lot of it had to do with just being exactly who I was, and this system not having frames or strategies for healing, people activating traditional structures to compromise my very existence, or to purge everything that I've done out of the system. I've outlived six superintendents, eight different department heads."

Not only did Chatmon see his weight balloon and his blood pressure dangerously increase, he actually was the target of death threats—two of them in the office's first three years of existence.

"One was a dude at a community meeting, a brother who followed me to my car. The other one was a phone call advising me to check under my car. I'm not a fighter; I'm a lover. I've always used my mouth to get me out of situations. But I was like, if you're going to do what you got to do, then come on, I ain't running. And so, at the community event, there was an elder who stood by while we allowed him to say and do whatever he needed to do. I was able to walk away. It's amazing to me that there would be all these different things that attack my person, all because of what I was doing for Black boys."

Even his family was targeted. His son, now 23, was attacked by a teacher when he was in middle school. Chatmon calls these attacks instances of the system "self-correcting." During his trials, he says he has benefitted immensely from his relationship with mentors like me and others in the CBMA family.

"I don't give up, but I was *struggling,* I mean in every sense," Chatmon says. "When I went to my first convening of CBMA, it just started to really open my eyes to the complexity of the work. It was validating. It was healing— the whole framing of healing the fish while treating the toxic ecosystem. I began to uncover and understand the complexity of this work, really through the Campaign for Black Male Achievement. The power of healing, the power of networking, and kind of understanding assets, right? I saw how CBMA, and Shawn were leveraging people, bringing them together, and I realized I knew the same kind of people back home who could do these things, like healing. I thought, *how do I leverage my people differently?* So, I created the same spirit here in Oakland, recreated these things in a local context."

He hired a woman in Oakland to focus on the healing of Black male educators, using tools like mindfulness and yoga to show them how to deal with the assaults on the spirit they would have to endure in the system. She's a big reason why the retention rate is at 93 percent. Chatmon didn't call me often, but when he did, I was glad to help. There was one vital phone call he asked me to participate in when he was talking to the interim superintendent about funding issues. He says my presence added to the credibility of the requests he was making.

"It's like the power of a quilt during the Underground Railroad," Chatmon explains. "They had a language within, right? There were certain quilts to tell you to keep on going. Quilts to tell you where to stop. Whenever I would go to the CBMA convenings, there were different patches I saw. And I got to explore the brilliance and beauty of that patch that somehow was connected to this convening. But I had to kind of figure it out on my own little journey and then figure out where I was. In the end, I got to understand clearly all of the patches that made up the quilt. I'm in a good spot now, but I'll never forget the support I got."

Through Chatmon's perseverance, he was able to get the state to establish a permanent funding stream in the Oakland budget for the AAMA department inside the newly created Office of Equity—which now also focuses on the needs of populations such as homeless youth and foster care youth. As of fall 2019, up to 20 school systems—including in places like San Francisco and Seattle—had implemented aspects of the AAMA model with varying degrees of commitment and success.

It is to lead young men like Romero to success that the Chris Chatmons of our movement endure the slings and arrows. Chatmon says he was taken with Romero from the beginning when he first got a sense of his remarkable poise and confidence shortly after Romero joined Muhammad's class.

"It was his persona—he just had a powerful spirit," Chatmon recalls. "Academically, he wasn't the strongest student. He wasn't a troublemaker, though he did have a spirited mouth. His comfort with referencing Jesus Christ was interesting because I didn't hear a whole lot of youth who would even mention going to church, let alone talking about it. He had lost one brother, and his younger brothers were actually in our system. His mother is definitely a matriarch."

While he was still at Castlemont High, Romero ran what Chatmon calls the largest Bible study course in the entire Oakland system, attracting big crowds of students and adults alike.

"He has a life force energy, man. Just someone that you knew that if given the continued support and just the right space, so to speak, he would thrive completely. So, here's a kid who is just still full of life and vibrance, and this school system, the longer you stay in it, what does it do? It sucks out your life, and actually, it dumbs you down. So, when you see that spark, you need to connect him to other folks who can support him. Romero hadn't taken on the position of the wilted flower. He hadn't internalized white supremacy."

Chatmon, in the beginning, fought with young men to change their language, to begin referring to each other as "kings" rather than "niggas." It was easy with young men like Romero to change their mindsets. Chatmon could see the impact it had on people outside the system whenever he would travel around the country with members of the Student Leadership Council he had established among the Black boys.

"Anytime SLC traveled east to a conference while I was leading it, we would always go to the neighborhood to get some food, always check out the local history. The thing that was extraordinary for all of us was the way people would respond when we traveled through airports, just 15 kings, myself, and another brother, Jerome. We would wear our suits and we would always get stopped. Everyone would say, what team are you? A football team? And we'd be like, No. Baseball? No. Basketball? Nah. We're an academic team. And people didn't know what to say. People would ask, 'Can we take a picture with you?' Black people, white people, it didn't matter."

Chatmon says a Black police officer outside of a Starbucks actually started crying when he was told they were an academic team.

"He couldn't believe it. He was like, an academic team? By the end, man, he was just in tears. He took pictures. He said, 'I've never, ever seen anything like this.'"

But as Romero is finding, Black male success from the cradle to career means a high school diploma isn't even close to the end of the road. There are so many more perils after you step out of the high school building for the last time. Romero isn't sure how school figures into his future. And he seems to be searching for the GPS navigation to direct the way. I am praying that he figures it out soon. Just as I took over The DOME Project as an adult, I could easily see Romero one day becoming a Chatmon-like leader, inspiring young people all over Oakland.

In fact, he is well on his way. Romero currently serves on the board of directors of Kingmakers of Oakland, the organization Chatmon recently spun off from the school district in 2020 to deepen the work and commitment to increasing the social mobility of Black boys in Oakland and across the nation. Chatmon often proudly introduces Romero as his "boss."

Chatmon points out that even when you make it out of the system and onto a prestigious college campus, you haven't made it. He tells the story of a talented young Black man from a high school in West Oakland who got a full scholarship to the University of California at Berkeley. But during the young man's first semester, his father began to worry because he hadn't heard from his son for weeks. It turns out he hadn't been in his dorm room for three weeks. When they found him, he confessed that he couldn't take the stress of being a lonely Black male on that campus. After California voters approved Proposition 209 in 1997, which prohibits the consideration of race or ethnicity in the operation of state institutions, the Black percentage in Berkeley's freshman class plummeted from eight percent to under four percent, where it has hovered ever since. Out of the 43,200 undergraduate and graduate students enrolled at Berkeley in fall 2019, just 600 of them were Black males, according to numbers released by the school. That's barely above one percent. This kid from West Oakland had no idea how to deal with such severe isolation. So, he dropped out. Now he lives in Atlanta, has a young daughter, and is trying to make it through community college.

"He didn't have a support system tight enough to help him," Chatmon says, shaking his head again.

Increasingly, the Oakland system has started to see a dramatic drop in the numbers of Black students because of rapid gentrification and soaring housing costs. When Chatmon first started AAMA, there were 7,000 Black boys in the system. In 2019 the number was under 3,000. Of course, Black girls have dropped in equivalent numbers. It's not hard to predict that these trends do not prophesy much good news for the Black residents of Oakland.

I know that I have to remain hopeful, even with all the challenges we face, but when I check in with young men, I hear harrowing tales of strife. Recently, I was in a room with about two dozen talented young Black men between ages 18 and 23 at the Black Men Excel Conference in Miami. They were all members of an organization called Brothers@, originally known as Brothers at Bard, which was launched by a young man named Dariel Vasquez while he was a Bard undergrad. The young men had all gone through a mentoring program with JP Morgan Chase called The Fellowship Initiative and all had matriculated to college. But when their masks fell away, they began to tell stories of having to drop out of college for semesters at a time because of financial shortfalls, family traumas, mental health challenges. Meanwhile, the people running the fellowship were raising a victory flag for the work they had done with these young men from New York, Chicago, and Los Angeles, successfully getting them from ninth grade to college. Listening to them broke my heart because it reminded me of the barriers they face even as young adults—most of whom were first-generation college students in their families.

There are so many Romeros out there—many who don't ever make it to a convening like our Rumble Young Man, Rumble at the Muhammad Ali Center in Louisville. They give up at 12 or 13, succumbing to the vacuum of the prison pipeline, the underground economy. As a leader in this movement, I feel the weight of that failure, all those young men that just drop away, never to be heard from again until a report on the evening news about someone being shot in the face. I don't want to feel like we're hydroplaning—looking good skimming the surface of the water but drowning below the surface.

I have been thinking more about the metaphor of Black boys running a race, thinking it's a straight sprint to the finish line. But then, suddenly, we realize someone has placed a series of hurdles in front of us that we weren't expecting. *Oh damn, I didn't practice for those,* we think. But we scale them smoothly and gather ourselves for another sprint. But suddenly, the track abruptly curves. It's not a straight sprint at all. We can't afford to slow down as we round the curve, but after a while, we do start slowing down. We start succumbing to the aspirational gravity pulling at us, the ghetto gravity. We start letting impostor syndrome creep in, pushing the sneaking suspicion that we don't belong in this race at all. We give in to survivor's guilt. Why am I still running, and all my homeboys disappeared a long time ago? Eventually the gravity can pull down even the strongest among us.

I've had Black men, leaders in this movement, crying to me on the phone because they feel like they can no longer do it, pushing forward with little support, no money, untold stress. When I read stories about the ways some of our heroes used the distractions of drugs or money or sex to survive, I can understand. *I get it.* They had to use whatever strategies, schemes, they could find to keep pushing themselves out of bed in the morning, to continue walking past the open windows.

But then I walk into yet another gathering of young men, and I spot a beaming flash of light. Another Jamare. Another Romero. Full of hope, brimming with promise, wishing that in me, he will finally encounter an adult who is brave enough to believe in him. Who is strong yet vulnerable enough to invest love and hope, wisdom and prayer? I smile back at him, shake his hand, envelope him in a warm hug. *Yes, I can love you. Yes, I can believe in you. Who am I to give up on you, young man? Let's do it. Let's go secure this future for you.*

Chapter 12: Where Do We Go From Here?

Speak what you seek until you see what you've said.
—Chris Gardner

I too have been that Black man on many occasions shedding tears because of the emotional labor that has inevitably come with leading the Campaign for Black Male Achievement since 2008. At no time though have my tears flowed as frequently and freely than during the first half of 2020 leading up to the May 1st decision to sunset CBMA operations due to financial shortcomings in the wake of a global pandemic. The future we seek to secure for our young men is often fickle and fleeting, fraught with disruption and setbacks, as the years of 2020 and 2021 have dramatically proven. This is one obvious reason why we stated in the Introduction that RESILIENCY is one of the main characters of this *I Too Am America* story.

While sunsetting operations was a very sour pill to swallow, as Dr. Henry Cloud eloquently writes about in his book *Necessary Endings: The Employees, Businesses, and Relationships That All of Us have to Give Up in Order to Move Forward*, "Endings are a part of every aspect of life. When done well, the seasons of life are negotiated, and the proper endings lead to the end of pain, greater growth, personal and business goals reached, and better lives. Endings bring hope." [4]

Hope? That surely was a far-fetched sentiment during the tearful and painful early days of the decision to sunset. Reconciling feelings of disappointing the many leaders in the CBMA network who looked to us for support and connection in our role as a catalyst in the BMA field, coupled with believing I personally let colleagues and partners down, was hard. I began to feed myself the story of "I failed." But thanks to the power of time and perspective, along with some stretching and soul-searching therapy sessions, I came to realize that

---

4   Dr. Henry Cloud, *Necessary Endings: The Employees, Businesses, and Relationships That All of Us have to Give Up in Order to Move Forward* (Harper Business, 2011) page 14

if you can reframe your seeming failure, you can reframe your future. Just as important, understanding that my mental health and well-being had to take priority over performing CPR on a not-for-profit organization whose season had come to an end.

The Campaign for Black Male Achievement was originally launched as a three-year initiative in 2008 and here we were 12 years later having helped to fuel a national movement for Black Male Achievement. That's far from failure. Yet, the need for the field- and movement-building that CBMA provided feels more urgent now than ever, calling for an answer to a very fruitful question: *What next?*

It's the question that keeps me staring up at the ceiling in the wee hours of the night. *Have I done all that I can do? What do I do now? What does the future of this movement look like?* The questions come hard and fast, waves of them that at times can be paralyzing. But they must be answered.

When you consider the future, of course, there is a great deal of uncertainty. *How can we know?*

But most of all, there is indeed hope that all that CBMA has invested in and built over the past dozen years can be parlayed into the next wave of strategies and innovations to support the positive life outcomes of Black men and boys.

The arc of CBMA's lifespan in many ways can be traced to two *New York Times* headlines. This whole thing began in 2006 with the front-page piece by Eric Eckholm that blared the headline, "Plight Deepens for Black Men, Studies Warn." That prompted Open Society Institute, later to become Open Society Foundations, to start having discussions about creating the initiative that eventually became the Campaign for Black Male Achievement.

Twelve years later in 2018, as I recounted at the start of this book, researchers from Harvard, Stanford, and the Census Bureau led by Raj Chetty issued a report revealing that a vast majority of Black boys end up in poverty as adults—no matter where they started. That *New York Times* headline read, "Extensive Data Shows Punishing Reach of Racism for Black Boys"—and it scared the hell out of every person working in the field. It was the bookend for CBMA, the exclamation point adding even more urgency to our days. And more sleepless nights.

The question I ponder now is, *What will the 2030 New York Times headline be for Black men and boys in America?*

The corollary question is, *What role will the network of leaders and orga-nizations that CBMA supported play in crafting that headline?*

Love

As I think about the things that Black men and boys desperately need in our lives, I keep coming back to *love*. That is the super vaccine that can inoculate us from so many of the social ills and viruses that have infected us over the last 400 years. Yes, even through a world-changing global pandemic that shifted the plot and progression of the story we set out in 2019 to tell in this book. It is like a protective blanket that can shelter us, uplift us, heal us, especially in the places where we hide our hurt. Whatever the field of Black Male Achievement is and will be over the next decade, it has to include massive doses of love.

The importance of love is summarized powerfully in this chilling anal-ogy: *If Black boys don't get the warmth they need from the village, they will burn the village down in order to be warmed by the fire.* That encapsulates so many of the programs and approaches we have tried to support and nurture over the years.

We have seen how vital it has been for us to help create that warm, loving village and to support the leadership that is out there on the ground, providing our men and boys with the caring embraces that let them know they are loved. Over the next decade, I am certain we must continue to pour into the leader-ship, to keep them strong and flourishing. We will give even more strength to the power of positive deviance, knowing that the solutions to most of our prob-lems are sitting right in front of us, in the brilliant actions and designs of the intergenerational leaders in our communities.

Like many African Americans, I traveled to Ghana at the end of 2019 to participate in the powerful and emotional "Year of the Return" festivities. I did a great deal of reflecting while I was there and on my way back. I was struck by the collective talent and drive of the couple hundred people just on the flight back to JFK—not to mention the thousands who gathered with me in Ghana. It became clear to me that one of the most vital roles the Black Male Achievement field can have over the next decade will be building partnerships that provide Black people the cover, the connectivity, the support, and the space to do their multi-faceted racial and social justice work. We need to be in the business of lifting up the models of success in the field and spreading the word among the flock, like a farmer planting and harvesting.

In the process of providing cover, I am certain we have to continue to give leadership a place to be vulnerable. I am so proud that we have been able to create an environment at our convenings where men and women—especially men—can feel comfortable and safe saying to each other, "I love you." Knowing that it's okay to cry together "Cry Like a Man," as Jason Wilson wrote in his important book.

Though this love ethos may sound like a no-brainer in this space, I think there are plenty of folks who are doing this work and don't love Black men and boys. They go through the motions and perhaps collect a check, but their hearts are not committed to it. It's not the work they would elect to do if they weren't getting paid. They wouldn't be volunteering their time and talent to bring about change. You can sense who these people are in short order. The passion just isn't there. A prominent, national leader once told me that no major change happens in Washington, DC, until somebody gets obsessed. I see every day the people doing this work who are obsessed. And I see the ones who aren't. I'm not implying that you must be obsessed to be doing the work, but it sure as hell makes a big difference.

The Reverend Al Sharpton addressed this eloquently in his book, *The Rejected Stone: Al Sharpton and the Path to American Leadership*, which he co-wrote with Nick Chiles.

"I think some of the most disappointing moments of my career have come when I met leaders who were leading people they didn't even like," he wrote. "Forget love—they see their flock as just props, extras to help them reach their life goals, backdrops in their photo ops. I think that when you have those feelings about your constituents, they can feel it. You can only fake the affection for so long. People know." [5]

While obsession is important, however, as I have spoken about earlier, there can be a danger when you become obsessed. You can get burned out, you can get disillusioned and frustrated by the slow pace of change, and, worst of all, you can work yourself to death. Over the next decade, I want to go even further

---

5   Reverend Al Sharpton with Nick Chiles, The Rejected Stone: Al Sharpton and the Path to American Leadership (Cash Money Content, 2013) page 43

in creating an ecosystem that takes care of the leaders who are taking care of Black men and boys. *Do you have a 401K? Do you have health insurance? Are you getting regular checkups? Do you have savings? Do you have a plan for your retirement? Do you have a mentor? Do you have a coach? Do you have a therapist?*

As I have gotten to know a lot of the leaders in my network, I see that too many of them do not have satisfactory answers to these nuts-and-bolts questions. For instance, a one- or two-year transition fellowship would be fabulous for those seasoned BMA leaders who might want to move on but are not financially situated to do so and/or aren't sure what their next chapter looks like.

Joyce Johnson, the co-founder of the Beloved Community Center in Greensboro, North Carolina, told me once on a conference call that we must do a better job as leaders in the social justice movement to share the baton with the next wave of leaders. Not pass it, share it. I feel really good about how much effort CBMA has put into pouring into the next generation of leaders. I have tried to be as honest as I can with young leaders who may see me as a mentor. I have shared my struggles and fears of trying to create a sustainable organization that would still be around when I have moved on to my next chapter.

I did get a cautionary note, however, when I asked Rashid Shabazz about his vision for the future of our movement. He pointed out that there is a dearth of leadership in his age cohort, which we refer to as Generation X—those born between 1965 and 1980. There's an abundance of the Baby Boomers like myself and the young folks, known as Millennials, but not enough rising leaders in between, who would be expected to take up the mantle next.

"I haven't seen a strong emergence of Generation X," Rashid said. "I don't know why that is. I see it having a detrimental impact on the field. But eventually, the young people will come along."

This focus on nurturing leadership has not been one that I have come to without a great deal of angst. In philanthropy, there has long been a relentless push for large-scale projects that can boast of population-level outcomes. *What metrics can you point to that demonstrate your organization has affected large numbers?* That is the central question at the heart of most conversations about funding. For a long time, I wanted CBMA to be one of those organizations that could brag about big effects. Many of the directional tensions between me and my board of directors centered around this question: What are we doing to make large-scale change? Where's the data? In the foundation world, the thirst for data is unquenchable. This issue has created existential crises for me over the last several years, as I have been pulled into two different directions—focusing on programs that would yield population-level outcomes or focusing on a love ethos that nurtured and supported leadership networks. The challenge now with answering the "where do we go from here?" question is manifesting and meshing a both/and answer to these strategic direction questions.

Hovering over my head and in my heart has been my relationship with my long-time mentor and board member, Geoffrey Canada, whose Harlem Children's Zone is probably the national prototype for an organization focused on population-level outcomes. Of course, I never expected CBMA to be as enormous as HCZ, but as a former longtime HCZ staff member, I couldn't help but be deeply influenced by HCZ's reach and impact on the Harlem community and the rest of the world. To his credit, Geoff told me on more than one occasion that I needed to make decisions about CBMA's focus not to please him or replicate HCZ but because I truly believe that is the right direction for me and the work I've been called to do on behalf of Black men and boys.

"Shawn, you have to do what you want to do," he said. "You don't have to worry about whether you're letting me down or disappointing me."

It took me two years after hearing those words from him for me to finally accept them.

To get the big dollars from funders, you have to have data. Making CBMA a foundation that focuses on being a catalytic force, bringing together leaders for nurturing, support, development, is not going to yield the kind of data that will bring in big dollars. At some point, I had to accept that reality and come to terms with it—and let go of my need for external, extrinsic approval and validation. I had to ask myself, *Where's the self-compassion? Why aren't you acknowledging and paying honor to all that you have done? Stop trying to* be *enough and just trust that you* are *enough.*

I can now say with confidence that we created a space and ethos of love, safety, and belonging, not only for Black men and boys but for all the leaders of this movement. I go back to a line that Jamare uttered in chapter 1, explaining how he went down the wrong path and hung out with the wrong kids: "I figured since I didn't know myself, I thought that like maybe I could be like them." I had to do the same, to figure out who I was and what I wanted this organization to be. We're not going to worry as much about population-level outcomes because there is no logic model for love.

Still, I won't forget the cautionary words of my former board chair, Tonya Allen.

"Chief Evangelical Officer is probably a good description of Shawn," she said. "And I do think that is necessary. But I think it's hard to think about how to invest dollars in that space when you're not clear about how those dollars actually translate into supporting people on the ground. Emotionally, I think I understand it and I know it's true. Hurt people hurt people, right? If you're healed, you have a greater power to create healing. But you know, quite honestly, and we all know this, that is not a part of our American psyche. And so, it's a counter-narrative about how change is created. I think we've yet to prove it to be true, but we haven't proved it to be untrue either. And so, in that space, it's very difficult to get people to believe that that's the pathway to actually create Black Male Achievement at scale."

I also would like us to become even clearer and more transparent that our ethos includes love for every type of Black male who exists in our community. Over the years we have received criticism that CBMA has lifted up a hyper-masculine, heterosexual ideal that doesn't leave enough space for same-gender-loving Black males. We must be more intentional about correcting that perception. If we don't, we are denying the power of our loving embrace to a significant portion of our community.

"When we talk about Black men and Black male identity in this space, we must acknowledge the diversity," said David Johns, executive director of the National Black Justice Coalition (NBJC), a civil rights organization dedicated to the empowerment of Black lesbian, gay, bisexual, transgender, and queer (LGBTQ) people. "One of the things that comes up for me in my work is the disproportionate rate at which Black males who are gay or believed to be gay are dying by suicides. Suicide rates for Black kids increased over the last couple of decades while they decreased for others. Some of that I'm convinced based on my experience and engagement with young folks is because of us not having conversations about diversity specifically concerning identity orientation and expression. We need to leverage the foundation provided by CBMA and organizations doing this work to clear those conversations, complicate things, and otherwise provide space for Black boys who also show up as same-gender-loving or gay to feel affirmed and safe and whole."

Money

Can't get away from this word. This is America, after all. Money is the blood that flows through every sector of American life, creating lines of inequity and division, walls of separation, lives of lack, and lives of plenty—demarked by race.

If someone had told me in 2008 that over the next 11 years CBMA would put a quarter billion dollars on the ground, I would have been impressed—and would have assumed it would surely lead to a quantifiable change in the lives of Black men and boys. But it's since become apparent to me that in the grand scheme of this 400-year assault on Blackness from white supremacy, $250 million is a minuscule amount. That's the impetus behind my desire to transition to the Corporation for Black Male Achievement. Back in 2011, it dawned on me that philanthropy is fickle; she is not a reliable patron. We didn't get to this point as a community overnight, so I asked myself what would a sustained, long-term entity look like? That's when I began to say that America didn't need a Campaign for Black Male Achievement; what we really needed was a Corporation for Black Male Achievement, which would serve as an endowed philanthropic social enterprise that leans into this issue for the long haul. It could have been Obama's My Brother's Keeper Alliance, but that hasn't really happened.

In our capitalist society, Black men have long been wealth generators. Look at the world of sports, or music, or entertainment. We generate many, many billions of dollars, but we are not often enough the primary beneficiaries of that wealth. We must begin to reclaim and take our assets and generate wealth for our communities. We will accomplish that by bringing folks from different sectors together because we have everything we need.

Tonya Allen said we should not be relying on philanthropy to do this work. "This is work that the government should be doing," she said. "It's not to suggest philanthropy doesn't have a role in it. But when that becomes the whole entire strategy, it's flawed." Tonya adds that Black men need to let go of the notion that we alone are the ones who must solve the problems of Black men.

"Black men, in particular, believe that they have to own the work when they actually haven't been the people who created the problems," she said. "The challenge to me is, how do we make sure that Black men don't feel responsible for the conditions in which they are in? The way that we approach Black Male

Achievement is that we end up beginning to own this country's shit instead of holding the country accountable to addressing and to changing it."

Jamare and Romero

In 2030, as Jamare and Romero approach the age of 30, I picture them both as self-sufficient, productive Black men who have tapped into their G-spot—their Genius-spot, their Gift-spot, their Great-spot, their God-spot. I see them pouring into not only their children but also children that don't share their last name. They will be able to sit down with a 15-year-old in their city—a child who was born in the last five years—and say, "You know what? I was exactly where you were at 15 and this is the path that I took."

They will be able to chart a path to success for that kid that resembles their own. While we all know that the peril boys face isn't going anywhere anytime soon, I would like to see over the next decade an exponential increase in the choices available to Black boys that lead to prosperity. Yes, we will still face the choices of peril, the choices of self-destruction, the choices of self-sabotage, but if we're playing the numbers game, we must get to the point where prosperity outweighs peril. If in a decade the perilous choices outweigh prosperity 10 to 1—as they do in many communities in 2020—we're never going to win.

I spoke in an earlier chapter about how profoundly disturbed I was when I saw the television report in Detroit of the two young Black men caught on surveillance cameras as they robbed a man at a gas station and shot him in the face. If these young men had been presented with an abundance of choices that would lead them to prosperity, would they still have wound up at that gas station? Of course, we'll never know, but those are the kinds of questions that gnaw away at me.

When we're talking about Jamare and Romero and the millions of other young Black men like them who have so much promise, we have to discuss the economic situation they face. At age 30, my prayer is that Jamare and Romero will have found their way to living-wage jobs. The future of work in many ways paints a scary portrait for young Black men. But the past wasn't exactly rosy for young Black men either. When we gaze at the iconic photograph of the Memphis sanitation workers in 1968 carrying the picket signs declaring "I Am A Man," their strike—passionately endorsed by Rev. Martin Luther King, drawing him to Memphis on that fateful day in April—was about their ability to support their families. Here we are, more than 50 years later, and we're still pushing for the same cause. In a decade, I want us to have made progress toward a point where we are in control of our own lives and destinies—enough that we don't have to carry picket signs asking someone to pay us a living wage or take to the streets to remind people Black Lives Matter.

Shawn Dove

In 2030, at age 68, where will this winding path called life have taken me?

The one thing I can say for certain is that I will continue to grow, to evolve, to move closer to the most actualized version of Shawn Dove. Maybe that more actualized version has been ignited with the sunsetting of the Campaign for Black Male Achievement and my response to launch the Corporation for Black Male Achievement in 2020. It is not the endowed philanthropic social enterprise I originally envisioned, but rather a publishing and consulting enterprise that curates community-building and leadership development engagements that elevate stories of loving, learning, and leading by and for Black men and boys, with a special sweet spot focus of empowering young men between the ages of 18 – 25.

"This work keeps evolving," said Regina Jackson, CEO of the East Oakland Youth Development Center. "The way Shawn showed up to the work is not who he is today. He has had to transform through the work as well. Like the snake, you got to keep shedding skin, to keep reinventing yourself, and recognizing the ways in which you must change to continue to be that light for the kids because the circumstances keep changing. The way we were reaching out to our kids 5-10 years ago is not the way we need to reach out to them today."

To Regina's point, the way we show up in 10 years will be different than how we work with them today. Jennifer Jones Austin, Chief Executive Officer and Executive Director of the Federation of Protestant Welfare Agencies (FPWA), a prominent social policy and advocacy organization based in New York City, told me a few years ago that I needed to figure out whether I'm a dean or a doer—meaning whether I will be talking and writing about the work or doing the work. I have always seen myself as both a dean and a doer. Perhaps a decade from now I might be leaning a little more toward the dean.

When I think back on that night I decided to throw my hat in the ring and become director of The DOME Project, it boggles my mind that more than 30 years have passed by. *What have I done with the 30 years? Have I done enough?* I am reminded of the famous Ralph Waldo Emerson quote, "Do not go where the path may lead, go instead where there is no path and leave a trail." I believe that at age 68, I'll look back and know that I've helped to inspire and fuel a long caravan of effective leaders who are walking confidently, blazing their own leadership trails.

However, I don't want to spend too much time trapped in assessing past work because there is so much more to do now to ensure a more prosperous future for Black men and boys in America; I want to keep running—and not because I have to, but because I want to. My dad still teaches dance, something he loves to do and has done well for over a half-century. He still teaches dance at 81 because he is clear on his gifts and purpose. And while we never had the ideal father/son relationship, watching him dance with his destiny has inspired me to do the same. I think over the next decade the frontier I want to tackle is building wealth to bless others. I don't need to be the multi-millionaire if I'm leveraging my talents to bring a group of multi-millionaires together to work on behalf of Black people.

Correction: Not just to *work*, but to *dream* on our behalf.

"We need to stop going for small things," Tonya Allen said. "This country knows how to put men to work. This country knows how to build wealth for people. We've set public policy in this country that has actually worked. Black men and Black people were excluded from that. I think our flaw in this field is that we keep asking for potatoes when we need to be asking for a full meal. And so, my aspiration is by the time we get to 2030 we've gotten ourselves clear on what the policy agenda is. That it is not a policy agenda that asks for mentoring programs to boys; it is a policy agenda that rewrites the rules so that we can have more equitable outcomes in every sector that would be able to support Black Male Achievement."

So here we sit in 2030, flipping through the New York Times on our hand-held device, perhaps popping the caffeine pill which contains all the ingredients and taste sensations we used to get with our morning coffee. We come across a headline that draws our attention—and brings a broad smile to our face. It reads:

For the First Time in History, the Nation Clearly Sees More Promise Than Peril in the Life Chances for Black Boys

Manifesting this headline is possible, but it will require increased levels of collective leadership, organized resources, and capacity-building for the leaders, organizations and networks committed to improving the life outcomes of Black men and boys. It will require many intergenerational heads, hands, and hearts to shape the next wave of Black Male Achievement work over the next decade. It will require a racial reconciliation that can only happen when America consistently remembers and reconciles its shameful history of white supremacy and racial oppression. This uncomfortable rumbling within the soul and consciousness is what is required for us— together—to truthfully realize the racial reckoning that so many prematurely declared during the racial justice protests of 2020.

With this in mind, and in the community-building ethos that my leadership journey has infused within me, we chose to conclude the book with the curated voices and ideas of a batch of leaders who have sought to answer the question, "Where do we go from here?" with mini-manifestos that we pray will serve as mission fuel for igniting and creating the future we're seeking to see.

Towards Our Shared Future

By Dr. Jackie Bouvier Copeland

I am proud to have worked with Loren Harris in 2007, then of the Ford Foundation, to design a national fund for Black Male Achievement that we called My Brothers Future that ultimately influenced the movement as well as eventually President Obama's initiative of the same name. On the one hand, it is a shame that it took well into the 21st century for philanthropy to recognize that Black men's rights were a legitimate focus for social change funding. It is even worse that I needed to do a special study to make the case as to why addressing the systemic barriers to Black male success was in society's best interest. On the other hand, it was a culture shift that had been in development for decades with the work of so many Black men and women in the field of philanthropy, who often risked their careers to promote funding to BMA-oriented initiatives, including Bobby Austin formerly of The Kellogg Foundation; Lynne Huntley, formerly of the Ford Foundation; Ike Tribble of The Florida Education Fund, and many others.

The Campaign for Black Male Achievement (CBMA) under Shawn Dove's pioneering leadership was the tangible result of these decades of struggle, risk-taking, advocacy, research, and design by many people. Its creation marked the formal development of a legitimate BMA field, recognizing that the racial oppression of America's centuries-old caste system plays out in gender-specific manifestations. CBMA ushered in a Movement. Movements transcend individual organizations. And the organizations that emerge during the early phase of a movement often close and morph as the movement matures. Having legitimized the need for a cross-sector movement focused on justice for Black men, it is time for the BMA to transition to a new phase for the times.

Justice for Black people requires a nuanced, intersectional gender lens, recognizing the specific impacts for men, women, as well as queer people, are interconnected. All humanity, and certainly all Black humanity, as Dr. Martin Luther King reminded us in 1967:

"We are all caught in an inescapable network of mutuality, tied into a single garment of destiny. Whatever affects one directly affects all indirectly. We are made to live together because of the interrelated structure of reality."

This Black intersectional philosophy, developed by our activists and social theorists such as Kim Crenshaw and John Powell, is critical to avoid the gender divide and conquer pressures that can still play out in the general movement for Black liberation. The COVID Era and recession provide a clear case example of how critical it is that every person advocating for Black social justice also be an advocate for the full humanity of all Black people, male, female, and queer. A full third of all COVID deaths are Black, equally impacting all genders. Black women are especially hit hard as primary family caregivers, but Black people, in general, have a higher rate of pre-existing conditions and work in frontline occupations that make them more susceptible to the pandemic. There is a mental health epidemic in our community made only worse by the public lynchings of our men and our women. Black trans people, including youth, are being executed at alarmingly high rates. As a result, our children are experiencing new traumas that will continue to undermine their lives for decades to come. The same patterns are playing out for Black people worldwide during this pivotal historical moment.

This is a time of emergency for all Black Movements equivalent to the post-Civil War period in its historical import. As the BMA Movement enters its next phases, it is critical that it continues its leadership spotlighting the plight and potential of Black men in the context of the Movement for All Black Lives. In fact, all gender-specific fields in the Black Racial Justice Movement must take very explicit steps towards intersectional action to dismantle anti-Black racism and proactively promote equality for all Black people. CMBA has shown a path towards how to begin this inclusive advocacy while remaining rooted in the unabashed effort to liberate Black men. The Movement for Black Lives is very deliberately attempting to integrate the Black male achievement, feminist, womanist, and queer movements into a unified American and indeed global Black racial justice movement.

Instead of an "oppression Olympics" focused on proving that Black males suffer more than Black females or vice versa, the next phase of the Movement should resist this unproductive tendency, instead focusing on how all are distinctly disadvantaged by a racialized caste system that ultimately leads to the death of spirit or body of Black people of all backgrounds. As many effectively argue, strict, binary genders are not indigenous to Black cultures but largely a result of mainstream, white constructs of gender advanced during transatlantic slavery and colonialism. Instead of pitting Black male, female, and queer liberation against each other, a unified Movement would cry out for justice of state-sponsored or tolerated murder of Black men, women, and trans people, advocating equally for justice of the many George Floyds, Breonna Taylors, and Tony McDades of our country. In a true Movement for Black human rights, every Black feminist would understand that they needed to be a BMA advocate; every BMA advocate would know that their freedom requires a Black feminist lens; and everyone would be a proponent of Black queer rights. That Black people are the canaries in the mine of the mass breakdown of our environmental, social, health, and economic systems is obvious in the COVID Era. There is no possible scenario in which we can thrive in the future unless we are all free.

Having established that Black men face gender-specific barriers to equal opportunity, CBMA and the work of its precursors have succeeded in a once impossible task. Now there is a framework and strategy to care about and impact the plight of Black men. Let us continue to build the field as a key component in the long struggle for dignity and justice for all Black people in

America. We need each other's voice because none of us can be free until we are all free. The time is now, and the BMA Movement is primed to help lead the way.

> *Dr. Jacqueline Bouvier Copeland is a scholar-activist, environmentalist, and technologist committed to making the world a better place. She is also the founder of The WISE Fund and Black Philanthropy Month.*

The Birthing of Our Own Healing

By Greg Corbin

September 7th, 2020, at 2:00 a.m., my wife's water broke, fully opening the portal of life that is her womb. Over a 17-hour stretch of back labor, massages, prayer, meditation, mindful breathing, motivational whispers, a dope playlist, and hundreds of pushes, my wife surged to the completion of her pregnancy— and the beginning of our new life. Coached by our midwife, doula, her mother, and myself, my wife made eye contact as she inhaled deeply to push three more times. They say that when a child is born, parents are born, too. I looked down below the birthing stool just in time to see our child enter the world, born in the living room of our home. Our baby boy is named Noble Sage. An old soul at birth, his name means royalty and wisdom. We've decided that as long as we remind him of the power behind his name each time he is addressed, a charge of energy will remind him of who he is, and who he is meant to become. It is, for this reason, I feel each child born into this world actually chooses their parents.

As our first night as new parents began, our midwife attended to my wife and our new bundle of joy. Our doula helped clean up after the day's efforts and prepared a first meal with my mother-in-law for my wife to consume. Ironically, she had not eaten the entire day and sufficed with liters of coconut water to get through each push. The living room, now known as the birthing room, was quiet and everyone had retired to their resting place. After weeks of preparation, we gazed down at the baby's bassinet, our process now complete with our baby in it. Little did we know, it had all just begun.

After 24 hours of journeying through the birthing process, we finally laid our heads down for rest, thankful for what we just accomplished. Well, for what my wife accomplished. My wife now bed-ridden in her healing process, I was tasked with perpetual night duty. Responsible for helping her to the bathroom every 90 minutes, to change all the diapers, and to prepare the baby for breast-feeding at every interval. I laid my head down on a pillow with a smile on my face. I had a son. With each restful breath, I felt my body drop into a state of relief, shortly joined by a slight feeling of anxiety. A tremendous paranoia and nuanced fear heightened as my mind began to race.

Did we leave the blanket over his face?
What if he doesn't make it through the night?
Where is the pacifier?
Is he hungry? What if we mess this up?

I laid back exhausted, staring at the ceiling. One story, in particular, came back to haunt me. Through past memories, trauma can be triggered, causing the present mind to time travel. Fear is a time machine and in this moment I was traveling in ways I did not foresee. I somehow journeyed from a newborn parent in September 2020 back to an 8-year-old attendee at local daycare during the month of August in 1987.

While sitting crossed-legged watching *Thundercats* on TV at daycare, I was struck when Mrs. Antoinette ran down the steps with my 6-month-old sister clutched in her hands. She frantically screamed for help, repeatedly saying, "Simone's not breathing. Call 911! Simone's not breathing. Call 911! Help!"

I stared at her face in shock. I could see it was blue and her chest wasn't rising. Mrs. Antoinette began infant CPR while the ambulance was on its way. I watched Mrs. Antoinette breathe into her chest, her chest rose, but did not bloom on its own. The paramedics arrived and went to work. I had a glimmer of hope that everything would be alright. It was not.

While upstairs playing with cousins, the house grew in attendance. Eventually, my parents arrived at my grandmother's house sharing the heart-breaking news that Simone, my 6-month-old baby sister, had passed away. I did not know how to feel. Nothing more was discussed, and I completed my summer break and went back to school that fall. No one unpacked the events; eventually, we just moved on.

The images and storyline forever imprinted in my mind, serving as a beacon of detrimental and heart-staking possibility. Through my eyes, the frightening reality of death was first observed in these moments, only to rest as a bookmark in a chapter of unaddressed challenges that were never discussed. I can only imagine, and still only desire to imagine, what my parents were experiencing beyond the sadness. A child struggles to empathize with their parents because the dynamics, experience, and events in the backdrop are different. My parents, blue-collar, industrious baby boomers, a generation cultivated to build, worked diligently to build a foundation.

When I recently asked my mother about the loss of Simone, she recalled, "We worked through it. Yes, it was sad and painful, but we had to move on. Your father, I think, took it harder than I did. And of course, having your sister, Donna, shortly after helped. But you know, time heals all wounds. I don't wish it on any parent."

I responded, "Mom, did y'all think about going to therapy?"

Her response: "Therapy wasn't a big thing back then, especially for Black folks, so we didn't go. There's been a lot of progress with mental health, but we didn't have access to it. It was often seen as something for rich and crazy white folk."

I wasn't surprised to hear that. For many people in our community, a Black person's relationship with the medical system walks alongside a colonized version of healing. It has been shaky for centuries considering the American context and origin story for Black people is slavery. Slaves were often used as subjects for experiments and treatments before the medicine was offered to white people because plantation owners believed they were subhuman.

I decided to ask her another question. "Mom, would you go to therapy today if needed?"

"Well," she said, "I'm not sure if it's even necessary, besides digging up the old is a lot. I put my trust in God. He knows what's best."

Although there is a divine plan, Black folks do use religion to escape agency and responsibility at certain points. I often wonder about the repression and suppression of emotion and memories that my family has indulged in over the past. As the author of *Post Traumatic Slave Syndrome*, Dr. Joy Degruy, says, "The absence of opportunity to heal or access benefits in society leads to post-traumatic events."

And now I sit, sharing this story with my wife while she holds our newborn. At first, I felt ashamed to share this with her. As a new dad, I imagine she wants me to be strong, thorough, and all-knowing. I worry these thoughts make me look weak. Then I remember how much I've grown. I am surprised to find out that she also has concerns about being a new mom. Just like me, she doesn't want to make a mistake and as she navigates postpartum, she battles worst-case scenario thoughts as well. I am reminded, we are in this together. That I am not alone, and I get to define the kind of husband and father I want to be. Even when it's tough, I will lean into my support. As I heal through my past, I am healing my future. My son will know his dad, not just as an accomplished man but as a flawed human being that understands the power of perspective and self-awareness. He will also learn the power of emotional literacy and intelligence while fostering great communication skills so that he strengthens his ability to imagine and reimagine. Learn and unlearn.

My father was an industrious, blue-collar, spirited man who was great with his hands. He had the ability to fix anything in the house. A car. No problem. His bare hands were golden. A believer in independence, he taught me to never pay anyone for something you can teach yourself how to do on your own.

He would say, "If there is a book, there is information. If there is information and knowledge, there is power. If you have power, you have control of the decision."

A man of provision and protection, he missed some key moments to connect with me through conversation.

Healing is a lifelong process. There will be wounds. I'm not sure what to share about the wounded soul of America, but I am tasked to share the truth with him. With balance and intentionality, I aim to make sure he has the tools to express himself. Too many Black boys and men have been taught to repress their emotions, oppressing their humanity by numbing their authenticity.

Dear Black Boys: Get lost in your wonder. Know that questions are often more powerful than the answers you seek. Master your curiosity. Smile, and then smile some more.

Greg Corbin II is a poet, arts activist, and the author of "Breathing Ashes: A Poetic Guide to Walking through the Fire and Coming Out Reborn."

Where Do We Go from Here?
The Necessity of Critical Hope

By Judy Touzin

As Shawn and Nick wrote in the opening chapter, Jamare and many Black boys like him are carrying "the hope of generations." And yet, hope alone, as it is typically understood, will not ensure our boys overcome the various barriers they face as they strive to walk freely—boldly even—towards their aspirations.

Jeff Duncan-Andrade (2009) writes concerning the *critical* hope that is necessary for creating the conditions that allow the potential and promise our young men carry to be realized. To be sure, this brand of hope is not to be confused with the fugazi kinds. We are not talking about the "hokey hope" that would have us believe that if our boys "...just work hard, pay attention and play by the rules, then they will go to college and live out the "American Dream." Life has sadly taught most of us better than that. Further, we are not encouraging that "mythical hope," an equally fraudulent hope that seeks to amplify the success of a few to downplay the oppression of many. To quote Duncan-Andrade (2009), "...a single event cannot by itself, provide the healing and long- term sustenance required to maintain hope amid conditions of suffering."

Critical hope then, is hope that acknowledges and pushes back on the hard realities of today while gripping onto the possibilities of tomorrow. It is equal parts "...material, Socratic, and audacious" (Duncan-Andrade, 2009). *Material hope* compels us to ensure our boys have access to the resources they need to navigate their current context and overcome the obstacles they face. On a practical level this looks like safe housing, good teaching, healthy food, and quality health care. To acknowledge and not respond to the material need is to deal in "hokey hope."

The second element, *Socratic hope*, requires us to acknowledge and even embrace that our "...pain may pave the path to justice." It is a hope that holds space for young people to share and own their stories. It is an orientation to liberation that validates the righteous anger that awakens when our boys become aware of the intentional construction of their condition. Rather than dismiss or discipline this response we can help them channel and express it in ways that serve to amplify their voices and their humanity.

The third and final aspect of critical hope is *audacious hope*. Audacious hope is solidarity in motion. It is stepping into the pain and suffering of others, claiming it as our own, and then fiercely laboring to transform the systems that created such human suffering in the first place (Duncan-Andrade, 2009). Audacious hope gives us the courage to confront the conditions of today. It fuels the conviction that tells us it's all worth the fight even if we don't see the change ourselves in this lifetime. Our boys are worth it. Once armed with this critical hope, our mission must be clear, our work must be collaborative, and our effort must be consistent.

BE CLEAR

When I started The ExceptionAL Project, my mission was to actively push back on the stereotypical images and stories that characterize how society often portrays Black men and boys. At its core, The ExceptionAL Project was about narrative change. I wanted to help Black boys hold onto a strong sense of self and dignity while navigating a racist and often dehumanizing society. As I set out to do the work, I carried with me the faces and names of the brilliant boys I had been blessed to work and learn alongside as a public school teacher and principal in New York City.

Somewhere along the line my clear intentions grew fuzzy and started to fade. I found myself talking about college-going and goal setting. Some of the educators I partnered with suggested we cover topics like etiquette, communication, and hygiene. While there is nothing inherently problematic about the topics above, leading with these sessions implied that the struggles and low expectations our young Black men contend with are of their own doing; that somehow if they were focused enough, more goal oriented, and communicated in calmer, "less aggressive" ways, they would be safe in society. It was as if we too believed that if they *acted* "better," then their condition would *be* "better." I had slipped into pedaling a hokey kind of hope. This realization caused me to take an important step back to regain clarity on the purpose of my work.

If we are to realize the transformational impact we seek, we must periodically go back to our mission, and ask ourselves the following critical questions:

1. To what extent is the work we are leading aligned to our intentions to truly love, affirm, and support Black men and boys?

2. How, if at all, are our practices unintentionally reinforcing racist values and ideology?
3. Are we doing this work *to* and *for* Black men and boys or are we engaged in this work *with* them?
4. Where have we intentionally made the effort to center the voices and lived experiences of the Black men and boys we say we serve?

It can be easy to lose sight of our intentions, especially if our work is dependent on donor dollars. But all money isn't good money and the men and boys we say we serve are worth more than photo ops. Being clear can help ensure we stay true to our core purpose.

BE COLLABORATIVE

To achieve the scope and scale of transformation we envision, we must also be collaborative. Deepa Iyer (2020) describes the many roles that exist in the social change ecosystem. We can't all be *front-line responders* or *healers* and we shouldn't try to be. Driving social change requires us to acknowledge our interdependencies and commit to doing our part. We need co-laborers in every role if we expect to tear down the barriers that many Black men and boys contend with. We need *disruptors* working to dismantle the systems that created the conditions we face in the first place. We need artists and *storytellers* to capture the strength and resilience in our struggle. We need *visionaries* who can inspire us to reimagine what's possible and *caregivers* to foster communities of love, joy, and compassion. Finally, we need *builders* who can help create and sustain the infrastructure needed to create systemic change.

The roles described above are not necessarily fixed. We may play different roles at various points in our lives. In recent months, I have identified more and more as a storyteller and bridge builder. I regularly share affirming images and experiences of Black men and boys and create space for dialogue across racial lines. This is the work that feels right for me in this moment. This work is bigger and more important than any one role can adequately address. The part we each play is significant and without comparison. It will take all of us, working in collaboration, to ensure that Black boys born today inherit a more just world.

BE CONSISTENT

In addition to being clear and collaborative, we must be consistent. We cannot allow our efforts to wax and wane with every high-profile tragedy or blatant act of racism. We must remain clear and focused, even when Black male achievement is no longer the "sexiest" problem of the day. Consistency is required because the systems that created the challenges we seek to disrupt remain (almost) completely intact and will concede nothing unless pressured to do so.

In pushing for change, we must consistently center the voices and aspirations of our Black boys and young men. If we don't, we run the risk of treating them as a monolith; making assumptions based on the deficit-based narratives we may have internalized. It is easy to find and rehearse the stories of trauma and peril that our young men experience. But everyone is not from a single-parent home, with a dead or incarcerated father and failing in school. And even if those things are true for some, there is so much more to any individual than the list of their perceived challenges.

Finally, being consistent includes honoring the need to rest and refuel. In the past, I have done myself a disservice by neglecting my family and my health for the sake of my work. I have come to accept that I cannot pour from an empty cup or drive on an empty tank. My commitment to serving Black boys and young men now explicitly includes a commitment to taking care of myself physically, spiritually, mentally, and emotionally. It is the periods of rest that allow me to stay consistent.

If we are to make a profound and lasting impact with and for our boys, we must commit to being clear, collaborative, and consistent. I make this commitment as I hold on to the faith that one day the world will look at our boys and see them for the valuable human beings they are. This faith is the essence of my critical hope. I trust that God will continue to strengthen and guide us as we do our part and that my nephews, my godsons, and other beautiful, brilliant Black boys like them, will inherit a world that protects the fullness of their humanity, invests in their aspirations, and reminds them they were *born* worthy.

References

Duncan-Andrade, J. M. R. (2009). Note to educators: Hope required when growing roses in concrete. *Harvard Educational Review, 79*(2), 181-194.

Iyer, D. (2020, July 7). Mapping our roles in a social change ecosystem. Deepa Iyer. http://deepaiyer.com/2020/07/ mapping-our-social-change-roles-in-times-of-crisis/

Judy Touzin began her career as an elementary school teacher in the Harlem section of New York City in 2003. In her experience as a teacher, principal and coach for aspiring principals, there has been one constant—her desire to help create affirming learning environments for Black boys and young men. In 2016, Judy self-published ExceptionAL: Black Men Leading, Living, and Loving to help counter the prevailing image and narrative concerning Black men and boys in America. A year later she launched The ExceptionAL Project, an extension of that book. The book and project seek to amplify the beauty, brilliance, and humanity of Black men and boys across the country.

Never Get Comfortable

By Alphonso Mayo

"In life, we must leave things behind that we care about to grow. It may seem strange that growth comes with loss, but some losses are worth the victories that God has for you."

—Mayo

As a Black male, father, son, friend, leader, educator, husband, and mentor, I believe that most if not all Black men have carried the burden of being all that God is calling us to be on our own for far too long. God's word says that "Before I formed you in the womb I knew you, and before you were born, I consecrated you; I appointed you a prophet to the nations." Which means we were all born with a promise. Yet, we live in a world that has suppressed that promise for Black and brown people. Many times, causing me/us to believe that I/we can do it on our own, working in silos, pretending not to be hurt, working from a place of brokenness, working from a place of fear, and then you come across an organization like the Campaign for Black Male Achievement. You're met with the harsh reality that you can't do this work alone.

Where do we go from here? We never forget the promises that we were all born with. As a reminder, what you have experienced thus far didn't happen to you, it happened for you. I'll leave you with a few of the promises that were made.

Jeremiah 29:11: For I know the plans I have for you, declares the LORD, plans to prosper you and not to harm you, plans to give you hope and a future.

Joshua 1:9: Have I not commanded you? Be strong and courageous. Do not be afraid; do not be discouraged; for the Lord, your God will be with you wherever you go.

Philippians 4:6-7: Do not be anxious about anything, but in every situation, by prayer and petition, with thanksgiving, present your requests to God. And the peace of God, which transcends all understanding, will guard your hearts and your minds in God.

I was born at the height of the crack epidemic in 1987 to an addict mother who abandoned me in a drug house when I was six months old. Rescued by an aunt, I spent the rest of my childhood in a home filled with drugs and violence. My relationship with my father was particularly brutal, with relentless beatings and psychological games, yet somehow I was always reminded of the promise. There's a difference between knowing the promise and birthing the promise.

I gave birth to my promise after the passing of my grandmother. After dropping out of college and returning home in 2007, I learned that my grandmother was diagnosed with dementia and cancer. I, along with my big cousin India, became my grandmother's primary caregivers. Every day was an emotional battle, and I became profoundly depressed but was too stubborn to get help. Despite my grandmother's dementia, she is lucid about one thing—me returning and finishing college. Nearly every day, she pestered me about it. I would hold her hand each time and promise that I'll go back. What I learned is that God uses these moments in our lives to help push us to our promises if we can see past our pains.

Today, I'm a proud father of four, a college graduate from Stevenson University and Johns Hopkins University, and the Founder and Servant Leader of Mentoring Mentors. Like the students we serve and most of the people I know, I did not have the best support, was born into some daunting circumstances, and was diagnosed with a learning disability, causing me to struggle academically. Like many young African American boys, my intellectual disability was overlooked due to my athletic ability. Yet, I never got comfortable with not working towards the promise I knew was inside of me. I didn't understand God, better yet, I didn't even care for God, but there was and still is this little voice inside of me that is guiding my being. A part of me tells me that you too experienced that despite your challenges, upbringing, or current circumstances.

Listen to that voice. I'm proud of the connection I have with CBMA because, for a moment in time, everything that I could have ever desired in a community was presented to me. The truth is, I stumbled across the organization. The day that I learned about CBMA, I was busy trying to save Baltimore by saying yes to every community project I could. I didn't even have time to go to the convening, but a friend texted me and said he was looking for me at the event.

When I walked into the rotunda of Baltimore's City Hall, I was pulled by this energy and spirit. The convening reminded me much of the football comradery that I was longing for, but it was more graceful. That day I saw the power of love, brotherhood, healing, uplifting, encouragement, excitement, and peace. That day I experienced God in a room full of men and women seeking to bring change. I was sold. Then my reality came crashing down when I tried to connect with the 62 individuals I took cards from, and I waited on the 102 people that I gave cards to. What I expected after my experience made feelings of frustration and defeat set in as all the hope that I gained was lost. Despite that, I knew there was something profound about the work of CBMA. At the last Rumble convening, I was standing in the Muhammad Ali Center, taking in everything that I had just experienced.

As I stood there alone giving things to God, Shawn Dove walks up and put his hand on my shoulder. Before that moment, I never shared my gratitude for all that CBMA meant for me, but I also never shared the story of trying to connect with those people, his team, him, and feeling disconnected. Shawn looked me in my eyes and apologized and said, " Mayo, I promise moving forward you'll never have to worry about that again," and we hugged. Since that time, we text weekly, we email frequently, we have monthly calls, we have cried together on Facetime, we have shared our pains and love, Shawn has allowed me to be a part of speaking engagements, and he has become a mentor to the founder of a mentoring organization. I say that to say the promise was there; I just had to be patient.

Where do we go from here? We move forward with the promise by following the biblical principles that were set.

1. We love and trust God with all our heart, knowing that all things are working for our good despite our challenges and circumstances.
2. We love our neighbor relentlessly. Love with the same heart as young children have. Blind love is where you can be naked in the presence of God.
3. Add value to this world. Your life is not about you, it's about the choice that you make that will impact everything around you.

Alphonso Mayo is a servant leader native of Baltimore and founder of Mentoring Mentors, a community-based organization that envisions a world where Black youth have equal opportunity to reach their full potential and become leaders in their communities.

Sacred Ground

By Althea Allen Dryden

August 21, 1619. The first sunrise for twenty and some odd Africans. Our ancestors woke up and wondered, *Where are we? Where do we go from here?*

The birth of a nation.

March 12, 2020. The last sunset for Breonna Taylor. Twenty rounds fired. America woke up and wondered, *Where are we? Where do we go from here?*

The death of a notion.

Twenty Black bodies. Twenty bullets. 2020. *Where are we? Where do we go from here?*

Once, *here* were the shores of Hampton, Virginia. Now, *here* are the streets of Louisville, Kentucky. We stand at the crossroads and in the crosshairs of a nation.

This is sacred ground.

In 2011, the Campaign for Black Male Achievement held the first Rumble Young Man, Rumble—a yearly convening of leaders from around the country working to elevate and celebrate the lives of Black men and boys. From a boxing ring in the Muhammad Ali Center, Shawn Dove declared Louisville, Kentucky, the "epicenter of Black male achievement." While many would rightly contend our present practices, policies, and percentages counter such a claim, understanding how we got here—Louisville, Kentucky—will help us get where we must go. For reasons awful and awe-filled, we are meant for this.

This is sacred ground.

To declare Louisville, Kentucky, the epicenter of Black male achievement is to acknowledge the blood and bones of our ancestors who loved and lamented Kentucky as their home. It is to realize the cornerstone of white supremacy; the foundation stone of racialized oppression was masoned from Kentucky limestone and to recognize Louisville, still, hones the tools of its construction and houses the relics of its dead. Kentucky was the architect of an American culture. To declare Black male achievement at the core of this city is to lay claim to Black peoples' history of resilience and legacy of resistance. It is to prophesize a reckoning.

This is sacred ground.

Here is the origin story of the Black experience in America. Kentucky, the "land of tomorrows," whose motto, "United we stand; divided we fall," foretold the fate of a nation. Beneath the bloody and blue grass lies a mythic creature. She is both the Sankofa bird—flying forward, remembering the past, holding the future in her beak—and the Phoenix—regenerating out of ancient birth ash and rising to live again. Here is the setting, the characters, and the plot. Here is the conflict and the resolution. This story, the archetypal hero's journey, is an American horror story.

Technically a border state during the Civil War, Kentucky was philosophically in bed with the Union and the Confederacy bearing both Abraham Lincoln and Jefferson Davis. The legal ending of the transatlantic trade of enslaved Africans gave rise to a particularly heinous chapter in our American narrative. Kentucky created an industry of breeding Black bodies in its sheets and an institution of selling Black bodies in its streets.

Our ancestors were bred, born, and raised, then sold down the river from Louisville only to return generations later to escape the segregated South during the Great Migrations. True to her southern, tangled roots, Kentucky did not bother to ratify the 13th amendment of the Constitution, abolishing slavery in 1865, until 1976. Here, we live at the confluence of the troubled waters of history and our story.

Our people passed this way again and again. Nineteenthth-century Black bodies birthed generations of southern, Black people. They birthed the 20th-century Black families who later journeyed through her streets during the

Great Migrations. And those Black mothers and fathers bore the 21st-century activists organizing in living rooms, liberating in classrooms, and agitating in board rooms.

This is sacred ground.

Here, the Earth quaked as each police bullet entered the home and the body of Louisville's daughter, Breonna, the *exalted*. The aftershock was an assassination in the streets by the National Guard of Louisville's son, David, the *beloved*. After centuries of stress, the moral fault line of our nation fractures Kentucky's bones exposing the diseased marrow. The foreshocks, Trayvon, Mike, Sandra, George, were glaring warning signs. Here is the epicenter of a reckoning built on the lives of Black people. We were destined to erupt. We are determined to heal.

This is sacred ground.

The seismic waves of revolution and resistance are traveling around the globe. Here is everywhere. The world is shaken to its core. Paradigms shifting, institutions crumbling, ideologies melting. The egg in Sankofa's beak is broken open for all to see. The fiery feathers of Phoenix fan the flames of our nation's resurrection.

This is sacred ground.

Where are we?

Where do we go from here?

I am here. My heart is in my old Kentucky home beating fiercely for my brilliant, beautiful, Black children, Amari and Grayson. My head is in Louisville bearing witness to Breonna's revolution around the sun. My hands are in the work of Cities United, a national organization, which Shawn helped found, whose mission is to work with cities to reduce the epidemic of homicides of Black men and boys and whose vision is to create safe, healthy, and hopeful communities for all families. You don't have to be *in* Louisville to be *of* Louisville. Our ancestors were here. We are all still here.

This is sacred ground.

While there are pockets of promise across the country, no city is yet in a position where it can claim victory for its work improving the life outcomes of Black men and boys. Yet, if we act with urgency, match resources with smart people and plans—we can win.

—Shawn Dove, CEO CBMA

If we are to build a new foundation grounded in racial, economic, and social justice; if we are to write a new story centered on our promise and not our peril; if we are to claim victory for the work of improving the life outcomes of all Black lives, Louisville must win.

This is *our* sacred ground.

Althea Allen Dryden is a mother, writer, and solopreneur. Althea has an academic background in psychology and Black Studies and 30 years of professional experience in research, community organizing, marketing, and nonprofit management. She recently transitioned from her role as Director of Marketing & Storytelling at Cities United to start her own small business, Afromoon Collaborations. Operating as a "dream doula," Althea will support other creatives to build their brand and their business and give birth to their dreams.

Our Power Begins With Us

By TK Coleman

When I think about the question "Where do we go from here?" I can't help but ask "Wherever it is we intend to go, who will take us there?"

Most of us are familiar with the saying, "if you don't know where you're going, any road will take you there."

Well, the following is also true: "If you don't know who's leading you, any fool will do."

Even if our destination is good, our journey will be compromised if we pick the wrong people to lead us.

So, here's my question: Regardless of where you're trying to go, who's leading you? Will a great leader come along and guide us?

Yes, but that great leader has to be you and me.

If we are to truly achieve equity and economic self-sufficiency in this country, we can't afford to place our faith in a worldview that says, "Just wait until we get the right person (or the least evil person) into a position of power."

We must understand power as something that begins with us.

I remember hearing many of my colleagues and acquaintances express feelings of fear, disappointment, and anger after the results of the last presidential election. In an effort to muster up some feelings of hope, many of them said things like, "Well, at least we still have our creativity."

At least?

It's almost as if we see creativity as a bronze medal or a mere participation trophy. The real prize, we think, is when we vote the right leaders into office.

But what if we looked at things in the reverse order?

What if we saw the creative power of ordinary human beings as the gold medal and we saw everything else as a lagging indicator of the changes we create as individuals?

When I think of Rosa Parks, I think of someone who worked within a community of passionate and persistent believers to overcome structural injustice even when the most powerful political leaders were practicing open denial of their struggles.

When I think of E.D. Nixon and Howard Thurman, I think of leaders who invested considerable time trying to convince the people in their communities that they had more power than anyone realized.

They didn't treat our need to have faith in ourselves as some sort of second-rate consolation prize that only matters when we feel like the system has failed us. They treated it as if it were the very foundation of our freedom.

The message they embodied was this:

We should always feel a sense of urgency about challenging the status quo, coming up with alternatives, and refusing to accept our current reality as the final answer. We should always be striving towards new and better ways of getting things done. We should always be asking ourselves, "How can we make the world a better and freer place without requiring permission from authority figures?" We should always be investing time and energy into the process of subverting the forces that prevent us from living fully and freely. And we should always begin our efforts with self-reliance.

As long as we see our progress as being primarily dependent on political leaders, we are guilty of mistaking the cause for the effect.

Creativity isn't something we should settle for when life lets us down. Creativity is life itself.

There will always be people, situations, and events that we can't control. And there will always be creative things we can do to create a freer society in spite of those things. There's nothing wrong with being frustrated by an undesirable political outcome, but it only makes things worse when we use such situations as evidence that everything is inevitably going to hell regardless of the reactions and responses we choose to have.

We are not defined by the politicians who beg, perform, and plead for our votes. We are defined by the fact that we are a people with a voice, with the power to imagine, and with a capacity to innovate that can't ever be extinguished by any political regime.

Yes, I'm talking about you and me. We are the leaders who must change the world.

And by "change the world," I don't just mean "go vote for someone who promises to change the world." I mean "respect your own ability as an individual to do amazing things that don't depend on your favorite candidate winning the election."

Every election, people will tell us that this is our one big chance to make a difference. They're wrong!

Every single day of our lives is our big chance to make a difference, but we have to be willing to take ourselves seriously. We have to be willing to diligently entertain the idea that we are creative forces.

If your favorite candidate gets elected, what then? Are you going to sit back and expect the world to magically become more peaceful and prosperous all by itself? If your favorite candidate doesn't get elected, what then? Are you going to just sit around and complain about how stupid people were for voting in the winner?

It's okay to feel inspired by certain leaders, but at some point, we have to start respecting our own capacity to make history. We can only vote for politicians during election periods, but we can cast a vote for our own potential every single day of our lives.

We must ask ourselves, "How can I live more freely, and how can I help others do the same?" Then we have to start acting on that answer without waiting on political issues to get resolved first.

Where do we go from here?

We go to an entirely new stratosphere; to a realm of achievement, that's only made possible by our willingness to embrace the creative power of the individual.

And those individuals are us.

As Shawn Dove so often and eloquently says, "There is no cavalry coming to save us. We are the leaders we've been waiting for."

T.K. Coleman serves as the Education Director at the Foundation for Economic Education and is the co-founder of Praxis. He is also the founder of RevloutionOf1, a community that believes that "change doesn't begin with politics. It starts with you."

The Great American Reset

By Dr. Pamela Jolly

"During slavery, our ancestors were used for the benefit of others. We no longer want to be used. We want to be included."

—Pastor Grainger Browning

Time waits for no man; there is nothing new under the sun. And for me, this new decade reveals a cross-generational chance to turn the collective wheel of American change as it continues to move forward generation after generation. The exclusion of Black men in the historical turns of our wheel is a matter of inheritance. I believe it is time for Black men to come away from the circular pattern of denied access to acceptance and the opportunity to grow great wealth their way.

My work in the world of Black male achievement has blessed me with this perspective. The problems in America are not void of context. My great grandfathers, who were entrepreneurial men, did what they had to do so that their legacy could afford to do more in the next turns of the wheel. This context gives me the ability to appreciate the circumstances that the next generation, my grandfathers, navigated to turn the wheel that gave my father the will and insight to give my brother and me.

External perspective of internal progress always leads to miseducation and misinterpretation. History has required Black men to develop internal and external strength that only knowledge and appreciation of our past allows one to understand and appreciate the potential of what America has inherited in the Black men building, growing, and expanding today.

Three years ago, my research of thousands of Black men connected to the insight and experience of Shawn Dove and his work leading CBMA. Together, we focused on the internal expectation of a group of Black men in Detroit who came together to explore wealth from their perspective. The Black Male Equity Initiative demonstrated our ability to see what many in America have yet to develop the eyes to see—America's wealth-builders have always been Black men. Our collective look inward to the achievement of Black men, their legacy, and the wealth stored up in that resilient perseverance created the understanding that the Black Male Equity Initiative was the key to expanding the Black Male Achievement Narrative to include wealth creation as a legacy. Not as a beginning but as a continuation of our nation's wheel that keeps on turning.

My research with thousands of African Americans exploring ways wealth could be a standard in our community revealed a problem with America and her people's business context. Black people are the only people in America who were first capital before they ever made capital. Black men and their women were the first to be traded before they could trade, first owned before they ever could own. When you own something, you know it. Initially, you come to know how it works. As you build deeper relationships, you learn what it is capable of, and when allowed to grow and scale, you reap the benefits of its value. Appreciation for the asset in the ownership relationship requires acknowledgment of both the value created and your accelerated progress.

This fact makes it essential for Black Male Achievement to remain a priority for our American business model. There is unfinished business in the business relationship between Black men and America. This dysfunction is stunting the growth of all involved. History has proven that being the first is a journey along a road of tremendous thankless, unpaid work that leads those watching the opportunity to innovate and make things better for the business of themselves. In this way, Black men have been and are the cornerstone for America's business model, Black women birthed the economy, and the Black family keeps it honest about things the model may like to forget about its legacy and the way its first wealth was created.

It seems like we all need reminders of things that are worth never forgetting; the inclusion of Black men and their families is one of them. I am thankful to work with and come from many Black men who prove that America would not be the same without them. My prayer is that the elevation of their efforts and unique leadership lens remains a priority for us all.

When I think about where we go from here—the legacy must continue. The cornerstone must remain at the foundation for any and all change. The wheel can continue to turn along a road that leads to progress for the collective business model. This next turn is one that must be co-owned by the many American perspectives who have yet to inherit their seat at the equity table.

The last decade has shown what can happen with investment in Black Male Achievement second generational work of Shawn Dove and his colleagues such as Willie Barney, Trabian Shorters, Anthony Smith, and Ron Walker; each lead organizations that show what is possible when Black men continue the legacy of culturally relevant leadership.

I look forward to this next decade to show what happens further down the road beyond investment to increased Black male ownership and equity in every facet of our world's business model. The road ahead indicates it's time for the wheel to come full circle with one distinction—men whose families were owned some 400 years ago had no choice but to create wealth for others. Together we must choose to turn our wheel in ways that include the opportunity for those who have been disinherited to participate in wealth creation for themselves, their way.

I remain committed to supporting this turn of the wheel with the Black Male Equity Initiative and look forward to what is to come for us all because of it.

Dr. Pamela Jolly is the Founder and CEO of Torch Enterprises. She is a Wealth Strategist, committed to guiding men, women, business owners, pastors, and young professionals along The Narrow Road to legacy wealth. Dr. Jolly is also the founder of The Black Male Equity Initiative.

To Become Somebody

By John Simon

I started The DOME Project in 1973 to provide marginalized youth, especially marginalized young people of color, with an opportunity to resist and reject the internalization of society's destructive assumptions about them described so movingly by Shawn Dove in this book. When I remember Shawn from the time he attended The DOME Project, I see not only Shawn but Lincoln, David, Chris, Leonard, and Victor. Some, like Shawn, came from what would be called good homes; some from homes where there were "issues." Some of the boys were fairly successful in school, some less so, but when they first came to The DOME Project afterschool program, as Shawn mentions in this book, it was to play basketball, not to get help with their homework.

Many young people find themselves doing self-destructive things because of their need for approval and inclusion. Shawn didn't make his way to the corner of 80th and Amsterdam to sell loose joints because he needed the money or couldn't deal with life at home; he was attracted by the comradeship and excitement.

It was Shawn's good fortune to find an alternative to street life on the basketball court. And although he may have originally been attracted to The DOME Project by the prospect of getting new sneakers, once he and the others got there, they had to pay their dues by studying. We read together and discussed what we read. Our mantra became: "First hit the books, then bang the boards!" The DOME created summer jobs for teenagers in the neighborhood, too, empowering them to give to others some of what they had gotten from our staff. The mentorship our basketball players received from their DOME coach, Ed Scott, was passed on as they coached teams of younger boys in our summer league.

DOME participants knew they could come to the staff with their problems, and sometimes they did. Many of those problems concerned school. More commonly, it was the tension that arose as school, street, and home all pulled them in different directions. A few years before Shawn and his buddies showed up, three boys from the afterschool program had appealed to me to help them "get away" to school far from New York City. They were from strong, loving, immigrant families, but they felt they were at risk of failure and serious trouble if they could not escape the pull of the 'hood. I am a big believer in public schools but not in school systems defined by *de facto* segregation, inadequate resources, and a culture of failure. Despite my reservations about private boarding schools, I sought and found prep schools willing to take a chance on these boys. I felt obliged, however, to subject them first to an intensive year-long "orientation" in preparation for the culture collision they would experience. Learn all you can while away at school, but hold fast to family and community values.

Shawn, Lincoln, David, and Victor would follow those early escapees to boarding schools in Massachusetts and New Hampshire. I would have been happier if, together, we could have created a firewall right there in the city to counter the attraction of drugs, petty crime, collective misbehavior, and eventual failure, but we were neither clever nor strong enough. Chris didn't attend private school, but we helped him get away to college. Only Lenny left The DOME without having severed his ties to the street, or at least that was how it seemed to me at the time.

Why, in writing about Shawn, have I insisted on writing about all six friends? Because ever since leaving The DOME, they have carried on their own version of The DOME's work by helping each other. Shawn felt this was so important that a few years ago he got the idea of creating a documentary about how their friendship had helped them support each other in times of need. The film, *We Are Somebody*, took its title from my 1982 book, *To Become Somebody*. Its theme was how positive collective energy and mutual support worked to counteract distraction and the seduction of the streets' lowest common behavioral denominator.

No one absorbed that message better than Shawn himself. He has devoted the last quarter-century, through good times and bad in his own personal journey, to creating an ever-larger positive-energy resource to nurture the development of Black males in a decidedly hostile environment. First at the local level, then at the national, he did whatever it took to build this collective movement. In the process, he has been forced to confront his own weaknesses, and his willingness to do so has made his trajectory all the more impressive.

Recently, the six "DOME Buddies for Life" asked me to join their WhatsApp chat group. At an age where they no longer have to curry favor with anyone, these six guys chose to invite me into their inner circle, and that touched me deeply. I love them all and am proud of how each has lived his life.

Shawn calls me occasionally to discuss whatever is on his mind. Of course, he is the expert now, and my role is that of an interested and supportive listener. The Campaign for Black Male Achievement and the grassroots programs it has supported have touched countless lives. The national community it has nourished successfully multiplies the messages of pride and accomplishment Shawn picked up, on his odyssey from The DOME Project via Lawrence Academy, Wesleyan, Rheedlen, the Harlem Children's Zone, and the Beacon at Countee Cullen to the Campaign for Black Male Achievement.

Somehow I think the metaphor of six struggling adolescents and their mutual support and love through good times and bad has played an outsized role in shaping Shawn's vision of how Black male achievement can be realized. Create or reinforce a community to enable all its members to remain standing despite the gale-force winds gusting from every direction. Help others, and in doing so help yourself.

John Simon founded The Dome Project in 1973 on Manhattan's Upper Westside in New York City to provide young people with positive alternatives in their lives. He is the author of "To Become Somebody: Growing Up Against the Grain of Society" and "Strangers in a Strange Land"

Believe In Your Legacy

Dr. Dorian Burton

Where do we go from here? It was a question posed to Moses, to Martin, to Malcolm, and to be asked means someone thought you a leader worthy enough to follow or at the very least to have an opinion with some merit. There is a weight to this question, a laden burden passed by the inquisitor, that expects the answerer to know where we have been and to convey where to place our collective next steps. There is a special weight when asked by an elder and an inherent trust that signals the passing of the baton and gifting of the next leg of the race.

And so, just where do we go from here? It is a question I am always honored to be asked and yet in the same breath always feel wildly unqualified to answer. The truth is, I don't know. So, let's stick to what I do know. I know that for every leader there has to be a reckoning with "I" before we can fulfill the purpose of "WE." Sharing my own reckoning and continued journey, I have come to some of the following conclusions.

Don't divorce your leadership from your faith.
What is leadership? For me, leadership is a human art form, a creative balancing act that requires an individual to possess the sensitivity and humility to listen to others, the integrity and selflessness to act with morality, and the confidence and knowledge to make decisions in the best interest of the people that one is both accountable to and for. And while all that is all true, good leadership is nothing if you try to divorce it from the reason you lead or have the opportunity to lead in the first place.

1. Build your purpose and your work for an audience of one.
2. Orient your mind towards joy, and never compromise on your values.
3. Construct strategy on the foundation of love and compassion.
4. Make every decision based on love.
5. Don't be critical without a solution, and work with grace.

Don't let your libraries burn.
Amadou Hampâté Bâ said, "When an elder dies, a library burns." In the movement for Black male achievement, there are no easy answers. I have learned to:

1. Respect the map our predecessors have penned to get us to this point and forge the next leg of the journey with their knowledge in hand.
2. Realize that many of the questions we struggle with today have been toiled with long before we picked up the baton. There is value in not always starting from the beginning of the equation. If we are ever going to get to the finish line; starting from the beginning of the same question with a new generation might not be the answer.
3. Be discerning in your deference. Older does not always mean smarter, but it does mean they have had more opportunity to have more experience. These are experiences that have accrued and that have happened in your generation and in theirs; you cannot say the same.

Although deference is earned, you have something to learn from everyone.

Do believe you have a legacy to leave.
How many of you feel like you're not worthy of a legacy? If you asked me this five years ago, my hand would surely be raised. Now, however, I realize:

1. You are going to leave a legacy whether you want to or not. You get to choose if it is positive or not.
2. God does not choose the qualified, He qualifies the chosen. Get comfortable with being chosen to do great works for someone else.
3. You never have to rehearse to be yourself. Your legacy is your own to build and you can only do it by being authentic.

So where do we go from here? I am not sure; I know the destination is not as important as who you're able to help on the journey. Most importantly, I know I am willing and available to be guided and will put one foot in front of the other until we get there. Let's walk together and find our place to go.

Dr. Dorian O. Burton is a social entrepreneur, scholar-activist, philanthropist, and the founder of the Southern Education Reconstruction Fund.

Bonding Together in Imaginative & Prophetic Building

By Reverend Emma Jordan-Simpson

I feel like I have known Shawn Dove all of my life. It doesn't matter how long the intervals are between the opportunities we have to talk with each other, we always proceed as if we are just picking up the conversation from where we left off a few months ago. In that sense, we have been having one long conversation for maybe 17 or 18 years.

When we met, I was leading the expansion of Girls Incorporated's "Urban Girls" initiative. Its programs for girls across the country followed the "clubhouse" model. To reach girls in New York City, we were trying a new model not dependent on one clubhouse but rather focused on providing training and technical assistance to youth development professionals (leaders) to deliver the Girls Inc. programs in their organizations. In building this citywide network of organizations committed to positive youth development, age-appropriate, and gender-specific quality youth programs, I spent a lot of time dreaming with communities (parents, staff, management, board, facility staff—anyone and everyone considered a stakeholder in that community's success for girls) about the future they envisioned for girls.

During one of these workshops, I heard a plea from a grandmother that caused me to consider whether my own visions for my community were big enough. After the "Build a Girl" workshop, this grandmother was animated and excited about her organization's plan for the girls she cared about, including her own granddaughter. As we prepared to leave, her facial expression changed, and she grew somber. I pulled her aside to inquire about what she was experiencing.

The question she asked is the reason Shawn's vocation to do "Cavalry development"—inspiring, cultivating, and building the leadership we need to subvert the world order for Black boys—is critical. "I'm excited about what we will do for girls, for my granddaughter," she said. "What about boys? What about my grandson?"

"Why do you have to choose?" I said. "It's not Black girls or Black boys. It's Black children. What did you learn today about how you need to show up in the lives of girls that will change your approach in how you show up for Black boys?"

But when I left that workshop, I was restless. Who was investing in leaders and infrastructure specifically focused on Black boys? My colleagues and I were building the infrastructure of a movement for Black girls and investing in the leadership of Black women. Often, the women who were introduced to our programs in their capacity as youth development professionals experienced personal change and transformation as they began to advocate for themselves. They changed their own lives and their communities. Their work was bigger than a program.

And (not but), what about Black men and boys?

I went back to my office and began some informal research, looking for who was doing for Black men and boys in NYC what Girls Inc. NYC was doing for Black women and Black girls. After running into brick walls all over the place, I started a conversation with Ken Merin at the Charles Hayden

Foundation. It was at the Hayden Foundation's convening on boys programs in NYC that I met Shawn Dove.

What does it mean to call forth the Cavalry within the Black community? What does that look like today? Those questions are always agenda items three and four in our conversations after "How is your spirit?" and "How is your family?"

The Campaign for Black Male Achievement has been investing in the game-changing idea that Black boys deserve leaders who are invested in transforming their world, not just delivering good programs and good experiences here or there. Slavery made a world that continues to shape the Black experience in the United States—Black lives limited by mass incarceration, evictions, poverty, poor health outcomes, substandard education, and traumatized families. That world holds no space for Black leaders to imagine, dream, build, live, and love. The world that slavery made is ordered trauma. Trauma is killing us. And the incessant drumbeat of perpetual crisis means that very few of us have the bandwidth to try something new. That is probably the most egregious aspect of oppression and anti-Black policies and why the convenings the Campaign for Black Male Achievement has led over the years have felt like revivals.

In the world that slavery made, philanthropy funds not toward transformation, but to be "helpful." It follows the white supremacist reasoning and demands data. It has no patience for a different bottom line analysis—lives changed because perspective is changed. So, when Shawn, the Chief Evangelical Officer of the CBMA, sets out to create and resource healthy and protected space for Black men and boys to dream and to imagine, he is doing nothing short of subverting the claims the world slavery made and continues to make on the lives of Black men. Dreaming and imagining liberation should not be limited to the privileged.

His vision is dangerous because it is a distinctive and intentional departure from crisis leadership, deficit-based, "in the box that somebody else made" engagement of an entire field of CBMA leaders. He is banking on a generation who will see themselves (not just their programs) as the answer to the most important questions of our time. Like a good preacher, he is whispering in their ears and declaring the truth in prophetic poetry. We are the "iconic leaders" for whom we have been waiting.

Where do we go from here?

My thinking about the future is dominated by the face of an 11-year-old boy I met a few years ago. I was chairing a community advisory board for the New York State Office of Children and Family Services "Brooklyn for Brooklyn" project. Since the overwhelming majority of children detained in NY's juvenile detention facilities were Black, male, and from New York City, the aim of the project was to close upstate juvenile detention centers and bring those children closer to their homes. The vision was to provide services for children and their families at the same time. That vision was nearly impossible to achieve in New York's current system because that system was not designed to do anything more than what it was doing—warehouse Black boys in upstate communities dependent upon juvenile detention centers as contributors to those local economies.

My aim with the community advisory board was to engage community in ways that facilitated their remembering these children were ours. They were not super-predators, and they were not adults. They were Black children. They were Black boys. Our advisory board was meeting in one of the new local Brooklyn-based facilities one evening and we were interrupted by the arrival of a group of boys returning to the facility after an outing. They stopped into our meeting to greet us and I came face-to-face with an 11-year-old Black boy. He was slight in body. His eyes darted around the room and then settled on mine. My heart seemed to stop for a moment—as if to acknowledge that what I was seeing with my own eyes demanded an end to business as usual, that I stop and take a breath, that I remember this moment.

He was 11 years old. Forget the "system jargon"—he was incarcerated. I don't know why he was incarcerated. I don't know what he did "wrong." But the fact that he was incarcerated means that he—*at 11 years old*—was being held accountable for whatever his wrong was determined to be while there would be no real accountability for the adults and the systems that did him wrong *long before he was born*. This 11-year-old Black boychild carried a *Toy Story* Sherriff Woody doll. And detention was the best we could come up with in answer to whatever his infractions were? What a condemnation on us! Who are we that we have tolerated those who enslaved our ancestors to imagine "correction" for our children?

Where do we go from here?

We have to make a decision. Our investments must be in Black people's lives—not in propping up the systems that have failed them, the systems that we are always spending millions of dollars to "reform." What we spend on salaries for more police and corrections officers must be diverted as investments—including cash investments—into Black families. "Children don't come in pieces" is Marian Wright Edelman's reminder to us. To secure Black boys, we must secure their families and their communities. That security does not look like policing. It looks like food, shelter, employment, health, arts and culture, and education.

We must join with leaders like Shawn Dove as evangelists for a vision that sends a better letter to the future than the letter we received. Philanthropy, leaders, and communities that just want to be "helpful" cannot help us carry this new letter. We call for bold and courageous Dream Doers to answer the call. The most radical thing we can do in a world that hates and fears Black bodies is to resource and protect the warm loving spaces that nurture Black men, extend the joyous communities created by CBMA that bond Black leaders in imaginative and prophetic building, and stir up the spirit of revival so desperately needed for this movement to hold strength for a hopeful future.

Let's Lead with Love and Healing

By Richard Taylor, Jr.

Where do we go from here? This is a question that I often wrestle with. My honest to God answer with our current brewing climate is, "I don't know." As someone who delivers messages of hope and a better future, it pains me to say that, but it's my truth. In the hope of remaining optimistic I will say this: I believe that our "where do we go from here?" will be discovered in our "what do we invest from here?" approach. Shawn Dove has always reminded me that the cavalry isn't coming, but rather, it's already here. If we approach it from that lens then I believe that a lot of the answer we're looking for will come through self-reflection on what we have already poured out, how we need to be refilled, what we have left in our tanks, and what we have yet to tap into with our gifts/talents.

I'd like to start with the thought of "what we have already poured out in this work." Whether through our successes or failures we have contributed something to this work. Maybe in that, some of our expectations to affect change were met, and sometimes they weren't. If we're going to move forward effectively we must be able to look at the good and the bad as learning lessons while also showing ourselves grace. I think that grace is so important when we talk about moving towards a better future because we sometimes have a tendency to be our own worst enemy when it comes to the expectations we have set in place within our respective work. With the growing issues that we see through forms of trauma, violence, and destruction, it is very easy for us to feel as if we've missed the mark or that what we've poured out isn't good enough. This is the farthest thing from the truth. I think it's time for us to ask the question, "what have I poured out, and what do I have left to give?"

Just a thought, but what if what we have left to give is somehow tied into our personal healing from being burnt out, dealing with unmet expectations, or traumatic experiences? "Where do we go from here?" was a question I found myself asking 13 years ago. I was 19 and I had just tried to take my life for the umpteenth time. This tome was different because I almost succeeded. I felt completely lost, questioning my life's purpose, wondering how I had gotten to this point. I found myself taking a hard look at just how I let depression, anxiety, and suicide from my past traumas lead me to that point.

When I think about the notion of "Where do we go?" I'm immediately reminded of how easy it is to look at the thought of a better future as being impossible. It's not necessarily lacking hope or faith in it, but rather lacking the blueprint to what better could potentially look like. After my final attempt, I remember coming back to my college campus to the dorm room where I tried to end it all. The fear of relapsing was so overwhelming and evident. It's that very feeling right there that can start to cloud our judgment and haunt our thinking of where we go from here. The closer I got to that room, the harder it was to think about anything positive for forward progress.

I started thinking about all of the traumatic experiences from my childhood that led me to this space. Every childhood trauma, every bad experience, dealing with being bullied, the immense feelings of failure. All of these things played in my head as I got closer to that room. I didn't realize it at the time, but those thoughts were building a case that would make it harder to envision a hope for tomorrow. As we consider our approach to what we have to contribute to what's next, I'm reminded of one practice that helped me get over the hurdle of allowing my past to build up a case toward any hope for the future. That was to not allow the lens of the past to infiltrate lies of impossibility moving forward. It's very easy for pessimistic thinking to get the best of us in critical moments like this. Orally proclaiming our limited thoughts of what's possible because of the results of past investments into the work we have done to try and build a better America for Black men and boys.

As we deal with the issues that have led us to potentially pessimistic thinking, we have to address them head-on with grace and forgiveness. Grace in moments were maybe you felt like you could have done more or maybe missed the mark. And forgiveness in the moments where our investments weren't met with our desired outcome. When we do this, it opens the door for us to move forward with a clearer mind and a more hopeful approach in our personal lives. When we can practice these tools for ourselves, it will alo help us become better for those we serve. So, in your thoughts of how to move forward, I'd like to encourage you to ask yourself, "In what ways do you need to be refilled?"

Self-reflection is so important when we talk about being able to move and produce greater fruit for the future. Even in our work as heroes and influencers to others, it doesn't take away from the fact that we are humans that still need to be replenished and healed. So, I can't emphasize enough the importance of not only self-reflection but self-care that can lead to our own personal transformation. When we can be good to ourselves it helps us to flourish and how good we can be to others. I believe one way that we as leaders can effectively pour into those coming up after us is by making sure we ourselves have gotten the healing we need. One of the things that I've noticed from the past is that many times leaders with great intentions and great hearts who are hurting have a tendency to bleed out on those that they were meant to be a blessing to. Caring for ourselves is needed in order to effect change.

I believe we have to be honest with what we have left in the tank in order to determine what we can provide for the future. A lot of us are tired, sometimes even feeling defeated thinking that we've run out of options. I don't believe this to be the case, but I do believe that to overcome this thought process we must take time to truly reflect on the problems at hand while considering what we possess. This reminds me of a speech by Dr. Adam Clayton Powell, Jr., called "What's In Your Hand?" I think sometimes the answers that we look for when we ask the question, "Where do we go from here?" depends on what we believe is in our hands. And of course, the problems that we see our Black men and boys facing are definitely big and real. I think sometimes when we look at it from that lens we tend to give more power to the problem and not enough credit to what we possess to combat that problem. Believe that what we have left in the tank really does boil down to what's in our hands, no matter how big or small we think it is. We must challenge ourselves in taking what we have left and committing to it in order to see what can be produced from that small idea.

The final thought that I would like to give is how we choose to lead in love. Wherever we go from here, we must go by leading in love. This will be a true game-changer for the lives of our young Black men. Whether this comes through the form of our writing, programs that we create, messages that we put out, and the moments where we are face-to-face and have an opportunity to be love. I also want to encourage you all to be innovative in the ways you choose to create new systems, ideas, and platforms that can lead to changes of positivity for our Black men and boys. I truly do believe that there is a ton of things that we have yet to tap into when it comes to ways to connect and engage. However, you decide to do it, always check your heart and your motives. Consider how you would want someone to love you and help you if you were in their shoes. With that consideration, respond in that same light to those that you come in contact with. We must show grace even when it feels and seems hopeless. Remembering that we were once young and lost, thinking we had it all together and making a ton of bad decisions. From here we go up, but we do it by being more intentional than ever with every effort we put forward.

Richard Taylor, Jr. is a mental health champion, speaker, and the author of six books including, "Love Between My Scars" and "31 Days of Power: A Simplified Approach to Every Day Mental Health."

Co-Creating a World of Love, Dignity, and Justice

By Mark Leach

In Chapter 8, you say: *"...no matter how grand your plans, you must acknowledge that change happens on the local level, one person at a time."* It strikes me that this is true of both the "changer" and the "changed" (acknowledging the limits inherent in that binary) and sparks a number of thoughts that go to the heart of the stance and assumptions I bring to this more-than-usually-terrible moment and opportunity for reckoning in this nation's racial history.

At the level of the individual activist, all social change is autobiography [paraphrasing what Frederick Buechner said about theology], and inner work is one essential, foundational element for effective activism and enduring social change:

Effective, powerful, and enduring social change must come from the most loving and wise place within us (what different traditions and philosophies variously call "that of God in every person," "True Self," "innate, unborn awareness," etc.)

No matter our background, **our unhealed wounds from personal and systemic trauma and harm** (familial, racial, sexual, economic, and more)—and all the parts of us that keep manifesting to hide those wounds from ourselves and others (parts manifesting as defensiveness, addiction, un-skillfully channeled rage and attack energies, avoidance, fear, selfishness, etc.)—**are the greatest barriers to effective activism, collaboration, and systemic change.**

While others can certainly support and accompany us, **the inner work of connecting to our deepest places of wisdom and compassion and healing our wounded parts** (What Monica Dennis frames as healing from the four main disconnections of systemic racism: Reconnecting with our bodies, our stories, our emotions, and source) **is our responsibility** and is foundational to activism for lasting social change. **The inner work of white people, Black people, non-Black people of color, and Indigenous people is all different, but none of us are exempt from the need to do it.**

Individually and collectively attending to our physical, mental, and spiritual health is not something we just do for ourselves. When we neglect these, our resilience, creativity, and capacity to keep pushing are all reduced—and our families, communities, colleagues, and the work all suffer the consequences.

We're each good at what we're good at and not good at everything (white people, we need to give up our perfectionism around this!)

We know who we know, and do not know who we do not know, and we primarily trust and are trusted by the people with whom we have relationships rooted in authenticity, vulnerability, and proven integrity. **Social change is a collaborative effort, and collaboration and activism with people beyond this circle will be unavailable until we expand our circles of authentic relationships.**

As important as inner work is, it cannot be the end-all and be-all, or nothing of importance will get done. Putting this critical individual foundation in a larger context—my perspective on what is needed in this "moment of racial reckoning" can best be described by **working backward** from a vision of multi-racial activism and authentically co-creating a world of love, dignity, and justice:

- There can be no real just action without reconciliation and interracial healing...
- No real reconciliation and interracial healing without closing the racial wealth gap...
- No closing the wealth gap without a) reparations for stolen labor and lands (reparations are principally the work of white people at the direction of BIPOC folks); and b) de-linking Black wealth creation from dependency on white people and white dominant institutions...
- No reparations without truth-telling... (again, principally the work of white people)
- No truth-telling to others without first facing our own difficult truths and wounds... (work all of us need to do, but not necessarily all together)
- No facing our difficult truths without finding and surrendering to that deep well of wisdom and compassion that is always there but frequently covered over. (The work of all of us.)
- No surrendering to that deep well of wisdom and compassion without the experience of being held in the love and care of whatever we know as "source"— whether we find that in relationship and community, in spiritual benefactors and practice, in nature, in traditional religious communities and practices, in music, dance, poetry, or other expressive arts. (This is the work of all of us.)

And this is where I want to distinguish where I feel I have a responsibility—and legitimate place to stand—in naming and doing what needs to be done toward healing, reconciliation, and racial reckoning, and where I do not.

As a white person, I feel I have the responsibility to discern—guided by the perspective and thought partnership of Black, indigenous, and non-Black people of color—what white people most need to do now toward racial reckoning. White people are responsible for having created white supremacy and so we're the most responsible for taking it apart.

There are parts of this we can and should face and figure out on our own (for example through white caucus/affinity groups, taking a deep equity approach to transforming white-dominant social change organizations and spiritual communities); however, I do not trust myself or other white people to do this skillfully or without doing even more harm, unless we do it in authentic partnership with, and informed by the perspectives and priorities of, Black indigenous and non-Black POC.

Earlier in this book, Tonya Allen says, *"Black men need to let go of the notion that we alone are the ones who must solve the problems of Black men."* She goes on to say, *"Black men, in particular, believe that they have to own the work when they actually haven't been the people who created the problems. The challenge to me is, How do we make sure that Black men don't feel responsible for the conditions in which they are in? The way that we approach Black Male Achievement is that we end up beginning to own this country's shit instead of holding the country accountable to addressing and changing it."*

Two ways white people can answer this call to accountability and addressing and changing "this country's shit" is to own our principal role in creating this shit in the first place, and challenging ourselves and the leaders of white dominant organizations, movements, and networks to transform ourselves (through various kinds of individual and collective inner work) and the entities we have dominated for too long—including giving up our cultural tendencies to only value our own ways of knowing and expression and relinquishing or authentically sharing power and leadership.

When invited and challenged by BIPOC colleagues, fellow activists, and leaders to support BIPOC-led change initiatives, I see it as my and other white peoples' responsibility to both trust the wisdom of that invitation and leadership AND to do the inner work needed to confront whatever fears or biases are standing in the way of a "yes." And at the same time, making sure that the work we are being asked to do is aligned with our own true calling, and that a "yes" is being driven by our understanding of our own gifts, greatest contribution, and the joy of accompaniment, rather than by guilt or fear of being seen as racist if we say "no." At best, work that is not truly our own calling will be neither sustainable nor powerful enough to make a difference, and at worst results in toxic manifestations such as resentment, martyrdom, and paternalism.

The work white people have to do is different from the work Black people have to do to build a world of love, dignity, and justice, and some of that work we need to do in our own groups. And sometimes, and eventually, we must learn how to do some of this work together.

At this moment in history (and at this stage of my life) I have more questions than answers. How do we dance together? How do we move back and forth across the bridge that divides the world as it is from the world we want to see? How do we discern when it's time to be with the communities we were born into and when to be with other communities in accompaniment, support, and solidarity? How do we know when to DO, and when to just BE?

As a recovering white man, I am slowly undoing my attachment to individualism, to a fix-it mentality to being an expert, and to the bizarre, self-aggrandizing, and delusional belief that I am able to and should know enough about everything to actually make a difference on my own. I'm looking forward to continuing on this path of unlearning and learning, and being around as we all uncover our own deep wisdom and compassion, our shared humanity, and our infinitely rich and varied individual and collective gifts. I no longer know as much as I used to or with such certainty, but I do know it will take all of this, and it will take all of us.

> *For 40 years **Mark Leach** has worked in cross-cultural collaborations to advance social and economic equity, as a consultant, coach, researcher and writer. As Interim Co-Director at Change Elemental he gratefully works alongside loving and visionary people, organizations, and networks to pre-figure a world of love, dignity, and justice. Mark is sustained in this work by his family, friends, and co-conspirators, faith and practice communities, and by nature, music, and poetry.*

Where Do We Go from Here? From Pandemic to Promise

By Ron Walker

This critical question, *Where Do We Go from Here: Chaos or Community?* posed by Rev. Dr. Martin Luther King Jr. in his final book still endures today. As the founding Executive Director of the Coalition of Schools Educating Boys of Color, this question has continued to consume many minutes, hours, days, weeks, months, and even years of my life. Where Do We Go from Here? Moreover, what role must I play in getting to a destination that supports the affirmative social, emotional, cultural, and academic development of Black boys?

I speak as a man whose life trajectory was shaped by historical events. I remember like it was yesterday the horror felt when I opened the *Jet* magazine and saw the grotesque mask which was the pulverized face of the teenaged Emmett Till.

Fear overwhelmed any understanding that my nine-year-old mind could conceive. When I asked my mother, what happened to that Black boy in the magazine, she, herself a migrant from the dangerous nation called the Jim Crow South, said he was accused of doing something he was warned not to do. She ended her cryptic explanation without further explanation. That day, I promised myself that I would never go to Mississippi. But little did I know that my steps were already ordered.

In 1967, I was a junior at Lincoln University, the great HBCU that educated Black icons like Langston Hughes and Thurgood Marshall. It was a fall afternoon when I heard a lecture delivered by James Farmer, who was a leader in the civil rights movement and served alongside Dr. Martin Luther King Jr. Farmer headed the Congress of Racial Equality (CORE) and organized the historic Freedom Rides of 1961.

Professor Farmer gave an inspiring lecture. He challenged the class of Black males to consider becoming active in the movement to support the end of segregation and inequality in the deep south. He encouraged us that we stood on the shoulders of others who made a way for us. Professor Farmer, with passion in his voice, described his work to end segregation on buses traveling to the South.

He also talked about an emerging campaign to feed the hungry Black families who lived in the Mississippi Delta area. Senator Robert Kennedy was also poised to make a trip to Mississippi to dramatize the unrelenting poverty and hunger in the lives of unemployed Black farmworkers. Between Professor Farmer's challenge to do something and the Kennedy trip, a decision was made. Though I promised myself that I would never go to Mississippi, at the age of 20 I was bound for Mississippi with five other classmates.

What I saw forever changed me. I saw poverty, I saw hunger, and I witnessed and experienced the depth of racism and dehumanization up close and personal. I now realize the coincidence that the year Professor Farmer lectured us about going to Mississippi was also the same year that Martin Luther King Jr. wrote, *Where Do We Go from Here: Chaos or Community?*

After graduation and with the images of Mississippi seared in my memory, I went on to become a teacher, returning to the very same Philadelphia junior high school that educated me. I was blessed and fortunate to be a young teacher supported and mentored by the dozen or more Black male teachers who taught at a school with a one hundred percent Black student body.

I was a teacher anchored to the belief that a Black empowerment and liberation mindset were essential in the teaching of Black students. After all, I was nourished as a college student by the writings of **Frederick Douglass**, the poetry and music of **The Last Poets**, campus visits by activists, **Stokely Carmichael** and **Don L. Lee, now known as Haki Madhubuti,** and classmates with **Gil Scott-Heron** and future Black Panthers **Ericka and John Huggins.**

I am now in my fifty-fourth year as an educator and social justice warrior. As I reflect on Dr. King's essential question, Where Do We Go from Here? I offer forth a new title, Where Do We Go from Here: Pandemics to Promise. I speak from a deep well of experience educating Black boys and young men. I advocate for a bold agenda. Such an agenda, I submit, must rest firmly on a foundation grounded in the indigenous teachings of the ancestors and Babas who guided boys to manhood.

This core principle, the Rite of Passage, is critically important to Black male development and must be deeply rooted in the soil of our homes, communities, and schools that are committed to the full and complete education of Black boys and young men. The development and institution of this **Rite of Passage Pathway** should begin from the cradle to Grade 12. I think about this process of deep identity building and cultural immersion as intentional steps in positive immunization of the mind, spirit, and body of Black boys and young men. Collectively, as a village, our boys and young men must receive regular doses and booster shots of the **Sankofa Serum** to strengthen their immune systems from the attacks of racism, injustice, and dehumanization. **The Sankofa Serum** will enable them to engage consistently in the habit of culturally looking back, in order to go forward. This habit will increase their powers of discernment and will facilitate their full understanding and appreciation for their own genius and the dynamism of Black Culture.

I believe this to be critical to our ability as a people to survive, heal and thrive. This proposed agenda, I believe, is but one element in the vision of an ongoing and comprehensive movement for Black Male Achievement. It will undoubtedly go against the grain of the status quo. Historical, emotional, physical, cultural, and spiritual dehumanization has been a coordinated strategy for four hundred years. Therefore, the process of reclaiming our people's humanity and dismantling all forms of systemic dehumanization against Black boys must begin early.

Lastly, the glue to adhere this notion of a **Cradle to Grade 12 Rite of Passage Pathway for Black Boys and Young Men** must be bound by a **New Trust Compact**. Building a covenant of trust that lifts up the collective "We" rather than individual "Me" is the core work of the Village. I can imagine this as an opportunity to imagine, conceive, and create a cross-generational initiative leading to the **Ultimate Ubuntu**.

The perils of the pandemics faced by Black communities have been ubiquitous across the four centuries since our arrival to these shores. But in spite of racial violence and injustice, economic pain, social and emotional trauma, and health disparities exacerbated by a deadly virus, Still, We Rise! It is the hope of the slave that reminds us to never give up. The Promise that will overcome fear and pandemics will be manifested in the dreams and fulfilled aspirations of our children, youth. Onward and upward!

Ron Walker is the founder of the Coalition of Schools Educating Boys of Color (COSBOC) and the author of "Solomon's Plan: A Gift of Education from a Father to a Son."

Afterword

There is no greater agony than bearing an untold story inside you.
—Maya Angelou

Telling my story and sharing my life's work exemplifies the mission of the Campaign for Black Male Achievement—to love, learn, and lead Black men and boys. In the Introduction, I referenced Brene Brown's quote, "Owning your story and loving yourself through the process is the bravest thing you will ever do," as one of the inspirational mission fuel mantras that focused me during the writing, editing, and publishing process of this book—what I have described as an excavation of the soul.

I wanted to be a beacon of bravery, offering this book and my story to light the path for other Black men and boys to tell their "I Too Am America" stories. I realize now that there is an even braver step we can take beyond Brene's inspirational declaration. Yes, owning our stories and loving ourselves through the process is a brave act, but the ability to relive and reframe our stories with curiosity, transparency, and grace while learning, loving, and leading ourselves through the process is a loving leap forward on the path to self-compassion, self-awareness, and ultimately healing.

The mini-manifestos you just read were intentionally forward-thinking, designed to consider the question, "Where do we go from here?" within the field of Black male achievement. I wanted to give these leaders a platform from which to share their vision from the proverbial mountain and inspire you to do the same. Moving forward, creating spaces to curate and share our stories, is a cornerstone of building the Corporation for Black Male Achievement vision. I've learned over and over through this process that in the spirit of Sankofa, we must go back in order to go forward. I know for certain now that sometimes going back is the only way to go forward and owning our stories is the only way to share them.

We all have impactful moments in our lives that continue to influence us long after they seemingly fade. I want to revisit for a moment a story I shared in part one of this book. For almost 50 years of my life, I have told myself and anyone else who would listen, especially my own children around the dinner table, about the day nine-year-old Shawn traveled the New York City subways for the first time by himself. Whether I called it the "Fur Coat Story" or the "Shawn Dove Kidnapping Story," I always framed it as my "Harlem Resiliency Story." That December day in 1971 was indeed the making of my Harlem Resiliency story, but I now know two things can be true; that was also my story of childhood trauma.

Our "I Too Am America" stories too often normalize trauma for Black people in this nation, tricking us into believing that the pain, the poverty, the violence, and senseless deaths are all normal parts of the Black experience. This is a lie. We must stop believing it ourselves and feeding it to others. The depth of this truth broke open for me, nearly 48 years later, in the Fall of 2019 amid the majestic redwood trees of Santa Clara, California. During a True North Leadership week-long immersion, I and 70 leaders from around the country, most of whom I'd never met, shared the crucible moments of our life stories. While in my small subset circle of five colleagues with whom I dared to trust a little more each day, I shared my Harlem Resiliency Story once again. I sobbed uncontrollably while sharing the story. It was at that moment while breaking down that I began to also break through and open. And through ensuing sessions in therapy, I began to unpack and heal from that traumatic experience in my childhood.

For close to 50 years, several of which were truly dark and dared me to end it all, not once did I ever see that frightening experience of getting lost then abducted as trauma. Not one traumatic thought ever occurred to me in the many retellings of that day. I was the hero—Super Boy—a survivor of the mean, gritty streets of early 1970s Harlem. That was my badge of honor that I was a "bad man" even as a scared nine-year-old boy. I could share the story over and over, but not once did I own it.

In therapy, I finally gave myself permission to witness that story in its entirety, realizing that two things can be true. Yes, it was my Harlem Resiliency Story. But it was also a story of my childhood trauma. I could have easily wound up as that missing child on the side of a milk carton—big Afro, cute face, gone. I could have been harmed in so many ways, even killed. Slowly, week by week, I began to peel back the layers of the impact that one incident had on my entire life in ways I had not recognized or allowed myself to acknowledge.

I began to recognize that my penchant for wanting to prove I am responsible and can do the bold new thing; my tendency to not ask for help when I really need it; my lack of trust in others, yes, but even more jarringly in myself; the self-sabotaging of not completing assignments and not meeting deadlines—all have seeds that were sewn by this traumatic event and blossomed throughout my adult life. Fifty-seven-year-old Shawn cried more on that Santa Clara mountainside than nine-year-old Shawn ever did. As I began to peel the layers back on that frightful day, the unrecognized and unreconciled trauma that served as a silent narrative threaded through my soul—that still small voice ain't always God beckoning to your higher ground. Without a discerning ear, that still small voice is sometimes the soft soundings of our shadows and secret subconscious source of our sullen days and nights.

I rarely speak to a group of people, Black people especially, without urging them to have a mentor, an executive coach, and a therapist because I understand therapy is not about fixing a "broken" me; it is about uncovering and discovering how to live my fullest, whole self. Only with heightened self-awareness and unwavering self-compassion can we become the catalysts for our own healing. It was with this newfound belief and capability that I decided to become an active change agent in my own healing.

On Easter Sunday, April 4, 2021, I traveled from my home in Piscataway, New Jersey, to 174th Street and Bryant Avenue, my childhood block in the Bronx, to re-enact my 1971 solo subway journey. I parked about 30 feet from the entrance of my old building and walked to the elevated number 2 train at the 173rd Street and Boston Road station. Childhood memories meandered through my mind, some like friendly ghosts, as I recalled the many times I traveled those three blocks between the train station and my building as a boy.

I took pictures along the way retracing my roundtrip train ride to Harlem, getting off at 116th Street and Lenox Avenue, now also known as Malcolm X Blvd., and walking to Lel's stoop at 100 West 119th Street where, as children, we began so many games with the refrain of "Engine, engine number 9 going down Chicago line, if the train fall off the tracks, do you want your money back?"

I stood staring at the top of the stairs leading to the Downtown platform on 116th Street, remembering that day, when on my first solo subway ride, I inadvertently went down those steps and boarded a train in the wrong direction. This time, guided by a purposeful, pregnant pause, instead of going down those stairs I crossed Lenox Avenue as I should have 50 years ago and went down the stairs to the subway to begin my trek uptown back to the Bronx.

In a surreal moment standing on the platform, I was Big Shawn holding hands with nine-year-old Little Shawn, telling him that he would be okay. Letting him know that he made a mistake that day, that it was okay. I told him that his getting lost and the ensuing victimization wasn't his fault. It was no one's fault. It was life. Big Shawn told Little Shawn on that platform to forgive himself and to realize how blessed he was a half-century later to be the catalyst of his own healing.

Through my own adult trepidation, I boarded the number 2 train wondering if routes had changed in all those years. Was I even on the right train or should I be on the 5 train instead? The trepidation faded as the train rattled from Harlem to the Bronx to my stop at 173rd Street. I walked the three blocks back to my car and exhaled with puddled eyes feeling the unexpected relief that I finally completed the trip. I thought of Melvin Miller, who reminded me on a Mohonk Mountain retreat that "I have nothing to prove. Only gifts to share." That seems truer now than ever. I could not help to think also of Arundhati Roy's reminder that "Historically, pandemics have forced humans to break with the past and imagine their world anew. This one is no different. It is a portal, a gateway between one world and the next."

On that Resurrection Sunday, *my* Resurrection Sunday, I stepped through the portal and imagined my world anew.

Epilogue

I want to start out saying that I love Shawn Dove. Over the years, he has been a mentee, brother, friend, godson, and boss. With that said, I found out more about Bro. Dove in the chapters you finished reading. The book helped put together for me the pieces that can be called his life's puzzle. I was there, just off-stage, for most of Shawn's experiences after he graduated from Wesleyan. I was there for the ups-and-downs during his maturing process. Shawn had a persona that was at once inquisitive, engaging, and fun-loving—and a smile, sometimes mischievous, that can still light up a room. We spent time learning new things, laughing at each other's jokes, and crying. I was honored when he asked me to add my behind-the-scenes perspective to this work that will live longer than all of us.

The Campaign for Black Male Achievement doors closed while this book was near completion. There was nothing like it before and I can only pray there will be something like it moving forward. While this is not an epitaph for CBMA, it is important to say that this organization, no, more like this movement, tapped into the reality of addressing one's spirit needed to do the work of youth and community development, while fighting for asset-rich social and education policies. I reference spirit not in the religious sense, though some brothers and sisters came to CBMA events in need of revival. I am referring to spirit that is needed to motivate self as well as others. Let me take you back a decade plus when Shawn asked me if I would consider being a reference for him as he competed for the CBMA director position. At the time, I was vice president of the Fund for the City of New York. There were few persons of color in philanthropy at the time I was hired, and even fewer males. I knew what Shawn was in for; I also knew he was not the "classic" foundation candidate. I said to his soon-to-be supervisor, "If you hire Shawn Dove know that you are getting a social entrepreneur with a big vision as to what is needed in the field."

I had first-hand knowledge of Shawn's entrepreneurial spirit through his work at Rheedlen (later became the Harlem Children's Zone), when he rallied young people fighting themselves, the crack epidemic, and rival street gangs, to put down their guns and pick up pens to write for the youth-driven newspaper *Harlem Overheard*. The success of *Harlem Overheard* brought creativity, opportunity, and supports, all steeped in the principles of youth development, coupled with adults proactively involving youth rather than doing for youth. Shawn knew how to make work fun, uplifting, and transformational (I know Salahadeen Betts, one of Shawn's early mentees, would testify to this fact). It did not stop there. Shawn created a series of mini-books called Pocket Magic Books using voices from the field, all unpublished, to address pressing issues (one edition was geared to help parents raise their children). It was during this same time (he was prolific) Shawn invited me to a recording studio on 145th Street and Broadway. He wanted me to record a special Y2K (remember that?) message about faith, hope, and a vision of the future that I free-styled. It was not important to him that I had never been in a recording studio before. Shawn had a way, back then, and right now, of pulling the best out of people.

Another one of Shawn's ideas was starting a newspaper out of his house in 2006 called *Proud Poppa*. It was written to be a resource, a mirror, and inspirational guide for fathers who were doing, or wanted to do, the right thing for their children. As I was putting this closing together, I came across the one-year anniversary edition of *Proud Poppa* with father and son Eddie and Gerald Levert splashed across the front page touting their book, *I Got Your Back*. Shawn was able to pull people like Susan L. Taylor, Kirk Franklin, and the late Phillip Jackson out of Chicago, to contribute their time, talent, and treasure in order to further the cause. I want to offer an excerpt from a column I wrote for the first anniversary edition of *Proud Poppa* titled, "Are You A Be Back Brother?"

> *I called Shawn Dove and asked him what does this issue's theme of* Proud Poppa, *"I Got Your Back," mean to him?*
>
> *He replied, "Do you remember what you felt back in the day when a brother said, 'Don't worry, I got your back?'"*
>
> *I smiled after recalling how this "old school" street pledge that no matter who, what, when, or where, the vow giver would stand by his word to protect you. We both laughed, but probably wanted to cry because of the growing number of struggling fathers [and their children] who never hear, "My brother, don't worry, I got your back." Let*

me take this to another level. Some of you may be familiar with the parable of The Good Samaritan. Just in case you are a tad hazy, allow me to offer this modern version of the story:

A brother on his way home from the check cashing spot one late Friday night was dragged into a dark alley and jacked for his money. A stranger passed by and his fear would not allow him to intervene. After the beat down artist fled, another man stopped, looked, and felt pity for the brother but left because he did not have time to get involved. A third brother passed by and heard moans coming from the alley. Without hesitation, he comforted the injured man and called for help. The good brother followed up days later and found out that the badly injured man would need time to heal (he lost his job at the car wash). He gave money to the injured brother's wife so she could feed their children and pay the rent. He said to the sobbing pair that he would be back next week to take care of any loose ends.

The takeaway from this urban parable is that the helper did not know the brother or his family but intervened nevertheless and kept his word to return, thereby earning the honor of being called a "Be Back Brother." A Be Back Brother is inner-directed to help by giving either time, talent, or treasure. A Be Back Brother's word is his bond. (Do you remember back in the day saying, "My word is bond"?) It is clear that we need strong, focused, and spirit-fueled Be Back Brothers to step up to the plate because there are many unmet needs in our [young people], families, and communities...

Rumble Young Man Rumble (RYMR), CBMA's signature program, started out with both of us writing letters of encouragement back and forth to each other inspired by the relationship between Muhammad Ali and Drew Bundini Brown. We had sent several exhortations to each other via email, but the effort died a natural death. We did not try to resuscitate it—but a decade later, it was resurrected and was situated at The Muhammad Ali Center in Louisville, Kentucky. As a participant, adviser, facilitator, and elder in the RYMR village, I can say that there has never been anything like the experience (a special shout-out to CBMA staff—ALL of you!) that took participants to the place he or she needed to go in order to Love, Learn, Lead—and I add, Heal. There were exciting speakers like Ambassador Shabazz (Malcolm X's oldest daughter), who dropped knowledge that would lift the entire room to a higher level of consciousness. It is rare that young people from middle school to college are invited to adult events. Youth (Flyweights) were expected to attend RYMR and have their voices heard by their mentors (Heavyweights), parents, and other helping adults in the room. I loved the opportunity to address all of the attendees and conduct the morning spirituality sessions (even though the 7:00 a.m. start was difficult. to say the least).

I still remember RYMR Nine, when the spirit of healing, recognition, love, forgiveness, and support took over the 120 Rumblers of all ages gathered in the room. The session started out with a brother from Baltimore who just returned from doing a bid in prison. Through his tears, he recounted how his teenage son pulled a knife on him during a disagreement that escalated out of control. The next speaker told the harrowing story about how his son was killed while filling his tank with gas because a man in another car argued that the music his son was listening to was too loud. Last, a sister known for her spoken words found words to talk about her life in foster care and sexual abuse that occurred. Through her tears, she focused on not being believed. I was bent over in tears and could not stop crying. I thought I was picking up on the raw outpouring of pent-up emotions. It came to me while I was sobbing that I did not get the chance to mourn the passing a month earlier of my sister-in-law. I had to hold my family together, look out for my older brother, and do her eulogy. I believe there were many reasons why the other mentors and mentees, sons and daughters, mothers and fathers—in short, the RYMR family—were all crying. I think I speak for everyone in the room saying the memory of this indelible moment will last a lifetime.

Shawn and I have tried to meet every other month or so over a meal so we can collect ourselves, process our lives, share visions (we LOVE doing that), and speak truths into each other's spirit. When Shawn went into drug treatment back in the 80s, I sent a short poem to encourage him. The fear that he lost it all—his standing in the community, family, and some friends—was real. One day, as we reminisced over lunch about this dark and fearful time in his life, I was shocked to see him go in his wallet and take out a crumpled piece of paper with the words I wrote to encourage him several decades earlier. We cried as he read aloud:

the heart of it
find strength in your weakest moment
let the armor of self be stripped
expose the warrior
no longer wary of the coming engagement
combatant raise your eyes
strike the telling blow
shout
death
to
fear

—Rev. Dr. Alfonso Wyatt

Gratitude & Acknowledgments

Shawn Dove:

I am so grateful that God infused me with the purpose and fire to see this publishing project to fruition and for delivering the timely help of so many midwives and co-laborers along the way.

Eternally grateful to my friend and co-author, Nick Chiles, without whom this book would have not been birthed. Our more than 30 years of friendship was deepened and illuminated during the two years of this book project. Love you, my brother!

Many thanks to the team of midwives that enveloped me with love, patience and understanding during the writing and publishing process—and for calling an emergency C-section so that we could finally deliver this book to the world. Monica Michelle Cooper, Valerie Merritt, Althea Allen Dryden, Stephen A. Hart, Salahadeen Betts, and Janet Dickerson—we did it!

To Romero Wesson, Christopher Chatmon, Jamare Winston and Quan Neloms for generously giving us a glimpse into your lives and sharing your *I Too Am America* stories with the rest of the world. Jamare and Romero—I believe in you and your brilliant futures!

To all the coaches, mentors, and teachers who have infected me with the love, learn, lead ethos that has inspired me and so many others along my journey. Ed Scott, John Simon, Martin Tandler, Sue Carlson, Cliff Carlson, Richard Murphy, Reverend DeForest Soaries, Susan L. Taylor, Reverend Alfonso Wyatt, Terrie Williams, Dr. Derek Suite and Dr. Anne Elliott, along with a host of heads, hands, and hearts that have generously poured into me over the years.

To my DOME Brothers, Chris, Lenny, Dave, Lincoln and Victor, for 45 years of brotherhood, teamwork, forgiveness, and a lifetime of stories never to be told. Love y'all!

To Tonya, Trabian and the rest of my SOAR family for providing me with the mission fuel to keep loving, learning, and leading.

Special appreciation to all the bright lights who graciously illuminated the pages of this book with their mini-manifestos. Your contributions to this book were everything!

Thank you Maria Rodale for ushering in at the right time memories of our high school poetry classes, the purpose and power of publishing books, and the periodic pushes of encouragement that helped keep my eyes on the prize of completion.

To my mom, Deanna, for lining our living spaces with endless shelves of books, while lining my heart with your endless love.

To the Dove Nest, my wife Desere and my children, Nia, Maya, Cameron and Caleb, for the love, laughter, and tears over the years and for allowing me to vulnerably show up as your Hon and ShawnDaddyD!

Nick Chiles:

It has been an unabashed pleasure to write a book with one of my oldest and dearest friends, Shawn Dove. Our careers have been moving in tandem for the past three decades, always producing major fireworks when we dive into a project together. There will be no fireworks louder than this book, which feels like the culmination of our personal and professional lives as each other's cheerleaders and sounding boards. I love you, my brother. Continue to shine your dazzling and healing light on the world of Black men and boys.

I am so grateful to Romero Wesson and Jamare Winston—and their families—for letting us into their lives with such candor and transparency. You both are bursting with talent, charisma, and grace, with hearts as large as your smiles. I am anxious to watch you jump into adulthood and soar into the stratosphere.

As always, my children Mazi, Mari, and Lila provide me with the inspiration and drive to keep doing this. I am so proud and impressed with the man and women they have become.

My bride Sadiqa has been a constant source of joy and strength in my life. She makes every day a party. I can't seem to stop smiling in her loving presence.

My parents and my siblings have been there with me every step of the way, cheering me on and providing a shoulder when I need it. I would not be me without them.

Black Male Achievement Organizations To Support

BMe Community: An award-winning network of community builders known for defining Black people by their assets and building on those assets via the largest fellowship program for Black leaders. www.bmecommunity.org.

Brothers@: Brothers@ unleashes the power of young men of color by recruiting, training, and hiring collegiate men of color to serve as positive male role models to their high-school peers, and by creating pathways to full-time employment as professional mentors on college campuses, within local communities, and at non-profits serving young men of color. www.brothersat.org.

Cities United: Cities United supports a national network of mayors who are committed to reducing the epidemic of homicides and shootings among young Black men and boy ages 14 to 24 by 50%. Cities United works with cross-sector leaders to design public safety plans for cities to realize their vision of creating safe, healthy, and hopeful communities for young Black men and boys in America's cities. www.citiesunited.org.

Coalition of Schools Educating Boys of Color (COSEBOC): The mission of COSEBOC is to connect, inspire, support, and strengthen school leaders dedicated to the social, emotional, and academic development of boys and young men of color. www.coseboc.org.

CUNY Black Male Initiative: CUNY BMI's vision is to create model projects throughout the University that are intended to provide additional layers of academic and social support for students from populations that are severely underrepresented in higher education, particularly African, African American/Black, Caribbean and Latino/Hispanic males. www.cuny.edu/bmi

InDemand: A Detroit-based movement that seeks to connect Black men to opportunities to become teachers, mentors, and volunteers within Detroit's schools. InDemand leverages school and community partnerships to engage

Black men to serve as assets to Detroit's schools and community-based organizations. www.iamindemand.com.

Kingmakers of Oakland: Kingmakers of Oakland originated in the Oakland Unified School District's Office of African American Male Achievement (AAMA) and supports school districts across the country to improve the educational and life outcomes of Black boys by "healing the fish while treating the toxic ecosystem." www.kingmakersofoakland.org / info@kingmakersofoakland.org.

Mentoring Mentors: Baltimore-based organization that supports young people through an intergenerational, near-to-peer model that promotes interdependency, long-term relationships, and commitment to the community. www.mentoring-mentors.org

National CARES Mentoring Movement: Works to secure, heal and transform the lives of Black children by inspiring, recruiting, and mobilizing masses of caring Black men and women to mentor and nourish them. Their national volunteer affiliate network connects adults to local youth-serving organizations. They envision a nation in which all Black children are loved, have access to quality, culturally competent education, and are supported by well-resourced families and communities. www.caresmentoring.org / info@caresmentoring.org